International Economic Issues

Contributions by the Commonwealth
1975-1990

Commonwealth Secretariat
London
1990

International Economic Issues

Contributions by the Commonwealth

1975-1990

The Commonwealth Secretariat
Marlborough House, Pall Mall, London SW1Y 5HX

ISBN 0-85092-348-4

Copies may be purchased from:
Commonwealth Secretariat Publications, Marlborough House, Pall Mall,
London SW1Y 5HX

Set at the Commonwealth Secretariat
Printed in England by
Black Bear Press, Cambridge

Contents

List of tables

List of boxes

Abbreviations used in the text

ACP African, Caribbean and Pacific States (signatories to the Lome Convention with the European Community)

CBI Caribbean Basin Initiative

CCGTM Commonwealth Consultative Group for Technology Management

CFCs chlorofluorocarbons

CFF Compensatory Financing Facility (of the IMF)

CFTC Commonwealth Fund for Technical Co-operation

CIEC Conference on International Economic Cooperation

CITEP Commonwealth Industrial Training and Experience Programme

CYP Commonwealth Youth Programme

DAC Development Assistance Committee (of OECD)

DCC directly contributed capital (to the Common Fund for Commodities)

EC European Community

ECA (UN) Economic Commission for Africa

EEZs exclusive economic zones

EFF Extended Fund Facility (of the IMF)

FAO Food and Agriculture Organisation of the United Nations

GATT General Agreement on Tariffs and Trade

GDP gross domestic product

GNP gross national product

GSP Generalised System of Preferences

IBRD International Bank for Reconstruction and Development

ICAs international commodity agreements

ICGEB International Centre for Genetic Engineering and Biotechnology

ICOs international commodity organisations

IDA International Development Association

IDU Industrial Development Unit (of the CFTC)

IFC International Finance Corporation

ILO International Labour Organisation

IMF International Monetary Fund

IPC Integrated Programme for Commodities (of UNCTAD)

IPCC Intergovernmental Panel on Climate Change

ITO International Trade Organisation

MFA Multifibre Arrangement

mfn most favoured nation

msl mean sea level

MTNs multilateral trade negotiations

MVA manufacturing value-added

NGOs non-governmental organisations

NICs newly industrialising countries

NIEO New International Economic Order

NTMs non-tariff measures

ODA official development assistance

OECD Organisation for Economic Co-operation and Development

OMAs orderly marketing arrangements

OPEC Organisation of Petroleum Exporting Countries

R&D Research and development

RTA Retroactive Terms Adjustment
SAF Structural Adjustment Facility
SAL structural adjustment loan or lending
SDRs Special Drawing Rights
STABEX Arrangement for stabilisation of export earnings of ACP countries
TNCs transnational corporations
UN United Nations
UNCTAD United Nations Conference on Trade and Development
UNEP United Nations Environment Programme
UNESCO United Nations Educational, Scientific and Cultural Organisation

UNFPA United Nations Fund for Population Activities
UNGA United Nations General Assembly
UNICEF United Nations Children's Fund
UNIDO United Nations Industrial Development Organisation
UNIFEM United Nations Development Fund for Women
UNPAAERD United Nations Programme of Action for African Economic Recovery and Development
VERs voluntary export restraints
WMO World Meteorological Organisation

Introduction
by Shridath Ramphal, Commonwealth
Secretary-General

This publication documents a vital aspect of the work of the Commonwealth over the past one and a half decades. It is a record of our contribution to global efforts to reshape international arrangements in the economic, financial and trade fields so as to make them more equitable and more conducive to worldwide progress. These global efforts—and the Commonwealth's contribution to them—continue; but 15 years is a sufficiently long span to warrant the assembly within one volume of information on the Commonwealth's work in these crucially important areas.

The period since 1975 has been both eventful and testing for the Commonwealth. Membership has continued to grow, though at a slower pace than in the 1950s and 1960s when decolonisation brought many countries to independence—and to Commonwealth membership—in swift succession. Political issues were prominent on our agenda throughout the 1970s; for example, the Commonwealth kept faith with the people of Southern Rhodesia, as Zimbabwe then was, as they fought and won their freedom. And, of course, the Commonwealth continued to honour its commitment to ending apartheid in South Africa and establishing a non-racial democracy there. Living up to these obligations has involved strains for the Commonwealth; but its principled stand has been increasingly and amply vindicated. It also involved much visibility for this side of our work; but much else was being done.

Challenges in the political domain were paralleled in the economic by the insistent call to the Commonwealth to live up to the commitment spelt out in the Commonwealth's first collective articulation of principles—the Commonwealth Declaration of 1971—to the 'progressive removal' of global economic inequalities. Developments in the early 1970s served to give this challenge a sharper edge. The emergence of OPEC as a major factor and a generally more co-ordinated approach by developing countries to the economic agenda marked a new resolve to press for reforms in global economic relationships. These demands were given their principal expression in the United Nations. The Commonwealth, whose overwhelming membership is of poor countries but which embraces countries at all stages of development and with varying approaches to development, could not however remain insulated from these pressures for change. Nor should it have sought such insulation. Indeed, it was seen as having a positive and practical role in facilitating agreement on the issues of world economic reform which had brought developed and developing countries to adversarial and even confrontational positions globally.

Discussion of key economic issues had been a regular feature of the meetings of Commonwealth Heads of Government and Commonwealth Finance Ministers. In the 1950s and 1960s, an important concern of these meetings was sterling area management; another was the potential impact on Commonwealth trade of Britain's entry into the European Community. But the first major discussion on what came to be termed 'North-South issues' occurred when Commonwealth leaders gathered in Kingston, Jamaica, in 1975. On this occasion the host Prime Minister, Michael Manley, recalling the Singapore Declaration of Principles in which Commonwealth leaders recorded their belief ''that the wide disparities in wealth now existing between different sections of mankind are too great to be tolerated'', called on the Commonwealth to help to find ''the techniques of political management of world trade and world finance that will lead to a progressive removal of those wide disparities''. Arguing that the world faced a choice between dialogue and confrontation on the demand for a new economic order, he urged the meeting to explore ways by which ''the scales of probability may be tipped in favour of dialogue''.

At the same meeting, the Prime Minister of Britain, Harold Wilson, made a strong case for measures to promote stability in commodity markets and to secure remunerative prices for producers as a way of improving the prospects for developing countries. Forbes Burnham of Guyana wanted movement over a much wider front than commodities. But it was clear that they had a shared objective—a more secure basis for developing-country efforts to reduce poverty and speed development. This identity of purpose was finally reflected in the Commonwealth's unanimous agreement that there was need for immediate steps towards the creation of ''a rational and equitable new international economic order''. Heads of Government then decided to ask a group of experts from the Commonwealth to draw up ''a comprehensive and inter-related programme of practical measures, designed to promote development and to increase the transfer of real resources to developing countries, and directed at closing the gap between the rich and the poor countries''. The distinguished West Indian economist, Alister McIntyre, then head of the Caribbean Community Secretariat, was appointed Chairman of the Expert Group. That was the meeting at which I was appointed Secretary-General. There could be no doubt about Commonwealth priorities in the period ahead.

The McIntyre Group signalled the start of what was to become a new dimension of the Commonwealth at work. The groups set up as a result of this and later initiatives have been drawn from a representative range of Commonwealth countries selected to ensure that the experts themselves bring a diversity of view to bear on the issues. All members were invited to serve as individuals eminent in their own right; not as spokespersons for their countries, governments or institutions. That they would be sensitive to the national interests of their countries was a strength; yet they were not under the constraint of briefs prepared in their capitals or of the compulsions of official negotiating positions. At the same time, they worked and reported within the intergovernmental framework provided by an official mandate—a unique combination of individual professional judgement and broad international interests.

The calibre of the individuals serving on these groups was of paramount importance. The list of members of the different groups, which appears in an appendix, is a roll call of citizens—from countries large and small, developed and developing—who have distinguished themselves in a wide range of occupations and positions: politics and government, public administration and diplomacy, banking and finance, business and industry, the professions, international organisations, voluntary bodies and trade unions. The contact and the experience of having worked together, provided by these meetings to members of the experts groups, were to forge and strengthen a vital Commonwealth link of value beyond the immediate tasks.

The work of each of the Commonwealth Expert Groups which has functioned since 1975 is discussed in a separate chapter in this book. The circumstances leading up to the decision by Commonwealth leaders to have particular issues examined are set out; the main conclusions and proposals of the groups are indicated; and subsequent developments in relation to the issues addressed are outlined. Each chapter thus goes beyond the work of the Group concerned to give a wider perspective of the particular issue.

The range of subjects these groups have been commissioned to study covers most of the major issues which have thrust themselves on the economic agenda of the world community over the last two decades. They include matters of long-standing concern like commodity prices, protectionism, reform of the multilateral financial institutions and developing-country debt, as well as issues which have come to the forefront of world concern more recently, such as the impact of 'frontier' technologies, structural adjustment as it impinges on women, and the global environmental threat of climatic change and global warming. Not every subject studied by these groups falls under the rubric of North/South issues or ranges developed and developing countries on opposing sides. But the countries more acutely affected by high unemployment among the young or more exposed to the vulnerabilities associated with being small tend to be developing countries, and the amelioration of their difficulties would be hardly possible without significant North/South co-operation.

Even on those issues which bear the 'North/South' label, the arguments for change within the Commonwealth have not come entirely from developing member countries. There has been a general appreciation that most of these issues do not present zero sum situations where the benefits of change will flow in one direction only. Protectionism, for instance, is seen to hold out threats to the international trading system and the global economy and therefore to all countries that live by trade, though poor countries are naturally more vulnerable to the incidence and effects of trade barriers; it is significant that on the issue of the Bretton Woods system, the case for reform was argued most trenchantly by the then Prime Minister of New Zealand, Mr.Robert Muldoon.

While each group's work has been a discrete exercise, there have been many links and continuities. Several of the issues which the first group of experts covered in their report on the New International Economic Order came to be explored in greater detail by later groups. The Helleiner Group (the groups came quickly to be known by the names of those who chaired them) focused on the Bretton Woods institutions, for instance, and the Campbell Group dealt specifically with commodities. There were many strands linking the Arndt Group's report on the world economic crisis in 1980 and the work of the Cairncross Group on protectionism in 1982.

Over this period, I have myself had the opportunity of participating in the work of several Independent Commissions dealing with such matters as development, disarmament and the environment.* This afforded me a unique opportunity to facilitate a two-way flow of information and perceptions, assisting a process of interaction to the benefit of both sets of activities. On more than one occasion, the International Commissions with which I was associated were able to draw on work in progress within the Commonwealth's ambit. In the same way, I was able to appraise Commonwealth Expert Groups of the outcome of investigations made by these Commissions, often to the advantage of the Commonwealth endeavour.

The Commonwealth framework in which our groups were created has not in any way circumscribed their broader international scope. They addressed matters of worldwide relevance and their mandate was essentially to propose measures not for Commonwealth application but which the Commonwealth could offer as a basis on which global consensus could be built. Each report represented a consensus reached within a diverse group. Given the heterogeneous composition of the groups, reflecting the diversity within the Common-

---

* These included: (i) The Independent Commission on International Development Issues (the Brandt Commission) 1980, 1983; (ii) Independent Commission on Disarmament and Security Issues (Palme Commission) 1982; (iii) World Commission on Environment and Development (Brundtland Commission) 1987; and, (iv) the South Commission 1990. (Years refer to year of publication of the reports).

---

wealth, such consensus inevitably implied a substantial measure of give and take, of trade-offs between divergent interests, of compromise and accommodation, and of pragmatism. In this quality, combined with the standing of the individuals forming the groups, lies their principal value to the world community. It explains the wide impact they have had and the contribution they have been able to make to the evolution of thinking and discussions on the issues concerned.

In many instances, the recommendations made by Commonwealth groups have reinforced, or were reinforced by, other impulses within the international arena, and have contributed towards specific action. A notable instance was the proposal for a Common Fund to promote stability in commodity prices. The study made by a group of experts under Lord Campbell in 1977 led to a Commonwealth Ministerial meeting which looked at ways of accelerating progress in the negotiations. That it took several years for the way to be fully cleared for the Commonwealth Fund's establishment does not detract from the catalytic role the Commonwealth played in these early stages. The Clark report's proposals on improving the North-South negotiating process were acknowledged as timely and valuable by many participants and continue to remain relevant. It generated significant interest in other international organisations including the UN and the OECD and has been of great influence on subsequent reports on the issues concerned. The Lever report on debt was among the first to highlight the particular problems of low-income debtors, a theme taken up by successive meetings of Finance Ministers and providing a background to the Toronto/Berlin initiatives on official debt a few years later. The Holdgate report on climate change and sea level rise became an important input to the work of the Intergovernmental Panel on Climatic Change which is—at this moment—preparing the ground for a Global Climate Convention.

Another example is the sequel to the Helleiner Group's report in the form of sustained Commonwealth efforts to initiate a dialogue on the Bretton Woods system and its institutions. These were undertaken at the direction of Heads of Government and Ministers of Finance, by specially constituted Consultative Groups representing Commonwealth governments, with the support of the Secretariat. They involved the Commonwealth in a series of interactions with the key policy-setting committees of the IMF and the World Bank. This is one of the several areas where the Commonwealth expert groups' work in clarifying issues has helped to heighten the quality of discussion, and nudge the process along.

Not least among the achievements of the reports is that they have had an important bearing on how the Commonwealth Secretariat itself operates. The Jha report on industrial co-operation led to the establishment of the Industrial Development Unit. The report on the vulnerability of small states provided a powerful intellectual rationale for the operational emphasis of the Secretariat, including the CFTC, on small states' problems. It has helped to confirm a leadership role for the Secretariat in the international articulation of small states' issues. The study on structural adjustment and women emerged from, and reinforces, the work of the Secretariat on gender issues as well as on adjustment. The Menon report on technological change has led to the establishment, after Kuala Lumpur, of the Commonwealth Consultative Group for Technology Management, a network designed to provide advisory services to governments in the field of technology forecasting and assessment and R&D management. The Lever report on debt provided a powerful stimulus to the Secretariat's technical assistance work on debt management and its bulletin on capital markets.

As Secretary-General, I have had the opportunity to be associated closely with the work of all these groups. It has been my responsibility to set them up; to convey to them at the outset of their work the background to their appointment and the expectations of Commonwealth governments; and then to bring the reports to wider public attention within the Commonwealth and outside it.

In all of this I have had the good fortune to have had in the Secretariat's Economic Affairs Division a pool of professional officers, drawn from all parts of the Commonwealth, of extraordinarily high technical calibre and an equally high level of commitment to the Commonwealth's goal of responding effectively to the challenge to narrow the disparities in wealth between different sections of mankind which are too wide to be tolerated. To the Division's four Directors in the years of the Expert Groups' work—Frank Rampersad, Bimal Jalan, Vishnu Persaud and Vincent Cable—we all owe an immense debt. I know it has been a specially rewarding experience for them—as it has been for me—to witness the steady growth in international regard for the work of the Commonwealth to which the expert groups made such a substantial contribution.

Few organisations have the capacity and attributes to discharge the function the Commonwealth has assumed in seeking to bridge differences between the North and the South on economic issues and be a catalyst for global agreement. Outside the world forum of the United Nations, it is the Commonwealth that reflects most of the world's diversities and disparities. It has a strong interest in international issues, especially those concerned with poverty and development. At the same time, it functions with a degree of informality and understanding, based on common traditions and language. It is thus uniquely equipped to try to build bridges between the North and the South. These factors themselves justify the Commonwealth's commitment to this function —despite what appears to be less than encouragning progress in some areas.

Indeed, that insufficiency of progress enlarges our Commonwealth obligation to try harder. Some powerful trends have emerged in the decade and a half since the expert group mechanism was first employed. Some developing countries, especially in Asia, have made great strides in development. But the 1980s were a time of immense difficulty for the great majority of developing countries, particularly in Africa and Latin America. In many cases, domestic problems were aggravated substantially by weak commodity prices, protectionism in industrial countries, growing debt service burdens, and by negative net transfers of finance. In some countries, the gains in standards of health, education and social welfare achieved over previous decades were eroded and even reversed. The disparities which Commonwealth leaders found to be too great to be tolerated in 1971 have now become greater and less tolerable.

Industrial countries have been more resilient. They recovered from the recession of the early 1980s and have achieved a long period of uninterrupted growth. But growth is threatened by continuing imbalances in trade and inflationary pressures. Friction between major trading partners has been worsening. There is therefore continuing need to improve the functioning of the international economic system.

While these serious problems remain, there is a dearth of multilateral commitment to resolving them. Where industrial countries have come together to co-ordinate their efforts in economic management, their efforts have been directed largely to safeguarding their own interests, not promoting the interests of weaker nations. Multilateral institutions, which could have become a source of more effective support for developing countries, have been weakened by the lack of commitment to multilateralism by major countries, and inadequate financial support. The need for greater market orientation in economic organisation is erroneously seen as requiring less development co-operation. Moreover, the difficulties faced by developing countries in managing their balance of payments problems within a much harsher external environment have often been used to impose, as a price for limited international support, conditions which have brought severe hardship for their people.

Other developments are taking place whose significance for North-South relations can as yet be only dimly perceived but is potentially startling. The fundamental changes in Eastern Europe and the ending of the cold war have immense potential for creating a world in which there is less fear of conflict and less diversion of resources into armaments; but in the short term, development could become a global orphan. The already inadequate flows of investment to developing countries could be consciously diverted for geopolitical and market reasons. There has been a sea-change too in attitudes—worldwide—to politics and economics. The current enthusiasm for personal freedoms and democratic structures is welcome—even if not yet accompanied by a matching zeal for a democratic world structure. Similarly the broad emerging consensus on the need for a greater role for private initiative and for market-based economic systems has the potential to improve economic prospects in developing, as in developed, countries. But the process of political and economic reform in many developing countries is being severely undermined by adverse, sometimes hostile, international economic circumstances which little is being done to address. Another major change is the growing awareness of environmental problems, particularly enlarging global threats such as man-made climate change. The environmental crisis offers the potential to add a new dimension to North-South co-operation as its management requires the co-operation of all countries. But that need itself may not be perceived if developed countries fail to appreciate the extent to which poverty causes environmental stress in developing countries and therefore the degree to which poverty alleviation must be at the heart of our global response to the environmental crisis.

The Commonwealth has a unique opportunity to build on its efforts to nudge the world towards better management of its economic affairs in the interests of all its people. Such management requires greater sensitivity to global needs; it cannot, therefore, emerge from direction by a small group of the powerful. It must be fashioned by nations acting in partnership to secure their common future. In the absence of consensus, no change is durable. The reality of growing economic interdependence is making itself increasingly felt. The Commonwealth has the experience and capability to remain in the forefront of change. It has been an enduring example of voluntary international partnership encompassing almost as much variety as the world at large, and it has an inescapable obligation to point a way towards the larger partnership the world so desperately needs.

I hope the account that follows of the work of Commonwealth expert groups over the last 15 years will help to enlarge the potential of that work for solving the problems it addressed. But, more than that, I hope it will provide encouragement and reassurance that those problems can be solved. The consensus which the Commonwealth groups attained is within our wider human grasp.

Shridath S. Ramphal

Marlborough House,
London.
April 1990.

Chapter 1
Towards a New International Economic Order

In the immediate post-war period, significant steps were taken with the establishment of the Bretton Woods institutions – the International Bank for Reconstruction and Development (IBRD) and the International Monetary Fund (IMF) together with the General Agreement on Tariffs and Trade (GATT) to promote international co-operation in the economic field. These institutions and arrangements, however, reflected the political and economic realities of the time and their establishment did not involve the developing countries to any significant extent; nor were they structured to address the development needs of these countries. It was in the 1950s, with the progress of decolonisation, and mainly in response to the developing countries' expressed concerns and interests, that there was a shift in international attention to development needs through both bilateral and multilateral assistance programmes. Industrialised countries initiated aid programmes; the focus of the World Bank's operations changed from post-war European reconstruction to global development; and the United Nations technical assistance programme was established. Nevertheless, developmental issues remained peripheral in international economic relations.

In the mid-1950s developing countries began to perceive the need for unity among themselves to bring about a new type of relationship with the developed countries. The 29 countries which met at the Afro-Asian Conference in Bandung in 1955 called for "prior consultation of participating countries [amongst them] in international forums with a view to furthering their mutual economic interests". Coincidentally, 1955 also saw the beginning of a rapid increase in Afro-Asian membership of the United Nations, which stimulated awareness of common economic interests and of the need for a more co-ordinated approach in tackling development problems.

Developing countries began to perceive that they were not sharing sufficiently in the world's growing prosperity. Recognition that the terms on which they were participating in the expanding world trade were inequitable lay behind their call for a United Nations conference specifically to address trade and development issues; this led, despite opposition from some major industrialised countries, to the first United Nations Conference on Trade and Development (UNCTAD I) in Geneva in 1964. The Conference highlighted the need, inter alia, for a "very tenacious campaign to stabilise and increase the developing countries' income from primary commodities, to expand their exports of manufactured goods and to make more capital available for development programmes".

Experience of working together at the Conference enhanced the developing countries' appreciation both of their common interests and of the value of a united stand in advancing these interests. At the end of the Conference, they formed the Group of 77 – so-called because of their number at the time – to work for "the adoption of new attitudes and new approaches in the international economic field". The group pledged itself "to maintain, foster and strengthen . . . unity" and "to adopt all possible means to increase the contacts and consultations among themselves".

During the 1960s, Third World countries became increasingly conscious of themselves as an economic entity and a political force. Their perception of the international economic system, with its unequal distribution of decision-making powers, as being fundamentally inhospitable to their interests also increased and so also did their willingness to work together for structural changes in the world economy and reform of the institutional framework governing international economic relations. They began to co-ordinate their positions on economic issues and present a united front at multilateral fora; using their newly attained majority in the United Nations General Assembly, they succeeded in shifting the focus of the UN so that development became one of its primary concerns, a fact increasingly reflected in the UN resolutions of that time.

However, despite being in the majority in the UN fora, developing countries lacked the economic weight to oblige developed countries to engage in serious negotiations on structural changes in the world economy. Developing-country demands at that time were mainly directed at obtaining a substantial increase in aid and other financial flows on appropriate terms; establishment of institutional and other arrangements to stabilise and increase their export earnings; and provision of technical assistance. These were met only to the extent that they did not affect the fundamental interests of developed countries or were warranted by considerations of cold war politics. For instance, industrialised countries failed to meet the targets for aid which they had accepted in principle. Developing countries which had campaigned for a Special United Nations Fund for Economic Development, an international arrangement free of great power domination, had ultimately to be satisfied with the International Development Association (IDA) created as part of the World Bank Group, where the weighted system of voting left its control in the hands of developed countries. The proposal for a comprehensive international trade organisation was accommodated by conceding a Secretariat (UNCTAD) with, at that time, a limited budget and little operational capacity. When the

United Nations Development Programme was established, in 1965, developed countries ensured that they did not lose control by securing equal representation for developed and developing countries on the organisation's Governing Council.

Quest for change

During the early 1970s, developing countries became able to support their arguments with a degree of bargaining power they did not have before. While the Non-Aligned Movement and the Group of 77, founded in 1961 and 1963 respectively, increased their cohesion as a bargaining group, the steady dispersion of economic power and gradual emergence of a multipolar international system weakened the leadership role of the United States and encouraged disharmony in approaches to international economic problems. The breakdown of the international monetary system, raging inflation, a commodity boom, and, most of all, a fourfold increase in the price of oil created a crisis of economic management in the industrial countries. For the first time in the post-war period, developed countries were made strongly aware of the need to involve developing countries in efforts to resolve international economic problems.

The decision by the Organisation of Petroleum Exporting Countries (OPEC) to act jointly to raise the price of oil was the important new factor in the North-South equation. It was the first time that exporters of a major commodity, as against those who sell manufactured goods, had successfully set the price for their product in the world market, thus upsetting an important feature of existing trading relationships. The OPEC action hurt developed as well as developing countries which were not themselves oil producers. But the latter nevertheless drew encouragement from what the oil producers had achieved; they saw it as an effective use of economic power by a group of commodity producing developing countries and an example for other developing countries which as major producers of commodities may also have similar power.

The OPEC action raised the possibility of confrontation between developed and developing countries in the struggle for a new balance in economic relationships. It increased the significance of OPEC in the international economic system and induced some willingness on the part of developed countries to engage in a dialogue with developing countries. OPEC members, in a common front with non-oil developing countries, refused to discuss the issue of energy except as one of a cluster of issues of importance to developing countries. The fourth Non-Aligned Summit (Algiers, September 1973) outlined the conceptual framework of a New International Economic Order (NIEO).

These demands led to the convening of two Special Sessions of the UN

General Assembly - the Sixth Special Session held in March-April 1974 on the subject of 'raw materials and development', and the Seventh Special Session held in September 1975 on development co-operation.

The confluence of forces and events that led to the convening of the Sixth Special Session made it possible for the developing countries to get a Declaration adopted on the Establishment of a New International Economic Order setting out the basic principles for redressing the imbalances in the relations between developed and developing countries, together with a Programme of Action to make those principles operative.

The Declaration set forth the principles that should govern international economic relations in important areas including:

(i)   control over natural resources;
(ii)   regulation of the activities of transnational corporations;
(iii)   equitable prices for primary commodities and other exports of developing countries;
(iv)   reforms in the fields of money and finance;
(v)   access to markets for products of developing countries; and
(vi)   strengthening the science and technology capabilities of developing countries.

It also called for full participation of all countries in tackling world economic problems and strengthening the role of the United Nations in promoting international economic co-operation.

The Programme of Action envisaged measures to assist developing countries secure a substantial share in world industrial production and trade in manufactured products, effective control over their natural resources and greater participation in international decision-making processes. It also included measures to reform the "rules of the game" governing international economic relations in the fields of trade, technology, money and finance.

Immediately after the Sixth Special Session, the General Assembly adopted a Charter of Economic Rights and Duties of States, reinforcing the call for new "rules of the game", particularly with respect to sovereignty over natural resources and the authority of countries over economic agents operating in their territories. The Charter also designated resources outside national jurisdiction (e.g. on the seabed) to be exploited for the benefit of all states. The Charter was adopted after 79 different votes were taken. It encountered considerable opposition from developed countries.

The developed countries were, however, divided both in their opposition to the developing countries' demand for structural changes, and in dealing with the energy crisis which the developed countries regarded as much more critical than other issues. Their differences on the issue of energy helped the OPEC and other developing countries to consolidate their solidarity and insist on a link between energy and development issues. They soon reinforced the linkage: at a ministerial meeting in Algiers (January 1975), OPEC members emphasised that in return for any guarantees and commitments they were required to make on energy, developed countries would have to make major commitments to developing countries; and at a ministerial meeting in Dakar (February 1975), developing countries decided to adopt a united position at the special Conference on International Economic Co-operation (CIEC) held in Paris from 1975 to 1977. CIEC was itself a consequence of the greater influence OPEC and other developing countries had been able to achieve in international discussions. It envisaged negotiations between developed and developing countries in a representative forum of manageable numbers - 19 countries from the Third World (including eight from OPEC) and eight from the developed market economies (counting the European Community as a single entity). And although the prime interest of the developed countries concerned raw materials and, especially, energy, the conference adopted an integrated approach to problems and also covered money, finance, trade and technology.

The Third World's united stand led to a process of reassessment of their own position by developed countries. This process was given further impetus by the deepening world recession following the oil price increase and disturbances in the international monetary system. The developing countries were, of course, severely debilitated by the recession. The prices paid for most of their commodities—the mainstay of many countries—had collapsed; the terms of trade had turned sharply against them, squeezing their external purchasing power; and their payments deficits had become unmanageable. Industrialised countries, although better able to withstand the recession, had to contend with very high inflation, disorder in exchange markets and unemployment at levels unthinkable a few years earlier. The problems were so formidable that even in leading industrialised countries there were stirrings of doubt about the capacity of the world economic system to cope with the crisis and to engineer a recovery. There were also glimmers of recognition that constructive North-South co-operation and economic expansion in the Third World could help put the world economy back on a path to healthy growth.

Developed countries came round to the view (at an OECD meeting in July 1975) that confrontation with developing countries should be avoided and that efforts should be made to ensure that the Seventh Special Session was a success. But their commitment to structural reforms in the international economic system varied.

The Commonwealth gets involved

This was the setting when Commonwealth Heads of Government met in Jamaica in May 1975. The recession had damaged the economies of all their countries. Nearly a quarter of the developing member countries, with some 700 million people, were on the UN list of the most seriously affected countries. While there was a common interest in securing an early recovery from the recession, the new setbacks the developing countries had suffered had deepened their disenchantment with the workings of of the existing economic order.

The tone for the customary discussion on economic issues at the meeting was set at its opening session by the host Prime Minister, Mr Michael Manley. He recalled what Commonwealth leaders had said four years earlier in Singapore, in their Declaration of Commonwealth Principles, about the wide disparities in wealth between different sections of mankind, and went on to suggest that the call for a new economic order was a challenge to the Commonwealth to help in finding the techniques of political management that would lead to a progressive removal of those disparities.

Mr Manley said that the demand for change in the economic order confronted the world with a choice between dialogue and confrontation, and urged his colleagues to explore ways by which a device in favour of dialogue could be made more likely. He argued that the Commonwealth could make a meaningful contribution by helping mankind to search for solutions and that it ''may be uniquely blessed for this effort''.

The issue of a new economic order was the main focus of attention when Heads of Government turned to economic matters as their meeting progressed. Heads from all regions of the Commonwealth took part in the discussion, with prominent roles played by the British Prime Minister, Mr Harold (later Lord) Wilson, and the Prime Minister of Guyana, the late Forbes Burnham. It was the unanimous conclusion of the meeting that there was a need for 'immediate steps towards the creation of a rational and equitable new international economic order'. The leaders reaffirmed the statement in their Singapore Declaration that their aim was the progressive removal of the existing wide disparities in wealth, and decided to ask a Group of Experts to draw up for their consideration 'a comprehensive and interrelated programme of practical measures', designed to promote development and to increase the transfer of real resources to developing countries, and directed at closing the gap between the rich and the poor countries. Heads of Government agreed on detailed terms of reference for the Group, and appointed Mr Alister McIntyre, then Secretary-General of the Caribbean Community, as its chairman. The other nine members were appointed by the Commonwealth Secretary-General in consultation with governments (see Annex).

At its first meeting, in Ottawa in July 1975, the Group prepared an Interim Report, as requested by Heads of Government, in time for the annual meeting of Commonwealth Finance Ministers in August so that governments could take account of the Group's views in preparing for the Seventh Special Session of the UN General Assembly in September. A special contribution of the report was that it represented one of the early attempts to formulate a programme of reforms for the international economic system. Although the developing countries had pressed for a new economic order they had given little attention to refining a programme of measures that could constitute such an order.

Finance Ministers gave their general endorsement to the report. They decided to make it available to the international community in the context of the Seventh Special Session, where it played a part in the emergence of a wider degree of consensus on a new international economic order than had been evident at the Sixth Special Session in 1974.

After their second meeting, in London in March 1976, the experts issued a Further Report. This addressed the main issues to be discussed at the Fourth Session of the UNCTAD (UNCTAD IV) in Nairobi in May 1976. Both reports were presented to the Conference by the Commonwealth Secretary-General, who addressed its plenary session. They proved of acknowledged value to Commonwealth delegations who held seven consultations as the Conference progressed. Given wide distribution at UNCTAD IV (and elsewhere), the reports were also seen as an important input to the wider debate. Commonwealth Finance Ministers considered the Further Report at their 1976 meeting and agreed that the Group's proposals should be given due consideration in framing national and international policies on critical issues.

The Group's Final Report, prepared at a meeting in Ibadan, Nigeria, in March 1977, incorporated material from its earlier reports and extended the coverage to several additional issues. It made a large number of recommendations in several areas: commodities, food, industrialisation, finance, invisible earnings, co-operation among developing countries, and international institutions.

The recommendations were set in the context of the Group's unanimous view that 'a new and more equitable economic order must depend on progressive and radical change in the distribution of economic activity throughout the world', provide for 'genuine equality of opportunity and rewards between states', and 'bring new relationships of interdependence in place of the older patterns of dominance and dependence'.

The report, *Towards a New International Economic Order*, emphasised that such disparities as were represented by a per capita income of $200 and one of, say, $5,000 were socially disruptive and no longer accepted within countries; they should no longer be tolerated between countries.

The overriding aim of development, the report observed, should be to ensure that all people had an acceptable level of food, clothing, housing, health care and education. Development to achieve the satisfaction of these basic needs for all mankind would require fundamental structural changes in the economies of developing countries. But these countries could not achieve the necessary transformation by their own individual or collective efforts; it would require 'a substantially different pattern of international economic relations'. This provided the rationale for a new international economic order. It was wishful thinking, the group said, 'to suppose that solutions to global poverty could be found in case by case adjustments of an essentially marginal character'. The world community had therefore to demonstrate 'a new resolve for urgent and imaginative action'.

The Group regretted that this sense of urgency had not been fully reflected in the discussions held since the Seventh Special Session in September 1975. Meanwhile the external environment was making 'questions of survival take precedence over the pursuit of development' in developing countries. The report accordingly urged a 'comprehensive and early consensus on major issues', pointing out that the effective implementation of a new order would call for 'firm commitments from all parties to match rhetoric with action'.

In reviewing developments in the global discussions on an NIEO, the Group noted that while some progress had been made, there remained a wide area in which conclusions or agreements were not in sight. Further, in many cases, the agreements reached so far had been concerned with establishing broad principles; ways to convert them into programmes of action had not been decided and, in some case, not even considered. In this regard, the Group made a particularly valuable contribution by examining the technical validity and practicability of these proposals, and by suggesting the possible meeting ground between the developed and developing countries. The Commonwealth's initiative in establishing the Group was, in this respect, particularly well timed : its combined expertise and North-South synthesis placed the Group in an important position to influence the course of international economic discussions. The report indicated the main areas in which decisions or action remained to be taken, and voiced the hope that the time lost in taking the basic initial steps towards the reconstruction of the world economy would be speedily made up.

A particular value of the Group's reports is the contribution they made to an understanding of the issues, especially within national administrations. For many years after its publication, the Final Report was treated by many Commonwealth officials as a handbook on North-South issues. A number of its recommendations remained active proposals for change long after they were made. In terms of practical achievements, an evaluation of the role played by the reports is very difficult. Over the years some significant decisions have been taken in international development co-operation, but it would be difficult to trace the factors influencing such decisions except to say that Commonwealth contributions by the McIntyre and other Groups would have played their part in the evolution of thinking and policies which led to them. For example, the IMF Compensatory Financing Facility was liberalised in December 1975. In July of that year the Group's Interim Report had given much attention to this subject and pointed to some of the directions in which the reform of the Facility was actually undertaken. Also in areas such as indebtedness and the role of services in development, later events confirmed the perceptiveness of the McIntyre Group's analyses and recommendations. The Group's comments and recommendations on specific aspects of international economic relations are reflected in the discussion that follows on the substantive issues in North-South negotiations.

Commodity exports

Commodity issues had figured prominently in North-South negotiations, with developing countries consistently advocating the need to reduce fluctuations in commodity prices and to strengthen long-term price trends. The disappointment with the working of the commodity markets had been long-standing and there was wide agreement that both producers and consumers could benefit from a reduction in short-term fluctuations in prices.

The Commonwealth Group's examination of commodity policies took place against the background of their considerable interest to all Commonwealth countries. Britain was a leading importer of commodities, and the other developed member countries were all significant producers along with developing member countries. Commonwealth producers accounted for the major, or a substantial part of world exports of tea, cocoa, bauxite, tin, jute, rubber, wool, copper and groundnuts. Commonwealth concern with commodity issues had been reflected in the prominence given to them in discussions at the regular Heads of Government and Finance Ministers Meetings.

The McIntyre Group stressed that it was a matter of importance to the world as a whole—and of sheer survival to many developing countries—that commodity-exporting countries should be able to count on a high degree of stability and certainty in their income and look forward to expanding their earnings. They needed this stability to be able to make long-term and sustainable decisions in almost every area of their economic and social activities. Other factors, for example, inadequate domestic processing and transfer pricing by transnational companies, also harmed developing countries, but the adverse effects were not confined to developing countries alone.

The traditional approach to dealing with commodity price instability had been for exporting and importing countries to establish international commodity agreements (ICAs) incorporating mechanisms for regulating supply and holding buffer stocks. However, developing countries were convinced that, in addition to such arrangements for particular commodities, a more comprehensive and integrated approach was required to deal with the persistent problem of price instability. They therefore sought to establish an Integrated Programme for Commodities comprising a Common Fund to support measures to stabilize commodity prices through a comprehensive set of ICAs and to promote stabilization and improvement in other ways. The creation of buffer stocks for storable commodities with financing from the Common Fund was seen as an important necessity by developing countries. (Commodities were the focus of another Commonwelth Expert Group, see Chapter 6.)

While fully endorsing these proposals, the McIntyre Group also stressed the importance of strengthening the schemes for providing compensation for shortfalls in export earnings, as an essential complement to commodity price stabilisation through the operations of the ICAs and the Common Fund. The Group was well in advance of UN fora and developing countries generally in assigning this importance to compensatory financing, and its analysis helped the developing countries to recognise the role of compensatory financing in addressing the commodity problem. The Group's position also provided a basis for the decisions taken by the IMF in December 1975 to liberalise and improve its CFF. In retrospect, the Group's recommendation on the subject turned out to be one of its most significant contribution to the problem of commodity price instability.

Mention has been made of the contribution of the Group's interim reports to the discussion at UNCTAD IV in 1976, where an agreement on the Integrated Programme for Commodities was reached. The Common Fund negotiations were concluded in April 1980. But the mechanism is expected to become fully operational only in mid-1990. More importantly, the Fund, as it emerged, is unlikely to have a major impact on the commodity problem, as it has official resources of only $545 million, compared to the $1 billion proposed by UNCTAD. The effectiveness of ICAs, which the Common Fund will work through and which in turn are its potential clients, has significantly decreased over the last decade. All but one (natural rubber) have been, in effect, shorn of their operative mechanisms for market intervention, as a result either of inadequate funds to support buffer stock operations of an appropriate size (tin and cocoa), or of their member countries' inability to agree on quotas (sugar and coffee). Very little progress has been made on the other elements of the Integrated Programme, e.g. measures to enhance the developing countries' share in commodity processing, marketing and distribution. Efforts to establish, as part of the IPC, a new financing facility to compensate for shortfalls in export earnings have proved to be a non-starter. In the meantime, while the conception of the IMF's CFF has been widened, it is becoming, in practice, more restrictive as a mechanism for stabilising earnings from the export of commodities.

The problems besetting commodity producers have continued to worsen. Non-oil commodity prices declined sharply and remained at record low levels for much of the 1980s; in 1987 they were lower in real terms than at any time since the Great Depression of the 1930s. Between 1981 and 1986 developing countries were estimated to have lost about $70 billion in their earnings from commodity exports; this amounts to almost two-thirds of such earnings in 1980. The terms of trade of sub-Saharan Africa, and of the fifteen most heavily indebted countries, worsened in the 1980-88 period by around 30 per cent; and of twelve major oil exporters by about 65 per cent. Non-oil commodity prices recovered significantly towards the end of 1987 and into 1988 but this revival was not sustained in 1989. Moreover, the long-term downward trend in and instability of prices of some commodities are likely to continue. The technological and structural changes in the 1980s in industrial countries made them more efficient in the use of raw materials and energy and less material-intensive in their production processes, depressing the global demand for commodities. At the same time, in developing countries, foreign exchange shortages, currency devaluations and continuing constraints on the expansion of manufactured exports have encouraged an increase in the supply of commodities for export.

Money and finance

International monetary and financial issues had been one of the most important areas in the North-South dialogue. The negotiations in the field of finance were broadly concerned with

(i)   ways to increase the flow of resources to developing countries, particularly through multilateral institutions; and

(ii)   more basic reforms in the system, and in the individual institutions to give developing countries a greater degree of power-sharing.

The first element included proposals to increase the resources of multilateral institutions, notably the World Bank and the IMF, as well as changes in their policies to permit more relevant use of these resources by developing countries, while the reform issues ranged from voting rights within these institutions to surveillance of exchange rate and other policies.

The McIntyre Group addressed these issues against the background of the financing problems faced by developing countries in the mid-1970s. Apart from asking for a substantial increase in IMF quotas to meet the liquidity needs of developing countries, it pointed out that many developing countries had not made use of the IMF's regular facilities despite severe payments problems and recommended that the IMF should urgently review the factors inhibiting use of its facilities and introduce amendments, including discriminatory treatment in favour of the least developed countries, to make the Fund more responsive to needs. The Group called on the IMF to make successive allocations of Special Drawing Rights (SDRs) on a ''link'' basis, giving priority to developing countries in place of the prevailing quota basis. It also suggested further sales by the IMF from its gold stocks, giving part of the profits to developing countries.

In the case of the World Bank Group, the Commonwealth Experts stressed the importance of accelerating the growth of operations of the IDA; urged a general increase in the World Bank's capital to permit its lending operations to increase in real terms; and suggested enlargement of the Bank's range of activities to include support for interregional projects and trade expansion and for meeting the social and basic needs of developing countries.

There were indeed some improvements in the operations of these institutions in the 1970s : the IMF established the Oil Facility and its Compensatory Financing Facility was liberalised. During the 1970s, the World Bank Group achieved a rapid rate of growth in its operations, with IBRD/IDA commitments reaching over $12 billion in financial year 1981. However, during the 1980s, the attitude of some major industrial countries hardened towards multilateral institutions as vehicles for financial transfers to the South. For a number of complex reasons, during most of the 1980s the Bank had not only to moderate but even to reverse the earlier trend of rapid expansion in its lending operations, as the major shareholders became increasingly reluctant to provide additional resources. The Reagan Administration, particularly during its first term, adopted what many considered to be an ideologically rigid stance towards the Bretton Woods institutions to reverse what were seen as their liberal policies. This was reflected in less support for the IMF's Extended Fund Facility which offers long-term finance to facilitate structural adjustment; and the introduction of greater conditionalities and reduction in the automaticity of the CFF. In the World Bank group, there was a significant reduction in the level of replenishment of IDA VII. In fact, at present one of the issues causing great concern is that for the last three fiscal years (FY 1987-89) the World Bank has been a net receiver of funds from developing countries—and likely to be so in the next few years. These industrial-country policy orientations also affected other multilateral financial institutions and indeed the whole question of financial transfers to promote development.

At the IMF, most of the debate has been over conditionality. The developing countries have generally considered IMF policy prescriptions to be inappropriate to their own circumstances and a major obstacle to full use of Fund resources. They have therefore pressed for changes in conditionality practices as well as for the expansion of unconditional or low-conditional facilities. Notwithstanding the creation of new facilities and liberalisation of existing ones, conditionality became even more stringent in the mid-1980s, mainly because some major developed countries insisted on borrowing countries adopting stringent structural adjustment policies, and began to re-emphasise the temporary nature of Fund support which was considered inappropriate for long-term requirements. More recently there has been some progress in adapting conditions attached to the Fund programmes to specific conditions in different countries. It has also begun to show more sensitivity to development concerns and the requirements of growth-oriented adjustment in developing countries. It is relevant to recall that the McIntyre Group advocated in the mid-1970s a growth-oriented approach while recommending structural reforms in the economies of developing countries.

Among other issues, the most prominent was the role of SDRs. In 1976, it was agreed in principle to make the SDRs the principal reserve asset in the international monetary system. In practice, there had always been difficulties in agreeing on fresh allocations of SDRs, and there has been no allocation in the last eight years. SDRs have now, in fact, declined considerably as a proportion of total international reserves. The 'link' proposal, which seeks to take account of different needs among countries for purposes of allocation, has long been pressed by developing countries but opposed by the developed countries on grounds of principle and as being inflationary.

Attempts to change the decision-making and negotiating process in the Fund and the Bank through the establishment in 1975 of the Interim and Development Committees have also not been particularly successful. The issue of control of Bretton Woods institutions, however, has long affected the North's attitude to negotiations in this field with the result that often negotiations did not succeed in going beyond the stage of stating the respective positions. The developed countries have generally been reluctant to discuss financial and monetary issues outside the confines of the IMF and the World Bank, where the system of weighted voting gives these countries a dominant position. Although China and Saudi Arabia have become members of the IMF/World Bank Executive Boards, major industrial countries continue to dominate their decision making process. In fact, in the IMF the developing countries have even suffered an erosion of their relative voting strength. The developed countries also resisted moves to increase the responsibilities of the UN or other specialised agencies with regard to monetary and financial reforms. This posture proved to be a major obstacle in reaching an agreement on launching the Global Negotiations in the 1980s. (For an account of Commonwealth initiatives to promote international monetary and financial reforms, see Chapter 4.)

Help from the rich

Even though the developed countries had made a modest increase in their official development assistance (ODA) disbursements in the 1960s, the McIntyre Group (in 1977) felt that their contribution was too small in relation not only to the needs of the poor but also to the capacities of the rich. The Group urged all developed countries with per capita income of over $2,000 to meet without delay the UN target of 0.7 per cent of GNP and to step up aid to 1 per cent by 1980. To do so, the experts felt, would not be an intolerable burden; developed countries would need to devote only 5 per cent of the increase in their GNP over the next decade.

The idea of an aid target was first raised as early as the 1950s and, after a recommendation by the Pearson Commission, the 0.7 per cent of GNP target for aid disbursements was adopted within the framework of the UN's International Development Strategy for the 1970s. Most donors eventually announced commitments to this target but failed to specify when they might achieve it. The US (and Switzerland) have not even formally accepted the target. Western industrial countries as a group now give on average only 0.35 per cent. Only Norway, the Netherlands, Denmark and Sweden have so far passed the UN target initially set for fulfilment by 1972-75. The rate of growth in aid flows in fact slowed down in the 1980s from an average 4.5 per cent a year in 1976-81 to 3 per cent in the 1980s. The Development Assistance Committee (DAC), at its meeting in December 1989, stressed that aid should become a more central political concern in the 1990s, but conceded that aid from its members in the coming years was likely to increase at the modest rate of 2 per cent which would mean no overall progress in achieving the UN target. There is also the fear now that aid may be increasingly diverted from Third World countries to Eastern Europe.

Apart from the 0.7 per cent target, most of the North-South discussions on aid policy were concerned with sectoral priorities and the special needs of particularly disadvantaged countries. These were in general less controversial than many other aspects of North-South negotiations, even though they have not always led to concrete improvements. For example, in Paris at the 1981 UN Conference on the Least Developed Countries some developed countries agreed to work towards providing 0.15 per cent of their GNP to these countries and others agreed to double their aid; and under the UN Programme of Action for African Economic Recovery and Development (UNPAAERD) 1986-1990, there was a commitment to providing increased financial assistance to sub-Saharan African countries. While these two groups of countries undoubtedly received additional assistance, the amounts were well below the agreed targets. ODA to the least developed countries remained sluggish during the first half of the 1980s and in 1985 averaged 0.8 per cent; and only seven DAC member countries met or exceeded the target of 0.15 per cent. Net resource flows under UNPAAERD to Africa increased from $17.9 billion in 1985 to $19.9 billion in 1986 and $22.9 billion in 1987; but, in real terms, they were lower in 1986 and 1987 than in 1985.

Caught in the debt trap

The debt issue had already become a matter of global concern when the Commonwealth Group began its work. It identified two groups of countries as having particularly serious problems : the very poor and most seriously affected countries, and those which had increasingly relied for some years on commercial borrowings. The Group thus clearly foreshadowed the impending debt problems of the 1980s. It noted that rising debt service payments in the first half of the 1970s had forced many countries to cut back on their economic growth in order to keep up debt payments and reduce their external deficits. While supporting the proposal that donor countries should convert the ODA debts of the poorest countries to grants, the Group asked the IMF to provide credit facilities to meet debt service payments on short- and medium-term private debt. It also proposed a number of steps to improve the arrangements for debt rescheduling, emphasising that development needs should be taken into account in debt renegotiations.

The debt problem has since assumed far graver proportions. As the second half of 1970s witnessed a substantial debt explosion, with developing countries meeting vastly increased financial needs through borrowed funds, debt relief measures became the subject of protracted negotiations within the context of the North-South dialogue. In the 1980s the problem became much more severe, even threatening the stability of the international financial system. A Commonwealth Group of Experts commissioned to examine it, described the world's financial safety as being "balanced on a knife edge" (see Chapter 5). Despite a number of international initiatives, and some welcome measures of debt relief being implemented, the problems of the two categories of countries identified by the McIntyre Group continue to persist, if not worsen. The ratio of debt to export earnings for the 15 largest commercial debtors increased from 203 per cent in 1981 to 300 per cent in 1988 (having peaked at 349 per cent in 1986); and from 179 per cent to 331 per cent for sub-Saharan Africa. The sub-Saharan situation is projected by the IMF to worsen further.

Barriers against exports

North-South negotiations on trade matters concerned improvements in trading opportunities for developing countries as well as long-term reform of the trading system as a whole. Developing countries need secure access to the large and growing markets of the North, and the confidence that it would be available on a stable and continuing basis. They had therefore pressed the developed countries to improve, or at least to maintain, the export opportunities available to them.

The McIntyre Group regarded adequate access to the industrialised countries as being indispensable to the industrialisation of developing countries, and advocated the removal of trade barriers against the exports of manufactures from developing countries. In view of the longer-term benefits to both, it advocated relocation of some industries from developed to developing countries and asked the industrialised countries to devise measures to ease the process of relocation. Some, and in certain respects significant, progress was made in improving on a secure basis the access to markets for developing countries in the 1960s and early 1970s. In June 1966, a new section, Part IV, was added to the GATT dealing specifically with the trading problems of developing countries. Later, the Generalised System of Preferences (GSP) was agreed at UNCTAD II in 1968 and implemented unilaterally by developed countries from 1971. It has proved to be of some help in raising exports from developing countries. But its limitations, in terms of product coverage and of discrimination with respect to eligibility for benefit, became apparent as time passed. In the Tokyo Declaration in 1973 (which initiated the Tokyo Round of multilateral trade negotiations), the special interests of developing countries were recognised, and the adoption in 1979 of the so-called Enabling Clause legitimised certain types of preferential treatment for developing countries.

However, until the Uruguay Round, launched in 1986, there was little negotiation involving the developing countries in the successive rounds of multilateral trade negotiations. Much of the bargaining took place on a bilateral basis or among small groups, and as they were unable to offer reciprocal concessions of any great value, developing countries were relegated to being passive participants. They only received unilaterally determined concessions, e.g. improvements in GSP schemes, apart from those arising from the application of the most favoured nation principle. The developing countries have, however, been playing an active role in the Uruguay Round negotiations, but have been, concerned about its lack of balance, with inadequate attention given to areas of particular interest to them, although the negotiations are now well on the way to their scheduled completion in December 1990. They have also been concerned about pressure to negotiate on new issues (trade-related aspects of intellectual property rights and investment measures, and services). Agreements on these issues which do not adequately reflect the particular concerns of developing countries could have far-reaching consequences, not only for these countries' trading interests but also for their sovereignty. It may be noted that in the mid-1970s, when these issues were not on the international trade agenda, the McIntyre Group had signalled the important contribution some service sectors could make to the development of developing countries. (This contribution is now receiving increasing recognition.)

The 1980s witnessed a marked increase in protectionism in the main industrial countries, with the majority of restrictive measures directed at products in which developing countries had a strong competitive advantage or were the major exporters. These measures were taken despite repeated commitments—at the 1982 GATT Ministerial Meeting, UNCTADs VI and VII, and in the Uruguay Round itself—to observe a standstill on new protectionist measures and to roll back existing ones. According to the President of the World Bank, protectionist measures by industrial countries now cost developing countries twice what they receive in aid. IMF data indicate that the industrial countries in 1987 had increased their resort to trade protection, while developing countries had on balance done the opposite. There has also been increasing erosion of the credibility of the GATT system, largely through a combination of increased bilateralist and regional approaches to trade problems and evasion of GATT disciplines by the major developed countries. The Uruguay Round provides an important opportunity to reverse these protectionist and other negative trends and move towards an open, non-discriminatory and GATT-based international trading system. But achieving meaningful and mutually acceptable results, particularly on some of the difficult issues, would require significant movement from present positions, and enlightened leadership and good example from the developed countries. Failure of the Round could increase the continuing danger of a slide to further bilateralism, regionalism and protectionism in international trade relations.

Commonwealth concern with the problems of the international trading system in the 1980s led to the establishment of an expert group to address these problems (see Chapter 7).

Transferring technology

Technical progress has figured prominently in the development aspirations of developing countries and there has been particular concern about the terms and conditions of technological flows to their economies. While recognising the contribution transnational corporations (TNCs) can make in providing capital, technology and know-how for development, developing countries have been concerned about the impact of TNCs on the economic, political and social fabric of their societies. They have therefore sought to control the activities of TNCs by formal agreements which would ensure that the latter's contributions were maximised and the difficulties arising from their operations and activities minimised. The main interest of TNCs and the governments of their home countries has, on the other hand, been to protect their foreign investments and to ensure the security of supplies, particularly of raw materials.

The McIntyre Group emphasised that the transfer of technology to developing countries should be undertaken in a manner consistent with the stage of development and internal requirements of the country. It also suggested that the conditions of access to technology should be improved and stressed the need for a code of conduct to govern the transfer of technology under private control. It also believed that for developing countries to avail themselves of the resources of TNCs in a manner consistent with their aspirations, appropriate codes of conduct should be established governing TNCs activities and their trade practices.

Negotiations on a Code of Conduct onTNCs formally began at the UN in 1976. The main issues concerned were the basic objectives of the Code, the respective rights and obligations of governments and enterprises, and the procedures for implementation. Although the negotiations had been protracted, considerable progress was made, with agreement on many of the provisions of the Code. However, unbridgeable difference remained on some issues including the question of nationalisation and compensation, the relevance of international law and obligations under the Code in respect of national sovereignty, and the Code's legal status (whether mandatory or voluntary). Efforts to promote the resolution of the outstanding issues have so far been unsuccessful. The potential benefits for host and home countries alike from a code are likely to be considerable, particularly in the context of the changing policy orientations regarding the role of direct foreign investment, and its growing interrelationship with foreign trade flows.

Earlier, in the 1960s, developed and developing countries began to search for means of regulating arrangements relating to international transfers of technology. They agreed in 1976 at UNCTAD IV that a detailed code should be drafted and recommended that the General Assembly convene a UN Conference to negotiate on the basis of the draft. Negotiations on the Code of Conduct on the Transfer of Technology began at the UN in 1978. The main issues included the treatment of technology transfers between parent enterprises and their subsidiaries and affiliates; the law under which technology transfers should take place and disputes be settled; the legal nature of the Code; and the rights and obligations of parties to technology transfers. The developing countries generally stressed the importance of state intervention and intergovernmental regulation to promote technology transfers. The developed countries, on the other hand, generally sought to preserve the freedom of action of private enterprises supplying the technology. Between 1979 and 1985 the UN Conference on the Code agreed on practically all the substantive provisions of the Code, except for two major clauses: one, on the manner of treating restrictive practices, and the other, on the relevant applicable law and dispute settlement. But there the negotiations stalled, and the deadlock continued. The advent of new technologies in the 1980s, which could have a revolutionary impact on the progress of developing countries, has increased the relevance of the issues about which the Code is concerned.

During the 1960s, the developing countries also became increasingly aware of the need for international control of restrictive business practices by TNCs. After eight years of discussion and two UN negotiating conferences, agreement was reached at UNCTAD in April 1980 on a Set of Multilaterally Agreed Equitable Principles and Rules on Restrictive Business Practices, including those of TNCs, adversely affecting international trade. The agreement, however, was not mandatory and also excluded the restrictive business practices arising from the activities of TNC affiliates or subsidiaries. Moreover, difficulties also arose at the 1985 UN Conference to review the effectiveness of the Set's application and implementation and to consider and adopt proposals for its improvement and development. The developing countries contended that host governments as well as TNCs were increasingly resorting to restrictive business practices in international transactions, thereby increasing protectionism, and that the developed-country governments had relaxed their application of controls relating to such practices. The developed countries, on the other hand, argued that the Set covered actions by enterprises, not governments, and thus protectionist actions such as voluntary export restraints fell outside its scope. Other points of contention related to the Set's legal nature; the type of institutional machinery needed to monitor and control its implementation; and the provision of multilateral technical assistance to deal with the restrictive business practices as called for in the Set.

Making the United Nations more responsive

In the early 1970s, the reform and rationalisation of the activities of the UN system concerned with international economic co-operation and development became an issue of high priority. However, for developed and developing countries, the grounds for, and the directions of, preferred change were very different. The developing countries have been dissatisfied with the capacity of the UN system to deal with the problems of international economic relations impinging on development, while the developed countries were unhappy with the lack of co-ordination and coherence in the growth of the UN system since its establishment in 1945 and in its working and efficiency. As to the direction of change, developing countries saw restructuring as a means of enhancing their collective influence on the working of the system, while the developed countries focused mainly on institutional rationalisation and more efficient resource management.

While the McIntyre Group was at work, an expert group established in 1974 by the Sixth Special Session made proposals on structural reform of the UN system to make it "a more effective instrument for the establishment of a new, more rational international economic order". The Commonwealth Group expressed disappointment with the slow progress in taking decisions on the recommendations to restructure the UN system. Although in the following years some steps were taken to increase the efficiency of the system, so far there is hardly any progress in implementing what many would regard as the main recommendations of the UN group. These would inter alia entail strengthening the General Assembly to allow it to function as the principal forum for policy-making in international economic and social matters, establishing overall strategies, policies and priorities for the entire UN system, and reviewing and evaluating developments in other UN forums. Nor has there been any real movement towards implementing other important recommendations such as enabling UNCTAD to play a major negotiating role in the field of international trade and related areas of international economic co-operation; nor in revitalising the United Nations Economic and Social Council (ECOSOC) to make it the principal arm of the General Assembly in economic and social matters.

In the 1980s, retrogression in international development co-operation manifested itself in many ways. The United Nations itself was denied sufficient funding even to undertake its approved programmes and projects. Prompted by budgetary constraints and pressed by major contributors, notably the United States, to agree on administrative and financial reform, the General Assembly unanimously approved in 1987 far-reaching changes in the UN planning and budgetary process. The new guidelines agreed for decision-making on budgetary matters gave more authority to the Committee for Planning and Co-ordination, on which the major contributors were well represented. The Committee would reach decisions by 'consensus', thus giving each member of the Committee a decisive vote. The UN also evaluated its programmes and projects, and took a number of economy measures to reduce its budget. It was expected that having obtained important changes in the budget-making process, member states in arrears would pay their dues in full. However, while some brought their contributions up to date, the United States is still in substantial arrears. The UN's budgetary crisis remains. The Organisation's ineffective role in promoting international economic co-operation is in sharp contrast to its success in recent years in dealing with many long-standing global and regional political conflicts.

Stalemate in the North-South dialogue

When Commonwealth Heads of Government mandated the McIntyre Group in 1975 to draw up ''in the context of the current international dialogue, a comprehensive and inter-related programme of practical measures directed at closing the gap between the rich and the poor countries'', the North-South dialogue was in its most intensive phase. As discussed above, for the first time in the post-war period, the developed countries found it harder to resolve international economic problems without seriously involving the developing countries. The latter's goal of moving towards a new international economic order was taken seriously. Thus the events leading up to the Seventh Special Session of the General Assembly assured it a measure of success: the issue was no longer whether but what kind of structural changes in international economic relations were required. The session ended on a positive note and the outcome was favourably received by both developed and developing countries. It is true that discussion at that stage was general. On the core issues in international economic relations (e.g. money and finance, trade, and science and technology), negotiations were still to come. Areas of disagreement were glossed over with expressions of general objectives or principles. Nonetheless, the session helped to identify the common ground that existed between the North and the South and to outline some directions for further discussion of unresolved issues.

But from then onwards the dialogue became progressively less productive. At UNCTAD IV in May 1976, although an agreement was reached to launch negotiations to establish an Integrated Programme for Commodities, the Conference achieved only limited results, particularly in relation to the expectations raised by the Seventh Session. The intermittent negotiations over two years (1975-77) at CIEC ended with largely symbolic commitments on the part of the developed countries on the Common Fund, on special assistance to oil-importing developing countries, and on development assistance.

Thus, by the time the Commonwealth Group prepared its Final Report, the climate for international co-operation was again becoming unhelpful, and the North-South dialogue was moving towards an impasse. During the late 1970s and through the 1980s many attempts have been made, without much success, to reactivate the dialogue and especially to launch a global round of negotiations: at the fifth, sixth and seventh UNCTAD Conferences in 1979, 1983 and 1987 respectively; at the Eleventh Special Session of the General Assembly in 1980, as well as at all its subsequent regular sessions; by the Brandt Commission through the publication of its two reports in 1980 and 1983; at the Cancun Summit in 1981; by the Non-Aligned countries, particularly at their Seventh Summit in 1983; and by the Group of 77 countries at several ministerial meetings. While it was possible to reach a measure of agreement on the need for strengthening international co-operation and reform of economic relations, there was no success in efforts to bridge the fundamental differences on the extent of change required in the existing international economic system and institutions, and on the process to bring about that change. (For an account of the negotiating process itself, see Chapter 2.)

The international consensus necessary to mount a comprehensive assault on the problems of poverty and development did not exist in the latter half of the

1970s and in the 1980s. As the global economic environment worsened further in the early 1980s, industrial countries failed to adopt a comprehensive approach of the type recommended by the Commonwealth Group and many others to deal with the interrelated problems in the areas of money, finance and trade. While progress was made from time to time in limited areas in dealing with specific problems, the fundamental problem of growing poverty in large parts of the Third World remained unresolved and indeed was aggravated as in the early 1980s the world economy plunged into the deepest recession since the 1930s and created an acute and prolonged crisis for development in the Third World.

A major factor was the increased emphasis given to anti-inflationary policies in the developed countries. This was successful in reducing inflation and although it caused much unemployment, it led to a period of sustained if moderate growth in their economies. The experience of developing countries has, however, been varied and on the whole much less satisfactory. For the bulk of them the 1980s were notable for a severe set-back to their development process. This was particularly the case in the highly indebted Latin American countries and in sub-Saharan Africa. A large number of them experienced negative or negligible growth; many suffered deep and widespread declines in living standards. The disparities in wealth existing between different sections of mankind, which in the early 1970s Commonwealth Heads of Government found were ''too great to be tolerated'', worsened in the 1980s.

There has, however, been a remarkable diversity in the experience of developing countries in the 1980s. In South and East Asia, including China, the growth of GDP in the period 1981-88 averaged 7 per cent, and improved living standards for a large proportion of the poorest populations in the world. On the other hand in Latin America and in Africa, per capita incomes declined in the same period by 1 per cent and 3 per cent a year respectively. Per capita incomes, consumption and investment in sub-Saharan Africa are now no higher than twenty years ago; in the 15 most highly indebted developing countries, they have even fallen—by around a third—since that time. It is estimated that the number of people living in absolute poverty has increased from 820 million in 1980 to about 950 million in the late 1980s. The number of countries categorised as Least Developed rose from 31 at the beginning of the decade to 42 at the end.

The development crises in the 1980s in large parts of the Third World were mainly due to structural changes in the world economy, domestic policy weaknesses and lack of effective global management. Major industrial powers, in their concern to deal with the problems of inflation and low-growth in the 1970s and recession in the early 1980s, and to improve their national competitive positions generally, pursued unco-ordinated policies without regard for their wider international implications. The structural changes taking place in the world economy in the 1980s also meant that the developed countries and a few developing countries have intensified the trade, investment and technological links among themselves, at the expense of a large number of developing countries. The latter, for their part, lacked the necessary bargaining power to negotiate and secure a less unfavourable international environment for their development.

From the late 1970s onwards, leading industrial countries have increasingly resorted to the use of fora like the Western Economic Summits, meetings of the Groups of Five and Seven, the OECD, the IMF and the World Bank, where the Third World is either unrepresented or lacks influence, to address contemporary economic concerns such as payments imbalances, currency misalignments and other monetary issues, debt and protectionism. At the UN General Assembly, UNCTAD and UNIDO, negotiations concerned with development co-operation have largely been reduced to an unavoidable formality.

A continuing crisis

Many developing countries continue to face a development crisis. Any significant improvement in their situation will at some stage require greatly enhanced international attention to their difficulties. The increased awareness of global environmental problems and the need for the co-operation of all countries to deal with them is bringing home to everyone the reality of interdependence. The developing countries themselves are now in a better position to define the kind of international system that will contribute most to their development. In the evolution of thinking on development and its international dimensions, the McIntyre Group made a substantial contribution. What is now needed is recognition by major countries that a more activist international approach is needed to effectively attack the major problems of poverty and development.

Chapter 2
Negotiations:
the process also matters

Since North-South economic negotiations began in the mid-1960s, much has been written about the substantive issues under discussion. However, until the early 1980s very little attention was paid to the negotiating process itself. Form and substance cannot be clearly separated in a negotiation; if there is political will to negotiate on matters of substance, improvements in the process are not likely to lag behind. Nevertheless, it is important that where the will exists, it should not be allowed to be frustrated by deficiencies and rigidities in the negotiating process itself. Consistent, dependable and effective results are not possible without an efficient negotiating and decision-making process. Such a process would not only enable the political will to be translated into intergovernmental action but, by virtue of its tone and encouragement to constructive interaction between nation states, could strengthen the political resolve itself.

When Commonwealth Heads of Government met in Melbourne in October 1981, the world was in its worst economic crisis since the Great Depression of the 1930s. In addition to continuing problems of massive poverty, the world economy was beset by recession, inflation, high interest rates, and high levels of unemployment. GNP growth in the industrialised countries had fallen from an annual average of 3.5 per cent in 1976-79 to just about one per cent in 1980 and 1981.

The poorer developing countries faced the bleakest of prospects. The World Bank projected an annual growth rate of only 1.8 per cent in the 1980s for the low-income developing countries in its more optimistic 'high case' scenario, and of a mere 0.7 per cent in the more likely 'low case' scenario. By 1990 four out of every five sub-Saharan Africans were expected to be living below the line of absolute poverty.

At the same time, the climate for international co-operation became progressively less favourable in the second half of the 1970s. The more hopeful climate for North-South negotiations reflected at the UN General Assembly's Seventh Special Session in September 1975 gradually changed as the impact of OPEC action on the economies of industrial countries eased. UNCTAD IV made some headway but the major industrial countries became increasingly concerned with their domestic problems of rising inflation and emerging recession and began to become more inward-looking in dealing with them. The North-South negotiations intermittently conducted over two years (1975-77) at the Conference on International Economic Co-operation (CIEC) in Paris began with persistent disagreements on both the agenda and the broader purpose of the conference, and ended with a largely symbolic agreement. UNCTAD V in 1979 was particularly barren of results.

Nevertheless, repeated efforts have been made, both within the UN system and elsewhere, to revive the dialogue. Following an initiative by member countries of the Non-Aligned Movement, the UN General Assembly (UNGA) in 1979 decided to "launch at its special session in 1980 a round of global and sustained negotiations on international economic co-operation for development". It was also agreed that the negotiations, which would take place within the UN system, should be action oriented and ensure a coherent and integrated approach to problems in the fields of raw materials, energy, trade and development, and money and finance. Despite concerted efforts during 1980 in the Committee of the Whole of the UNGA, which was designated as the preparatory body for the Global Negotiations, and at the regular session of the UNGA, agreement could not be reached on the procedures to launch the negotiations. The North-South dialogue reached a virtual deadlock with the failure of the Eleventh Special Session of the UNGA in August-September 1981 to agree to launch the Global Negotiations.

The Brandt Commission, in its report *North-South: A Programme for Survival*, which was published in 1980, was concerned with the need for a more active and effective dialogue. It proposed that a selective summit meeting be held involving leaders of key countries from both the North and the South. This should seek to bring about a change in the international climate and enlarge the prospects for global agreement, provide guidelines and a new impetus for future negotiations, and launch ideas for a world recovery programme. Following the proposal, agreement was reached to hold a North-South Summit of a representative group of world leaders from eight industrialised countries and 14 developing countries in Cancun, Mexico, in October 1981. The importance of this Summit was further enhanced by the deadlock on Global Negotiations at the UN after the Brandt Commission had issued its report.

The discussions by Commonwealth Heads of Government on international economic issues at Melbourne were influenced by the fact that this North-South Summit was to follow two weeks later, with a third of its participants drawn from the Commonwealth. Three months earlier, North-South relations had received significant attention at the seventh annual Western Economic Summit in July 1981 in Ottawa, largely at the initiative of its Chairman, Canadian Prime Minister Pierre Trudeau. The outcome of the Ottawa meeting was seen as raising the chances of success at Cancun; particular significance was attached to the association of President Reagan with the Summit statement which looked forward to "constructive and substantive discussions" with developing countries, and affirming readiness "to participate in a mutually acceptable process of global negotiations in circumstances offering the prospects of meaningful progress".

The Australian Prime Minister, Mr Malcolm Fraser, in preparation for the Commonwealth meeting, held discussions with Mr. Trudeau and with President Lopez Portillo of Mexico, who was to be Co-Chairman of the Cancun Summit. The Commonwealth Secretary-General, who was a member of the Brandt Commission, was also involved in the pre-Cancun preparatory consultations.

Commonwealth Heads of Government, recognising that they were meeting at a time of world economic crisis, emphasised "the importance of promoting rapid economic growth and development, and of pursuing necessary structural and institutional changes in international economic relations, in order to create a more equitable economic order". They were conscious of the significance of their meeting for the outcome of the Cancun Summit and expressed the hope that "Cancun would make a bold start by putting international economic co-operation on a new and constructive course, and that it would unequivocally reaffirm the commitment to Global Negotiations". They also resolved "to make every effort to remove obstacles to an early start of the Global Negotiations".

The Commonwealth initiative

At the Melbourne meeting, Australia circulated an informal paper on obstacles to the negotiating process. It argued that problems of substance were not the only source of rigidities in negotiations. The way in which the negotiating process developed had also sometimes created difficulties which were particularly severe when the negotiations were at the level of officials. Heads of Government felt that there might be merit in examining the negotiating process to facilitate more rapid progress. They requested the Secretary-General to convene a high-level group of Commonwealth experts to report on the matters involved.

The Group of Experts was constituted under the chairmanship of Ambassador B. Akporode Clark, the then head of the Directorate of International Economic Co-operation and International Organisations in the Nigerian Ministry of External Affairs. Its members (see Annex) had extensive experience in the North-South negotiating process, many of them at the highest level.

The Group prepared its report, *The North-South Dialogue: Making It Work*, at its third meeting in August 1982. It was presented to the Commonwealth Finance Ministers Meeting in September 1982, and to Heads of Government when they met in New Delhi in November 1983. Heads of Government commended the experts for their valuable contribution to the promotion of North-South co-operation.

As with earlier documents of this nature and in accordance with the wish of Commonwealth governments, the report was made widely available to the international community. At the request of the Permanent Representatives of five Commonwealth governments at the United Nations in New York, made on behalf of the Commonwealth as a whole, it was circulated as a document of the 37th session of the UN General Assembly.

The Group's report generated considerable interest in international circles; its recommendations received a favourable reaction and were welcomed as timely. It broke fresh ground, being the first major study by a group of developed and developing country experts on the North-South negotiating process itself, as opposed to the substantive issues. It was much discussed in intergovernmental groups, international agencies and amongst development specialists. Significantly, the Group's report assisted the Brandt Commission in preparing the relevant sections of its programme of emergency measures for world recovery, published as *The Common Crisis* in February 1983. It was made an official document of UNCTAD VI in June-July 1983; there was much informal discussion and expressions of appreciation of the Group's recommendations, although an attempt during the early part of the meeting by a developed Commonwealth country to have them formally discussed by the Conference did not receive adequate developing-country support. The report also attracted much attention in OECD, especially in its committees concerned with development cooperation. In addition it generated much interest among Permanent Representatives in New York.

In their report, the Commonwealth experts examined the principal obstacles which had limited the success of North-South negotiations; identified the extent to which they were the result of shortcomings in the negotiating process itself or in the institutions for negotiation; and pressed for a programme of action which called on both developed and developing countries to take steps urgently to overcome the obstacles identified. They advocated basic changes in countries' negotiating approaches and attitudes to the North-South dialogue, and recommended specific measures to deal with the most serious institutional and procedural obstacles encountered in the negotiations.

The Group believed that the GATT Ministerial meeting in November 1982, UNCTAD VI, and the Global Negotiations would provide an early opportunity to make a new beginning in North-South relations. It hoped that the international community would seize the opportunity and endeavour to conduct the dialogue with changed attitudes and approaches. It was confident that the recommendations, if acted on, would have a catalytic effect in building confidence and demonstrating to both North and South the mutuality of interests which characterise their relations. However, the impact of the Group's work on the negotiating process has to be viewed in the context of the state of the dialogue itself, which in the 1980s began to fade in significance.

Attitudes and approaches

The Clark report provided a careful analysis of the factors which had led to a largely sterile dialogue between North and South. It saw postures and attitudes adopted by both developed and developing countries that were not conducive to progress in the negotiatons. These were partly the result of the complex and dramatic changes in the pattern of international relations since the Second World War. With the progress of decolonisation, developing countries emerged in the 1960s as significant actors on the international stage. They began to perceive that existing arrangements to promote international co-operation did not fully address their needs, and that they were not sharing sufficiently in the world's growing prosperity. As North-South negotiations evolved, the developing countries began demanding far-reaching changes in the international economic system.

The developed countries, while remaining receptive to calls for facilitating development, resisted the demand for fundamental changes to the system. Favouring the status quo, they adopted a passive approach to negotiations, leaving the South to make proposals for change.

In making their proposals the developing countries were politically rather than technically oriented. Tending to see international forces as largely responsible for their economic problems, they sometimes played down domestic factors. They regarded positive intervention as an important means of correcting defects in the international economic system. Some of their demands arose partly from the need to maintain their group solidarity and unity in the face of a diversity of interests.

The developed countries merely responded with tactically improvised reactions, often exaggerating the proposals' technical defects and delaying the process by an excessive demand for studies. They saw many of the South's proposals as dirigiste in essence and as a disguised means of effecting a redistribution of resources.

These conflicting approaches and attitudes gave the North-South negotiations a confrontational character and acted as a constraint to progress. The Commonwealth Group believed that, even when there were conflicts of interest, a constructive and serious attitude to negotiations and recognition of the need to accommodate differences would help to improve the tone of negotiations. It suggested that the first step should be directed towards breaking the vicious circle whereby the behaviour of each side had progressively increased the suspicion and scepticism of the other, and proposed basic

---

Box 1: Recommendations for North and South

The Commonwealth experts suggested that the South should:

- adopt a more restrained, persuasive and factually based negotiating style, and present its case for international reform and co-operation in terms of the mutual benefits which could result;
- fully acknowledge that economic progress in developing countries was as dependent on sound domestic policies as on international action;
- seriously examine the forms and procedures of its group system so as to optimise the prospects of progress in negotiations with the North; and
- recognise that frequent resort to voted resolutions and majority decisions encouraged dissonance, and that consensus would be preferable for decision making at international forums.

As far as changes in the approaches and attitudes by the North were concerned, the experts suggested that it should:

- accept the reality of the Third World as a continuing, significant and organised political entity, and work towards improving the effectiveness of multilateral and group diplomacy;
- accept that the greatly increased interdependence of the world economy required co-ordinated international action, and that positive, flexible, timely and bold policies are more effective in dealing with genuine and powerful agencies of change in international relations than passive resistance;
- recognise the need to modify the operation of market forces in some circumstances in the international sphere, as in their domestic economies; and
- adopt a discriminatory approach to proposals for reform and give a positive response to sound proposals to strengthen the forces of pragmatism and realism in the South.

---

changes in the approaches and attitudes to the negotiating process required of both North and South (see Box 1).

The economic and political environment in the 1980s did not encourage the North to consider any change in its attitudes and approaches. Its fear at the start of the decade of a crisis in international economic relations quickly receded with the dissipation of OPEC's power. There was an internally generated recovery in industrial economies, helped by the prolonged depression in commodity prices; 1989 was the seventh year of sustained, non-inflationary growth. The threat of the debt crisis to the stability of the financial system in the North also declined. And the North saw its increasing market orientation as requiring a less active dialogue with the South. Accordingly, it gave low priority to North-South issues. Indeed, some major countries adopted what developing countries saw as an increasingly negative posture in international fora on issues related to Third World development.

At the same time, the worsening economic conditions in many developing countries considerably reduced the Third World's bargaining power. As international economic relations are basically a reflection of changing power relations, the South became more realistic and conciliatory in its approaches to promoting the dialogue.

In recognition of the new balance of forces, the developing countries of the Group of 77 made serious efforts to improve its practices and procedures. For instance, in preparation for UNCTAD VI in 1983, after extensive internal consultations, the Group prepared its positions with some care and presented draft resolutions on all the agenda items well in advance of the Conference. There was also a noticeable change in its tone and approach, with emphasis on consensus and cooperation.

The developed market economy countries of Group B, however, seemed unwilling to enter promptly into a serious dialogue. They did not establish their position on the substantive issues until half-way through the Conference. As a result there were hardly any real negotiations, let alone progress, during the first two weeks. Because of the wide differences in group positions, negotiations during the second half were slow and protracted, remaining in virtual deadlock till almost the scheduled end of the Conference.

UNCTAD VI not only produced meagre results but also highlighted the obstacles to the negotiating process itself. The experience made many participants acknowledge the urgent need for improving the process along the lines recommended by the Commonwealth Group of Experts. UNCTAD VII (July-August 1987) saw some improvements, albeit small, in both respects. Largely because of a more realistic approach by the Group of 77, the agenda was restricted to four substantive items. Four committees—each dealing with one item—conducted their negotiations in a less formal setting, allowing individual countries to participate beside their group spokesmen. UNCTAD VII also agreed on a consolidated document—The Final Act—in place of separate resolutions on individual agenda items which, at earlier conferences, had often been adopted with varying degrees of reservation on the part of major industrial countries.

In recent years, both South and North have shown greater willingness to work constructively at the UN, perhaps as a result of the improved international political situation. At a special session of the General Assembly in June 1986, the South adopted a constructive, and in some ways conciliatory, approach and the North responded positively in adopting the UN Programme of Action for African Economic Recovery and Development, 1986-1990, to deal with the economic crisis in sub-Saharan Africa. Agreement was also reached for holding a special session in April 1990 devoted to "international economic co-operation, in particular to the revitalisation of economic growth and development of the developing countries". However, the emerging revival in North-South co-operation has yet to permeate beyond the UN General Assembly and its largely unfruitful resolutions.

The power game

The resistance of the North to sharing power in the management of international economic institutions, particularly those dealing with monetary and financial issues, and in the international economic system generally, has constituted perhaps the most important obstacle to progress in North-South negotiations. For obvious historical reasons, developing country interests were not adequately reflected in the management and policy-making bodies of the Bretton Woods institutions and the GATT when they were established. But the power structures of the Bretton Woods institutions failed to evolve to reflect the wider dispersion of economic power globally, mainly because of the reluctance of major developed countries to share control. This affected not only the developing countries but also the less powerful developed countries, although the consequences were more severe for the former as they had special interests and needs which demanded urgent action.

Developing countries accepted that the principle of equality in voting could not be adopted in the Bretton Woods institutions, if they were to continue to attract strong financial support from the developed countries. What concerned them was the minimalist approach to sharing power in response to the evolution of a more pluralistic international system.

The Commonwealth Group appreciated that the principle of one-country-one-vote would not be appropriate for these institutions. But it urged the North to recognise the necessity of moving towards some synthesis between the principle of numbers and that of weight. Decision making in the IMF and the World Bank continues, however, to be dominated by the major industrial countries. Indeed, the developing countries experienced an erosion of their voting strength vis-a-vis the developed countries in the IMF during the 1980s because of the way quota increases were allocated among member countries.

Power relations created other obstacles to progress in the negotiations. The North attempted to keep as much as possible of the dialogue in those institutions, e.g. the IMF and the World Bank, which are congenial to its interests and amenable to its control. The South, on the other hand, favoured the UNGA and its subsidiary bodies, such as UNCTAD and the UN Economic and Social Council, where they command a majority of the votes.

These institutional preferences of the North and the South had wide-ranging and adverse effects on the dialogue. They prevented co-ordinated consideration of interrelated issues such as money, finance, trade and development, particularly within the general forums like UNGA and UNCTAD conferences. The relative neglect by the GATT of their interests had led the developing countries to demand the establishment of UNCTAD. But when the latter came into being, power relations and institutional rivalries prevented the two institutions from co-ordinating their efforts in dealing with closely related issues. Institutional growth in the international system also led to an overlap in their responsibilities and competence, sometimes resulting in parallel but unco-ordinated consideration of related issues.

The developing countries' perception that the Bretton Woods institutions had not adequately addressed their needs, and the unsatisfactory progress on global economic problems at the CIEC and UNCTAD V, prompted them to politicise issues by seeking the involvement of the General Assembly in their resolution. These developments gave rise to the demand for a Global Round of Negotiations. The North, on the other hand, tried to by-pass the General Assembly or at the least minimise its central involvement, and insisted on preserving the "integrity" of the Bretton Woods institutions on monetary and financial issues.

The Commonwealth experts highlighted the impediments arising from the existing institutional arrangements. They recommended that the specialised agencies and other international organisations should avoid duplication and conflict, and that the Administrative Committee on Co-ordination of the UN intensify its efforts to co-ordinate their activities. They also suggested closer co-ordination and co-operation between UNCTAD and the Bretton Woods institutions. Interrelated issues, they argued, should be treated in a comprehensive manner and not be allowed to fall victim to compartmentalisation and institutional rivalry.

The experts recommended that Global Negotiations should be launched as soon as possible and that the General Assembly, being the most representative body in the international system, should play a central role. To make this consistent with the role and competence of the specialised agencies, they suggested that the General Assembly constitute a small, representative and efficient negotiating and overviewing body that would attract representatives of high political stature and professional competence.

Although the interrelationships between monetary, financial and trade issues, and their interactions with the development process are self-evident, it did not prove possible to treat them, as the Commonwealth experts suggested, "in a comprehensive manner". The North resisted any meaningful involvement of the UN or other specialised agencies in monetary, financial and trade issues, and insisted on their consideration only in the Bretton Woods institutions.

Thus, at UNCTAD VI almost all heads of delegation, with the notable exception of the USA and the IMF, emphasised the interdependence of national economies, the interactions that existed between the issues on the Conference agenda, and the link between recovery in the North and revitalisation of development in the South. Yet the Conference could not agree even on a modest set of practical measures. This was not only because of the retreat from multilateralism by some major powers, notably the United States, but also because of the North's institutional preferences. It simply did not regard UNCTAD as an appropriate or competent forum for substantive consideration of issues in money, finance and trade.

The relative roles of the UN and the World Bank/IMF have been among the major obstacles in reaching an agreement on launching the Global Negotiations since 1980. At the Cancun Summit and elsewhere, the US repeatedly insisted that it was prepared to consider these negotiations only if the powers and functions of the Bretton Woods institutions were respected and decisions reached by them accepted as final. For the same reasons, agreement also proved beyond reach on a proposal by the Seventh Non-Aligned Summit (March 1983) for an international conference, with universal participation, on money and finance for development; and on another, in 1984, by the Commonwealth for an international conference on the world's financial and trading system.

Towards the mid-1980s, support for international co-operation declined further, with changes in the attitude to major industrial countries towards development matters; the UN system was denied funds even to carry out approved programmes and projects; the United States and United Kingdom withdrew from UNESCO; UNCTAD's role and relevance were questioned, and at times its very existence seemed to be threatened.

Groups in action

The group system, which provides the framework and structure for most North-South negotiations, also impeded progress in some ways. The laborious task of establishing group positions, which was further complicated in the case of the Group of 77 because of the existence of three regional sub-groups, often cut into the time available for actual negotiation. The negotiating process was also not adequately served by certain procedures of the Group of 77, such as limited flexibility in the brief given to its spokesmen and inadequate co-ordination of approaches between its chapters in different centres. The significant imbalance in the capacities of the North and South to support their respective negotiating positions severely restricted the latter's ability effectively to engage the former in a meaningful dialogue. The North had the benefit of technical support from a number of institutions to strengthen its bargaining positions. The South lacked a permanent arrangement to provide technical support, had only limited access to specialised information, and was ill-equipped to make prompt and necessary changes in its negotiating positions in response to Northern counter-proposals.

In the case of the North, its less formalised consultative practices and insufficient co-ordination of member countries' positions, made the Group an elusive target and made it easier for its member countries to avoid precise commitments. The position of Group B (the North), and within it of the European Community in particular, was frequently determined at ministerial level prior to multilateral negotiations, and obtaining any changes in those positions during the negotiations often proved difficult. In the case of Group D (representing the East European countries) non-participation at some negotiations, and passive participation at others, militated against obtaining multilateral consensus.

Given the large number of countries involved, the Commonwealth experts fully recognised the need for the group system in multilateral diplomacy. To remove or minimise the obstacles it presented to the negotiating process, they recommended that the Group of 77 establish its own Secretariat to provide support, which would enable it to adopt a more technically sound negotiating style. They also suggested that negotiations should be conducted in small groups rather than in plenary bodies, the enforcement of strict time-limits for completion of negotiations, the use of full-time professional chairmen, and the maintenance of channels of communication between groups and between individual members of different groups.

Apart from the Commonwealth Group of Experts, others, including Mr Shridath Ramphal (1979) and the Tanzanian leader, Mr Julius Nyerere (1982), advocated on strong intellectual and political grounds the establishment of a Third World secretariat to provide technical support on a sustained basis to the South. However some prominent member countries of the Group of 77 were initially sceptical about the value of such an arrangement. There were also concerns that a secretariat might reduce flexibility in the working of the G77, and that difficulties could arise over its location and funding.

More recently, there has been growing recognition in the Group of 77 of the need for technical support. Arising from the 1981 Caracas Programme of Action on Economic Co-operation among Developing Countries (ECDC), the Group decided that its Chairman in New York should be assisted by a 'Corps of Assistants', staffed by officials from the Permanent Missions in New York. An 'ECDC Account' was also established to finance the Group's activities, to which each member country expected to make a voluntary, annual, minimum contribution of $1000. However, it is widely recognised that these arrangements have proved very inadequate compared to needs; there is now wider acknowledgement of the need for a Third World secretariat, and the issue has been receiving prominent attention by the South Commission. There are strong indications that the early establishment of a technical support system for the South will be a major recommendation of the Commission.

The Clark team of experts argued strongly for an acknowledgement by both North and South that not all issues are best dealt with inside the North-South framework. They suggested that the group system should be operated with some flexibility. Where the interests of delegations and the subject of negotiations cut across the group structure, this should be reflected in the negotiating process. The emergence of sub-groups comprising delegations from competing groups should be allowed in order to build bridges, particularly when an impasse develops.

The Commonwealth experts' recommendation—an innovative one when it was made—on the flexible use of the group system has been extensively put into effect in the Uruguay Round of multilateral trade negotiations, arguably the most important negotiations involving developed and developing countries in the 1980s. Many coalitions of countries across North-South lines have emerged to pursue their common interests.

A coalition of several middle-sized developed countries and a number of developing countries played a critical role before and during the Ministerial Meeting in Punta del Este (September 1986) in promoting agreement to launch the Round. Subsequently, and more significantly, the 'Cairns Group' of thirteen developed and developing countries, with substantial interests in the liberalisation of trade in agriculture, have acted in concert—with some success—first to place agriculture on the agenda, and then to play an important part in the negotiations. Some members of the Group (e.g. Brazil and Canada) have strongly held divergent views on other issues in the Round, but did not allow those differences to come in the way of pursuing their common interests in agriculture.

A group of developed and developing countries with interests in natural resource-based products has been meeting informally to co-ordinate its positions on such issues as market access and tariff escalation, and on how to address the demands from major importing countries for access to supplies. Fourteen small and medium-sized developed and developing countries (including Australia, Canada, Malaysia, New Zealand and Singapore from the Commonwealth), known as de la Paix Group, co-operate closely to seek ways of promoting their interests in systemic issues in the Round.

New opportunities

North-South negotiations over the last fifteen years have been largely a frustrating experience. New opportunities are however arising for a revival of the dialogue, as some emerging developments in the political, environmental and economic fields strongly underscore global interdependence and the need for greater international co-operation. Growing recognition of the urgent need for such co-operation in the environmental field, for example, could provide a basis for linkage with other issues. Some governments—of developed and developing countries—feel that a limited North-South summit process should now be established. There is need for developing countries to take advantage of this mood by reformulating the dialogue's intellectual foundations and reviewing the strategy for reviving it, based on the South Commission's work. Ensuring effectiveness by securing the North in a constructive and productive dialogue would then be vital. In that process, apart from the important contribution that could be made by the work of the South Commission, the report of the Commonwealth Group of Experts on improving the negotiating process remains of great relevance.

Chapter 3
Crisis in the world economy

When Commonwealth Heads of Government met in Lusaka in August 1979, there was anxious questioning whether the world economy was not on the brink of a disaster comparable to the Great Depression of the 1930s; this was prompted by an unusual combination of adverse trends which constituted a veritable economic crisis for both developed and developing countries.

For the first time in recorded world economic history, there had emerged the phenomenon of 'stagflation' in industrial countries - the co-existence of double-digit inflation with high unemployment and a slowdown in economic growth. After a long period of liberalisation through the 1950s and 1960s, trade barriers were raised on a number of imports in the 1970s. Oil prices had increased sharply. There had emerged large balance of payments disequilibria, of an order scarcely imaginable a decade earlier. Meanwhile, aid flows had remained far below agreed targets; and massive debts were run up by many developing countries to finance the unusually large deficits they faced on their external payments.

Worries about the deteriorating global economic situation were reflected in the discussions of Commonwealth leaders. According to their Communique they noted:

> with deep concern the deterioration ... in the world economic situation. A continuation of this trend would pose grave problems for all countries. The developing countries, especially the poorest among them, were facing particularly grim prospects and there was a real danger that unless remedial measures were taken urgently, existing disparities in income and wealth between the rich and poor would widen further.

It was against this background that they called for a group of Commonwealth experts to investigate the factors inhibiting structural change and a sustained improvement in economic growth in both developed and developing countries; assess the importance of and the relationship between possible constraints such as protection and adjustment policies, inflation, subsidies both on production and exports, fluctuations in commodity prices, availability and cost of energy resources including oil, and factors inhibiting investment, transfer of technology and international flows of official and private resources. They also called for an identification of specific measures which the Commonwealth and non-Commonwealth countries might take as a matter of urgency to reduce or eliminate such constraints.

The Group of ten experts (see Annex) constituted by the Secretary-General had Professor H.W. Arndt of Australia as its chairman. It issued its report, *The World Economic Crisis: A Commonwealth Perspective*, in June 1980. Besides the contextual significance of the report, some of the major issues that engaged the attention of the Group remain of importance, both for the Commonwealth and for the world as a whole.

Developments in the 1970s

Economic growth in industrial countries, after staging a limited recovery from an output decline in 1974-75, the first since World War II, slowed down again markedly by the decade's end, raising fears of another recession. For the decade as a whole, annual growth in industrial economies averaged only 3.4 per cent against 4.8 per cent in the previous decade. In the 1950s and 1960s the world economy had grown at a brisk pace due to a clutch of favourable circumstances: the importance attached to economic growth in government policy; a rapid expansion of international specialisation via trade flows, facilitated by significant reductions in trade barriers and stable international monetary conditions; the opportunities for Western Europe and Japan to catch up with US technology; the large-scale movement of labour from low-productivity agriculture to high-productivity manufacturing; a substantial acceleration in the international flows of capital and technology; and relatively cheap energy.

These positive influences did not continue into the 1970s; indeed, developments in such areas as energy were actually stunting economic growth. The marked slowdown in industrial country growth directly hurt developing countries, in particular those which were not oil exporters, as demand for their exports dropped. Developing countries as a group, whose economies expanded by 6.3 per cent a year in 1960-73, saw their annual growth rate slip to 5.2 per cent in 1973-79. Towards the end of the decade, with signs of industrial countries' economies growing slowly, and with a (second) major increase in oil prices by members of the Organisation of Petroleum Exporting Countries (OPEC), the world economy appeared to be on the verge of a major recession, soon after it showed signs of having recovered from the recessionary conditions that had afflicted it only a few years earlier.

The slowdown in industrial economies during the 1970s took place against a background of galloping inflation - an experience totally new to them. Inflation in OECD countries doubled compared to the previous decade, with the rates in Europe moving from under 5 per cent to over 10 per cent. This pace of inflation was indeed so unsettling that from about 1975 it was seen in most of the industrial countries as the major constraint on stepping up growth.

While inflationary pressures were present before 1973 they became much more pronounced with the four-fold increase in the price of oil during that year. This unforeseen – and massive – increase created serious problems for oil-importing countries, particularly with regard to their balance of payments. Some countries – mainly the industrial ones – were able to withstand its impact partly by expanding their exports to oil exporting countries. But many oil-importing developing countries had no such resilience; nor were the additional official bilateral and multilateral credit flows – such as through the IMF's newly established oil facilities – adequate to meet their enlarged financing needs. Some resource-rich middle-income developing countries – as well as some low-income countries that had enjoyed temporary booms in commodity export earnings – resorted to borrowing from commercial banks; but, for many there was no alternative but to allow a sharp contraction in economic activity, including development expenditure. Non-oil developing-country debt to private creditors rose from $48 billion in 1973 to $214 billion in 1980. Those that borrowed large sums from banks were soon destined to run into difficulties with an increasing inability to service their debt – bank loans being on relatively short maturities – and to continue to secure funding. The balance of payments of many major oil-importing industrial countries also went into significant deficit after the rise in oil prices, but these countries generally did not find it difficult to adjust to their payments deficits or to increase exports to the oil producers. The higher real price of energy had major repercussions on consumer welfare everywhere, most of all in the poorest of the developing countries whose capacity to cushion its impact was extremely limited.

Annual growth in the volume of world trade slowed from 8.5 per cent a year in 1963-73 to 4 per cent a year in 1973-80. One factor was the slowdown in economic activity, especially in the industrial economies; this precipitated an inward-looking, defensive reaction, seen most clearly in what has come to be known as the 'new protectionism' (see Chapter 7). In a climate of rapidly rising unemployment and virtual stagnation in output, industrial countries were increasingly tempted to resort to measures to 'protect' jobs and industry, and to ignore the fact that protectionism was not only costly but would thwart the very 'adjustment' that was necessary to stimulate output in the long run and that ''beggar-thy-neighbour'' policies were, ultimately, self-defeating.

The 1970s also saw the beginning of the threat to the stability of the international monetary system, and of the global economy itself, that has been posed by large payments imbalances. In fact, the breakdown of the Bretton Woods system of fixed exchange rates in 1971 was attributable to the persistent US balance of payments deficits and eventual US eschewal of convertibility of the dollar. The escalation of the price of energy had an immediate, and large, impact on the payments imbalances of both developing and industrial economies. The continuation of these imbalances not only contributed to deflationary pressures in the world economy; they also made it difficult to strive towards exchange rate stability so that volatility and misalignment became persistent features of exchange markets.

On three broad development-related issues – official development assistance (ODA), food security, and earnings from primary commodities - the 1970s saw increasing difficulties on the one hand, and little effective action on the other. On ODA, the decade was disappointing. At its beginning as well as at its end, ODA was a mere 0.35 per cent of industrial country GNP, only one half of the internationally agreed target. Moreover, by 1979, there was little prospect for improvement as the onset of recession led to inflation-curbing measures.

The global food crisis in 1973-7 was felt most harshly in the poorer – and often foreign exchange reserve bereft – oil-importing developing countries, a large proportion of whose people were already at or near subsistence levels. The increasingly large balance of payments deficits faced by a growing number of developing countries meant that the problem of world food security was not eliminated even when international prices of essential foods returned to more normal levels; developing countries were experiencing declining food self-sufficiency, with increases in production failing to keep pace with demand.

The 1970s also saw extreme volatility in the prices of many primary commodities which were of major export significance to developing countries and which also influenced inflation in industrial economies. For many non-oil commodities, particularly minerals, the early years of the decade brought a significant upswing in nominal prices, largely as a result of high demand in the industrial economies. Within a few years, however, many of the gains had been reversed, while a significant number of commodities were caught in a secular price decline. Though international efforts resulted in the UNCTAD's Integrated Programme for Commodities (IPC) being accepted in principle in the mid-1970s, its potential for commodity price stabilisation, diversification and other commodity development matters had not been realised at the end of the decade as it remained unimplemented. Despite the establishment by the IMF of two oil facilities and significant improvements in its Compensatory Financing Facility (CFF), as well as enchancement of the export stabilisation scheme,STABEX,under the Lomé Convention, the capacity of developing countries to pay for imports was subject to wide fluctuations.

By the end of the decade, there was clear, and increasing, evidence of systemic threats, inadequacy or impotence in vital areas, exacerbated by some of the major economies attempting to seek 'national' solutions to externally emanating problems or being unmindful of the international effects of national actions. Indeed, seldom had so many problems arisen at the same time: a slowing down of economic gowth; growing barriers to trade; a sharp rise in oil prices; and diminished prospects for financial flows to developing countries. As economic growth slowed down, the world found it increasingly difficult to deal with the tasks of containing inflation, maintaining full employment, sustaining development and alleviating poverty.

The era after World War II was characterised by a rapid increase in global interdependence as a result both of technological developments, particularly in transport and communications, and of policy and systemic changes. The growth in interdependence was especially strong in international trade, finance and investment. While these developments brought enormous benefits to the global economy – albeit not accruing equitably to all its constituent parts – they also brought problems. Individual countries, especially those that were relatively weak and more exposed, became even more vulnerable to developments in other parts of the global economy. The management of national economies became more difficult as the international business cycles became more synchronised.

The concept of growing global interdependence and the need for remedial action in relation to the crisis was meanwhile gaining wider attention. The Independent Commission on International Development Issues (the Brandt Commission), which concluded its work* not long after the establishment of the Commonwealth's Arndt Group, emphasised that global questions required global solutions and stressed global interdependence, especially between the developing countries and their developed counterparts.

The need for global negotiations was also taken up by the Non-Aligned Summit held in Havana in 1979. Indeed, global negotiations were integral to the discussions held under the aegis of the UN since 1977 on the establishment of a New International Economic Order.

The Arndt Group's report

These developments formed the backdrop to the work of the Arndt Group. While the Group was concerned with global economic issues, its principal focus was on the implications of the world economic crisis for developing countries. The Group stated:

> The burden of our argument has been that it is always the poor who are most vulnerable. The consequences of inflation and recession, of high oil prices and balance of payments deficits are grave enough for the high income industrialised countries. They are liable to be catastrophic for the developing countries, and

---

* See the Commission's report, *North-South: A Programme for Survival* (Pan Books London, 1980).

most of all for the poorest and least developed among them.

Within this framework, the Group addressed a number of related themes, and made recommendations, many of which are still relevant today.

Balance of payments problems

In the light of developments in the 1970s, and its assessment of prospects for the 1980s, the Group was seriously concerned about the outlook for financing the balance of payments deficits of the developing countries. It noted that the picture that emerged in early 1980 was that the oil importing countries, particularly the low-income countries and those of the middle-income countries which were not in a position to expand their manufactures, would require substantial additional amounts of finance (of up to $ 5 to 10 billion) in the following two years beyond what was likely to be forthcoming. There were doubts about the capacity and willingness of official and private sources of external finance to provide the funds on the required scale.

The Group emphasised that if the large balance of payments deficits were not financed, it would involve a serious cutback in the growth of imports and economic activity in non-oil developing countries; this would have adverse consequences not only for developing countries, but for developed countries as well.

In view of this, the Group argued for expanded programme lending (i.e. non-project-specific) by the World Bank and the establishment of a special facility in the IMF to lend to the poorer developing countries on first credit tranche conditions (i.e. with little conditionality imposed). An interesting suggestion made in respect of the least developed and low-income countries, which the Group feared would not be able to afford credit even on concessional terms, was that OPEC should consider giving them a rebate on oil bills for a limited period, say five years.

Members of the Group felt that more far-reaching measures were needed to generate adequate finance in the longer term, to bring about structural adjustments:

> We strongly recommend that negotiations between interested parties should commence without delay to take the following steps: first, the provision of facilities for reserve diversification by the oil-exporting countries, whether through off-market transactions which would, in effect, create a tier of secondary reserve assets for the participating central banks or through the proposed IMF Substitution Account; second, the on-lending of such funds via the IMF to developing countries on suitable terms for financing their deficits; and third, consideration of possible ways of making this on-lending process the starting point for long term programme financing.

The financing arrangements, the Group thought, could be given effect through existing institutions (e.g. World Bank and OPEC Special Fund);

alternatively, they might provide the starting point for a new institution such as the World Development Fund proposed by the Brandt Commission. (A substantive Appendix to the Group's report was devoted to an elaboration of the proposal on the establishment of the World Development Fund.)

Growing protectionism

A related concern of the Arndt Group was protectionism. It believed that one of the most damaging consequences of the slowdown of economic growth in the North had been an inward-looking defensive reaction epitomised by the new protectionism, particularly against developing country products. The Group saw this intensifying dangerously, with harmful consequences for potential exporters as well as protection-imposing countries. It pointed out:

> Beggar-my-neighbour policies—and much of the resort to higher protection by OECD countries in recent years has been against one another—are liable to spread recession. At the same time, restrictions on imports, whether through tariffs or quantitative controls or other measures to protect high-cost producers, by raising domestic prices add to the forces of cost-price inflation.

The Group believed that protectionism had been exacerbated, and rationalised, by the belief that unemployment rates in developed countries were highly sensitive to competition from developing countries, even though recent studies did not confirm such a view. On the contrary, they showed that manufacturing trade between industrialised countries and developing countries tended to have a positive effect on employment in the industrialised countries.

While the Tokyo Round of Multilateral Trade Negotiations had, to a degree, liberalised international trade, the Group was concerned about the drawbacks of the results of these negotiations: the continued existence of significant barriers in developed countries to developing country exports in processed forms; and the persistence of heavy protectionism in temperate agricultural products, especially in the European Community. The Group urged new initiatives to reduce protectionism and to enlarge access in developed country markets to developing country exports. It believed that the time was ripe for a comprehensive examination of the whole problem and for negotiation of access for the exports of developing countries to the markets of the industrialised countries, and that the global round of North-South negotiations which was to start in 1981 provided an opportunity.

In this, the Group found strong support for its views in the report of the Brandt Commission:

> The great challenge for the North is to cope with the difficulties of adjustment so that world trade can expand; to see its trade with the South not as a threat but as an opportunity; to see it not only as part of the problem but as part of the solution.

... The industrial countries cannot expect their valuable exports to developing countries to continue ... if they do not permit them to earn their way by selling their manufactures in return. The challenge to the South is to develop the necessary expertise and trained manpower to ensure their own industrial development and to respond positively to the trade opportunities created by improved access to the markets of the North.

The energy issue

Recognising that energy had emerged as one of the dominant issues, the Group noted that the unforeseen, sudden and sharp increases in the price of oil had created major problems for oil-importing countries, not only through their effect on costs and prices of output but also by giving rise to balance of payments problems.

The Group emphasised the urgent need for financial arrangements to provide adequate balance of payments support to oil-importing countries. It believed that in the longer run, however, the solution to the energy problem must lie in increasing energy availability through an accelerated programme of exploration and development of all forms of energy and by reducing the consumption of energy per unit of GDP through conservation measures. The Group, therefore, gave consideration to issues related to the supply and conservation of energy.

Noting that the exploration of energy reserves in developing countries had been held back by the lack of adequate investment, the Group argued that in order to promote a fair sharing of the gains between external investors and host countries, there was a case for a wider adoption in concession agreements of a 'resource rent tax' principle and other similar arrangements. Among these might be provision of official funds on concessional terms to assist developing countries to survey and assess their energy resource potential before entering into contracts with external investors. It believed that a further expansion of the World Bank's energy programme would also be desirable.

The Arndt Group also stressed the need to improve energy conservation. It believed that, to influence the trend of energy use, an appropriate pricing policy for energy, especially petroleum products, was indispensable and urgent, above all in the major oil-consuming countries. There was considerable potential for conserving energy by applying improved technologies for energy conversion, distribution and utilisation, as around two-thirds of the caloric content was lost in these processes. Increasing public awareness of the progress of energy technologies, and of the ability to acquire, absorb and supply them, was also crucial to energy conservation. That demanded not only greater efforts by governments but also increased international cooperation to establish or strengthen energy technology training facilities and the R & D institutions in developing countries.

The Experts called for a global energy policy in which oil exporters undertook not to reduce supplies arbitrarily, or to increase prices unpredictably or suddenly, and importers made efforts to restrain their demand. They emphasised, however, that such a global energy policy could only be part of an agreement on a broad range of North-South issues.

Inflation

Accelerating inflation in industrial countries posed a problem to all countries, the Group said, as the policies adopted by industrial countries to counter inflation had implications for developing countries as well. The harmful effects of inflation had been aggravated by changes in the attitudes of governments, which had become increasingly willing to acquiesce in a slowing down of growth as a means of curbing inflation.

Agreeing that there was no universal or agreed solution to inflation or consensus on the correct mix of policies, the Group noted the two schools of thought that were then prevalent: those who favoured operating on the money supply as a means of resisting inflationary pressure, and, those who sought to operate directly on costs and particularly on wage settlements. The Group believed that the difference between the two views largely reflected different judgements about facts which were uncertain, though differences of analysis and 'paradigm' also played a part. But, in the context of policy, the underlying issue was at what cost inflation could be halted or at least slowed down.

Above all, the Experts emphasised, countries must not lose sight of the impact they have on one another. They said:

> Inflation ....poses a serious threat to the prosperity and growth of the world economy. It represents a failure of economic management that will be costly to remedy and the cost will not fall only on those countries where the failure has been the greatest. Each country has to wrestle with the problem in terms of its own local circumstances and priorities. But it is hoped that in their efforts to put an end to one evil, countries do not lose sight of their obligations to one another or of the even greater evils that might be let loose on the world by too single-minded, over zealous and wrong-headed remedies.

Global interdependence

A major theme of the Group, running like a thread throughout its report, was the increasing interdependence within the global economy. This interdependence had major implications, especially when the world was at the threshold of an economic crisis. The Group observed that the interdependence of the world economy was so strong that there would be a good case for collective action even in times of prosperity and growth; but in the crisis then prevailing the case for joint action was compelling. The issue, as the Group saw it, was whether the structural changes and adjustments necessary to solve the current economic crisis and the problems of development would be accompanied by economic confusion and chaos, with each nation struggling in isolation to maximise its own gain, or whether they could be achieved in harmony on the basis of a global consensus for the mutual benefit of all nations.

Indeed, the harmful effects of policies being pursued in isolation by governments in their national interests were a major concern of the Group:

> Many of the problems in the international economy cannot be solved by nations acting on their own or in small groups. Attempts by individual countries to maximise their gains or minimise their losses in isolation may reduce the welfare of all. Unfortunately, that is the direction in which things are moving. There is now a dangerous tendency among the world's leading nations to seek their own solutions. More urgent even than agreement on particular problems is progress towards re-establishing rules for collective decision-making.

The issue of interdependence was to acquire increasing recognition at the Western Economic Summits in the 1980s (see Box 2, pages 56-7).

Other issues

The Group picked several other issues for immediate attention: official development assistance (ODA), food and commodities, among others. It was concerned at the disappointing levels of ODA at a time when developing countries needed increasing amounts of financing; it was apparent, the Group said, that an increase in aid would not fuel inflation in the developed economies as they had significant unutilised production capacity. Like the Brandt Commission immediately before it, the Arndt Group noted that any transfer of real resources from the North increased the South's demand for imports from the North and trade between the two groups of nations in general. The Group urged greater effort in the 1980s by developed countries to reach the aid target of 0.7 per cent of GNP to which they were committed.

It also pointed out that in the 1970s food production in many developing countries had failed to keep pace with population growth, and that developing country dependence on food imports was rising. The low-income countries, in particular, were experiencing problems and there was a need for a dependable system of international food security.

Describing the slow progress in the implementation of the Integrated Programme for Commodities (IPC) as one of the major failures of international economic policy in the 1970s, the Group emphasised that:

> a world-wide programme to stabilise commodity markets remains a test of the collective will of the international community to create an effective framework

for self-sustained economic development.

It noted that subsequent to the McIntyre Group's Report (see Chapter 1, above), which had urged a considerable improvement in institutional facilities (principally in the IMF's Compensatory Financing Facility), there had been a significant enlargement in the availability of compensatory finance to cover export earnings shortfalls. The Group felt, however, that insufficient progress had been made and urged "full support" for the Common Fund, the effective operation of its Second Window; and action to remedy the identified short-comings of the IMF's Compensatory Financing Facility.

Developments since 1980

It is almost a decade since the Arndt Group surveyed the world economic situation. Since then significant developments have occurred on many fronts. The major crisis that threatened to overwhelm the global economy at the time of its report did indeed manifest itself in the severe recession of 1980-82. In 1982, following the adoption of monetarist policies by major industrial countries and the steep rise in interest rates, industrial country GDP fell; and world trade shrank. These developments were to herald a much more constrained economic environment in the 1980s than in the 1970s - something the Arndt Group had warned against. As it feared, in most leading industrial economies concern over inflation took precedence over all other objectives, including growth and the eradication of unemployment. Their deflationary policies had a severe impact on the economies of developing countries, causing significant declines in real commodity prices, substantial erosion in the terms of trade. With the significant increases in their debt service burdens, a debt crisis ensued and many developing countries were turned into net exporters of capital.

Indeed, deepening concern about the continuing deterioration of the international economic system - particularly with regard to finance and trade - led Commonwealth Finance Ministers in 1982 to call for an examination of the international financial and trading system; this was to result in the Helleiner Group Report, *Towards a New Bretton Woods: Challenges for the World Financial and Trading System* (see Chapter 4).

While the economic problems confronting developing countries did turn out to be overwhelming, to a degree not foreseen even by the Arndt Group, thinking on policy reform - and on steps needed to rehabilitate developing countries - did begin to reflect the Group's own views in some respects. Control of inflation remained a key objective of policy in industrial countries, but there was growing recognition by them that they should take account of the impact their policies could have on other countries. This was evident at the Western Economic Summits, and at the OECD ministerial and Heads of

---

Box 2: Efforts at economic co-operation among industrial countries

Due to concern over the marked slowdown in activity in the major industrial economies, the difficulties being encountered in reducing the major imbalances between them, exchange rate instability among the major currencies and increasing protectionist pressures, the leading industrial countries have shown an increasing commitment in recent years to co-ordination of their economic policies. Important developments in this area include the following:

Plaza Agreement (September 1985): The US, Britain, France, Japan and West Germany (G-5) launched a co-ordinated programme to drive the dollar down in relation to other currencies to let exchange rates reflect economic fundamentals better.

Tokyo Summit (May 1986): It was decided that the Finance Ministers of the Group of Seven (G7 - the G5 plus Italy and Canada), would work together more closely and meet more frequently between the annual economic summits. The G7 in conjunction with the Managing Director of the IMF would review their national economic objectives and forecasts at least once a year, taking into account such indicators as GNP growth, inflation, interest rates, unemployment, fiscal deficit ratios, current account and trade balances, monetary growth, reserves and exchange rates.

Louvre Accord (February 1987): The G-5 Finance Ministers declared that the dollar, which had fallen about 40 per cent from its 1985 peak, had declined enough. They agreed on steps to stabilize the dollar within a range but did not announce the range. Countries with external surpluses agreed to stimulate domestic investment and consumption so as to reduce their

---

Government meetings. It was also evident in action within the Group of Five and Group of Seven leading industrial countries, which intensified co-operation on exchange rate management (c.f. the 1983 Williamsburg summit, and the Plaza and Louvre accords).

Yet, co-operation is still at a very nascent stage. Effective surveillance of national policies by the IMF is far from being in place. The IMF, as part of its world economic outlook exercises, now assesses the consistency of policies among the major industrial countries, and also considers their impact on developing country prospects. While these exercises provide a background for discussions at the IMF's Interim Committee—and the G7 meetings—the

savings surpluses. The US, for its part, agreed to fiscal contraction to reduce its external deficit. Japan adopted a supplementary budget (approximately $40 bn) for additional public investment expenditure, and a major public works programme was announced in May 1987. Japan also launched a major plan to recycle a part of its surplus to developing countries during the next three years. The Federal Republic of Germany announced steps to stimulate its economy through a tax reduction programme phased over three years.

Group of Seven Meeting (April 1987): Finance ministers reaffirmed the Louvre Accord to stabilize exchange rates and pledged to adjust economic policies to reduce trade imbalances.

Venice Summit (June 1987): Heads of the G-7 nations endorsed the Louvre Accord and approved specific plans for policy co-ordination based on economic indicators.

Toronto Summit (June 1988): Heads of the G-7 nations reached a consensus on rescheduling official debt of the poorest countries, particularly those in sub-Saharan Africa. They also emphasised the undersirability of excessive fluctuation of exchange rates.

Paris Summit (July 1989): The G-7 leaders expressed concern about the threat of inflation; and stressed the need for further progress in adjustment of external imbalances, with surplus and deficit countries adopting appropriate policies.

Over the years, co-ordination among major industrial countries was thus intensified. But it still remains episodic rather than continuous and short-term rather than medium-term, with little or weak monitoring of follow-up action to commitments.

translation to policy implementation remains weak.

The trend towards 'new protectionism', against which the Group warned, was reinforced rather than weakened in the 1980s, as particular sectors in industrial countries sought to safeguard their employment levels. Indeed, the greater resort to protectionism was such as to deepen Commonwealth concern, resulting in the establishment of a Commonwealth Expert Group on that subject (see Chapter 7).

There has also been little cause for comfort over the provision of finance to meet balance of payments deficits, which in the event turned out to be far larger than foreseen by the Arndt Group. The drop in export earnings of developing countries, the steep rise in interest rates and the sudden contraction and cessation in net private capital flows following the Mexican debt crisis resulted in acute payments difficulties (see Chapter V). These could have been eased only by compensating increases in official finance. While some advances were made along the lines suggested by the Arndt Group, the scale of effort remained inadequate. The Group's suggestion for increased assistance, either through existing institutions or through a new institution such as the proposed World Development Fund, remained unfulfilled. OPEC countries, envisaged as one of the main sources of support for the Fund, found their supluses diminishing rapidly, as the oil price itself collapsed. Instead, a few industrial countries, mainly Japan and West Germany, emerged with large surpluses. The idea that a part of these surpluses should be recycled to developing countries has been put into practice only marginally; the large current account deficits which emerged in the 1980s in the United States absorbed most of these surpluses.

While the volume of resource flows urged by the Arndt Group was not forthcoming, there has been some recognition of the case – also pressed by the Group – for larger flows of concessional finance from multilateral institutions and of programme lending by the World Bank and others. In the early and mid-eighties there were major setbacks over concessional funding, especially with regard to the seventh replenishment of the International Development Association, but later, matters improved somewhat (see Chapter 4). The African Development Fund has been provided $2.7 billion for 1988-90, nearly double what was available under its immediate predecessor arrangement. Healthy as these developments are, they are still insufficient, given the acute financing needs of a very large number of low income countries. It is in this context that there was wide recognition of the need to increase ODA to assist the resumption of economic growth in much of Africa; in 1987 the UN's Wass Report identified a gap of $2 billion a year between available finance and what was needed to revive growth on a modest scale in sub-Saharan Africa (excluding Nigeria).*

There has also been growing awareness of the need for international action to harness private sector financing – largely in the form of direct investment – for development. The World Bank and the IMF, in addition to encouraging larger flows of such resources indirectly through their various country programmes, particularly those related to adjustment, have also become more directly involved (see Chapter 4). There is also a more receptive attitude towards private foreign investment in many developing countries. Direct private investment flows to developing countries had reached about $11

---

* United Nations, *Financing Africa's Recovery: Report and Recommendations of the Advisory Group on Financial Flows for Africa* (New York: 1986) pp.45-47.

billion in 1989, up from S5 billion in 1985 (at 1987 prices and exchange rates).

Complementing the Commonwealth's role in contributing to the search for international consensus on measures to spur recovery, the Secretariat has undertaken considerable work - through seminars for senior officials, a Small States Exposition in two major Canadian cities in 1987, and the publication of several country case studies - in the field of private foreign investment. It has also issued a report on mobilising private capital for development, which stemmed directly from a request by Commonwealth Finance Ministers in 1987 for a study of how Commonwealth capital importing countries could be helped to improve their access to private foreign capital. Finance Ministers at their 1988 Meeting accepted in principle the report's proposal for the establishment of a Commonwealth Equity Fund as a vehicle for private portfolio investment and asked for consultations to be held on its feasibility. This work was carried further. A fully commercial Fund, with a capitalisation of at least S100 million, will be launched in mid-1990 (see Chapter 8).

Among the other issues addressed by the Arndt Group, the decline in oil prices has pushed the energy issue from the forefront of global attention, and consideration of a world energy policy, as suggested by the Group, has not been taken up. Oil prices remain critical, however, and the wisdom of not addressing the issue as suggested by the Group is far from clear.

On commodities, there has been some progress on the the Common Fund whose treaty entered into force in mid-1988, and which is likely to become operational in mid-1990; it is however, doubtful whether the Fund will operate in the manner orginally envisaged (see Chapter 6). The IMF's Compensatory Finance Facility (CFF), whose scope the Group—and the Brandt Commission —wished to see expanded, has been ''extended'' to cover the excess cost of cereal imports. Despite this and other marginal improvements, only about one eighth of the $12 billion average shortfall in annual export earnings of developing countries from non-fuel primary commodities during 1981-86 was compensated for by the IMF facility and the EEC's much smaller STABEX/ SYSMIN arrangements. Under Lome IV, concluded in December 1989, the latter attracted additional resources, and assistance under these arrangements will now be on a grant basis.

In 1988, the IMF's Compensatory and Contingency Financing Facility (CCFF) was set up to embrace the CFF as well as cover other externally-emanating contingencies, particularly those associated with increases in interest rates. While in principle this is a welcome arrangement, it has the potential of reducing the already inadequate access for drawings to meet export earnings shortfalls.

Inadequate global and national action has resulted in increasing numbers of people in developing countries—now well over 700 million—living in a state of undernourishment. As the FAO has put it, there continues to be ''a paradox of hunger in the midst of abundance''; in the early 1980s world food stocks grew while many went hungry. While useful roles have been played by the International Emergency Food Reserve, the IMF's CFF, and multilateral and bilateral aid agencies, particularly in emergencies, these have not provided adequate food security. With noteworthy exceptions, largely in Asia, most developing countries still substantially depend on external sources for food or inputs and capital goods for producing food, and the generally unsatisfactory levels of foreign currency receipts have constrained the availability of food. Until well into the 1980s, a large number of developing countries maintained overvalued exchange rates, and paid unduly low prices for food purchased from farmers by monopoly state trading organisations. These cheap food policies, which favoured urban—and politically more powerful—people, held down food production. This was especially so in Africa, where the annual increase of 2.1 per cent in food production is well below its rate of population growth. In most countries, however, policy shortcomings are now being remedied, often in the context of Bank-Fund structural adjustment programmes. Nevertheless, several million people in developing countries continue to suffer from the lack of food security, because they are too poor. There continues to be a case for a dependable system of world food security based on externally provided resources.

Too few improvements

The Commonwealth's Arndt Group (like the contemporaneous Brandt Commission) was particularly concerned about the need for urgent and effective international action to avoid a major global economic collapse such as the Great Depression of the 1930s. The early 1980s witnessed an alarming deterioration in economic activity and trade and a concomitant rise in unemployment; an intensification of protectionism; a global debt crisis of unprecedented magnitude; greatly diminished commodity export earnings; further impoverishment of the already poor; a halt to the development process in many countries; and inadequate systemic responses. And subsequent years have seen little significant amelioration in many of these areas, and a deterioration in some. The improvements that have taken place—a number of systemic-related ones in the direction indicated by the Arndt and other Commonwealth Expert Groups—are as yet insufficient to restore basic viability to most of the large number of poor or heavily-indebted developing countries, let alone to restart the development process in many of them. As in the late 1970s, no less to-day, there is a pressing need for remedial action to be taken internationally—particularly on systemic issues—in the context of a genuinely global approach with particular attention to development problems, as urged by the Arndt Group.

Chapter 4
Money and finance for development

In the early 1980s, there was widespread concern at the disorder and recession in the world economy, as had been feared by the Arndt Group (see Chapter 3). The inadequacies of the world's monetary and financial system and institutions in keeping the world economy on an even keel became increasingly manifest. The growing pressure for consideration of long-term, systemic issues (see Chapters 1 and 2) acquired greater urgency in the light of economic events in the early 1980s. When Commonwealth Finance Ministers met in London in August 1982, the world's leading industrial countries were preoccupied with policies to curb inflation and inflationary expectations. Interest rates, raised sharply since 1980 as part of these policies, remained at historically high levels, at or above 13 per cent, in a number of these countries.

Industrial countries registered a fall in their combined GDP during 1982, and the volume of world trade contracted. Developing countries were inevitably caught up in this slowing down of the world economy; high interest rates and declining export earnings made the situation of some countries which had borrowed extensively to finance development particularly precarious.

At their 1982 meeting, Finance Ministers were therefore much concerned not only over the immediate world economic situation, but also over what they saw as the failure of the world's monetary, financial and trading institutions, i.e. the Bretton Woods institutions - which had their birth in the post-war years - to underpin stability. A widely shared view was that unco-ordinated national policies, together with the weakness of the international organisations, were responsible for much of the economic malaise in the world. The problems were most acute for developing countries that had to import oil, for whom the contractionary policies of major countries had brought declining commodity prices, lower exports and greatly increased interest payments on their external debt. In many countries, worsening economic conditions for large sections of the people had created a situation in which national political stability was itself at risk. It was felt that the failure to address the inadequacy of the existing system had been crucial and that this must be addressed immediately.

These concerns led Finance Ministers to conclude in their communique:

in view of the vast politico-economic changes which have taken place since the establishment of the Bretton Woods institutions, there was an urgent need for a new overall examination of the international trade and payments systems as a whole and in particular the role of the international economic institutions.

Ministers went on to call for an expert group to look into the possibilities for reforming the world's monetary and financial system. The Group of nine persons constituted by the Secretary-General in response to this call brought together knowledge and experience at the highest level in such fields as banking, investment finance and international economic policy (see Annex); Professor Gerry Helleiner of the University of Toronto, Canada, was its chairman.

The Bretton Woods system in trouble

The International Monetary and Financial Conference at Bretton Woods in New Hampshire in the United States in 1944 was a landmark event. Its objective was to fashion a financial and monetary system that would avert the kind of disastrous slump in economic activity which had engulfed the world in the 1930s and promote prosperity worldwide through the growth of world trade and investment, generation of high levels of employment and real income, and the development of the productive resources of all countries. With these objectives, two institutions, the International Monetary Fund (IMF) and the World Bank, were established; another—the International Trade Organisation (ITO)—was also conceived, to complete a triad of institutions, but non-ratification by the US Senate prevented its establishment. The General Agreement on Tariffs and Trade (GATT) was founded instead in 1948, but with considerably narrower scope than had been envisaged for the ITO.

The establishment of the Bretton Woods institutions and the stable system of exchange rates and the liberalisation of trade they underpinned contributed to a remarkable period of growth in the 1950s and 1960s, encouraging a level of international co-operation far in advance of anything achieved in the pre-war period. But with the onset of the 1970s, the system came under strain and soon collapsed.

There was growing support for the view that a new system, with reformed institutions, should be devised. The changes which made such a consideration necessary were several; some were of a long-run or a permanent character, while others were the product of more recent international events.

Among the long-term changes were those that had increased global interdependence, through the dramatic and sustained expansion in international trade, finance and investment, as well as in labour flows; and a rise in the number of countries participating in international economic organisations, and the emergence of a multipolar world. The Bretton Woods institutions, and their decision-making procedures, failed to keep pace with these developments. Solutions to global economic difficulties continued to be pursued almost wholly through independent national policies, as had been noted by an earlier Commonwealth Expert Group (see Chapter 3).

Superimposed over these long-term changes were those resulting from more recent events. The oil price increases of 1973-74 and 1979-80—and the deep recessions of 1974-75 and 1980-82—required structural adjustments in the economies of many oil-importing countries which therefore needed balance-of-payments finance on a much larger scale and over a longer period than the IMF had previously provided.

The multilateral financial institutions, notably the IMF, were able to respond only to a limited extent to the new needs for longer-term and expanded balance-of-payments finance. For the bulk of their new requirements of finance, developing countries turned to a previously little used source: commercial banks. These were at that time eager to lend to Third World countries.

As a consequence, there was a sharp increase in the external debt of developing countries, particularly to the commercial banks. As commercial credit was on the whole more costly and of shorter term than official finance, developing countries became vulnerable on two fronts simultaneously: the cost of debt, and increased vulnerability to the swings in confidence as to their creditworthiness. In 1970, the external debt of non-OPEC developing countries stood at $75 billion; this increased to $520 billion by 1982. The proportion of debt owed to private creditors increased from 49 per cent to 64 per cent in the same period.

Another major change—which had shifted the context in which the Bretton Woods institutions functioned—was the collapse of the system of fixed exchange rate parities—a key feature of the monetary system introduced at Bretton Woods—and the emergence of the multiple currency reserve system. While the new system of floating rates had undoubtedly introduced a degree of flexibility, and facilitated balance of payments adjustment, it had also brought unforeseen problems. Exchange rates came to be characterized by volatility and misalignment with economic fundamentals, as indicated by competitiveness and other long-term factors. Interest-responsive speculative capital flows came to have a significant impact on exchange rates.

The environment for world trade had at the same time deteriorated. A transparent, rule-based system of trade, under the aegis of GATT, had underpinned an expansion in world trade in the 1950s and 1960s. By the 1970s, however, there had been many developments in trading practices which were not anticipated when GATT was established—and there was concern that the established trading system was ill-suited to the resolution of the

---

Box 3: Interim and Development Committees, G10 and G24

The Interim Committee

The Interim Committee of the IMF is one of two committees that succeeded the Committee of Twenty in 1974. It advises and reports to the Board of Governors of the IMF on its functions in (1) supervising the management and adaptation of the international monetary system, including the operation of the adjustment process; (2) considering proposals by the Executive Board to amend the Articles of Agreement; and (3) dealing with sudden disturbances that pose a threat to the international monetary system. As part of its functions, the Committee reviews developments in global liquidity and the transfer of resources to developing countries.

Each Fund member that appoints an Executive Director and each group of members that elects an Executive Director is entitled to appoint one member and upto seven associates to the Committee. The Committee usually meets twice a year, normally once in conjuction with the Annual Meeting of the IMF and once in the spring. The Managing Director participates in the meetings and the Executive Directors are entitled to attend.

Development Committee

The second Committee that arose out of the Committee of Twenty was the Joint Ministerial Committee of the Boards of Governors of the Bank and the Fund on the Transfer of Real Resources to Developing Countries, usually known as the Development Committee. It was established to recommend measures to promote the transfer of real resources to developing countries, paying special attention to the problems of the least developed countries. As with the Interim Committee, each member that appoints an Executive Director and each group of members that elects an Executive Director is entitled to appoint one member of the

---

problems they posed.

As reduced economic growth encouraged protectionist sentiment in the industrial countries, trade came to be increasingly characterised by ad-hoc, sector specific, discriminatory and unpredictable measures, introduced unilaterally or bilaterally to 'order' markets. By the early '80s, only a little more than half of world trade was transacted on the basis of the unconditional mfn tariffs, on which the GATT system was centred.

The ability of OPEC countries to make sharp increases in oil prices had also brought attention to issues relating to the security and supply of energy at stable prices.

Committee and up to seven associates. Meetings of the Development Committee are usually held at the same time as those of the Interim Committee.

The Group of Ten (G-10)

The Group of Ten originated when the General Arrangements to Borrow (GAB) was set up to supplement the resources of the IMF. Its membership of ten countries – Belgium, Canada, France, Germany, Italy, Japan, Netherlands, Sweden, the United Kingdom, the United States – was subsequently expanded to include Switzerland. Representation at the meetings of the G-10 is at the level of Finance Ministers and Governors of Central Banks. The Group now has a broad mandate and is serviced by a tripartite Secretariat comprising the IMF, OECD and the Bank for International Settlements. It meets twice yearly in the spring and autumn, in advance of the Interim and Development Committee Meetings, to consider issues on the agenda of those meetings. Broadly, the Committee examines the effect on international payments of monetary, fiscal and other measures and consults together on policies to promote better international payments equilibrium so as to achieve sustained non-inflationary growth in the world economy.

The Group of Twenty-Four (G-24)

The Group of Twenty-Four was formed as the developing countries' counterpart to the Group of Ten. It originated out of the G-77 and could be considered its sub-committee on economic and financial matters, particularly issues related to the IMF and World Bank. It may be argued that while the G-10 was set up as a steering committee, the G-24 is essentially a pressure group. The group was constituted to include eight members each from Africa, Asia and Latin America.

The Group usually meets twice a year, in advance of the Interim and Development Committee meetings. Ad hoc meetings have, however, been called to discuss matters of special importance to the developing countries.

The economic troubles of industrialised countries during the early 1980s, coinciding with the dominance of strongly market-oriented ideological trends in some of them, also led to a diminution in the support for internationalism and multilateralism that underlay the Bretton Woods system and post-war support for development. Industrial countries became more inward-looking in their policy orientation, without due regard for the impact of their policies on other countries, including poor countries, as exemplified by the increase in non-tariff barriers, evading GATT provisions and defying its principles. There was also a decline in their support for development, especially through multilateral agencies.

The Commonwealth intervenes

Commonwealth Finance Ministers were not alone in seeking a review of the Bretton Woods system in the light of these developments. Their call for reform of the system was echoed in a number of other fora. In March 1983, the Non-Aligned Summit called on the 1983 September Bank/Fund annual meetings to begin preparations for an international conference on money and finance for development. In May 1983, reflecting growing unease over exchange rate volatility, France urged the Williamsburg Summit of the seven largest industrial countries (Group of Seven) to consider another international conference along the lines of Bretton Woods; the Summit asked the G7 Ministers of Finance, in consultation with the Managing Director of the IMF, to define the conditions for improving the monetary system and to consider the part which might, in due course, be played by an international conference. The Williamsburg decision was followed up in the Group of Ten industrial countries (see Box 3).

The Helleiner Group thus commenced work against a background of an increasing acceptance of the need for reform in the global financial and monetary system. The perspective of its work, in its own words, was:

> We have not interpreted the call for 'another Bretton Woods' as simply a call for another conference. A premature and ill-prepared conference could easily be counter-productive. Rather, we have interpreted it as a call for renewed work towards agreed international objectives, in the same spirit of optimism and creativity and with the same awareness of the costs of non-co-operation as were shown at the Bretton Woods and Havana conferences nearly forty years ago.

It was in this spirit that the Group set out to examine a set of issues, medium- and long-term; and the question of how to provide an impetus for a process of reform.

These two aspects—the issues and the process—are, of course, intertwined; the process itself was likely to gain momentum as consensus developed on what needed to be done on specific issues. The Group thus sought to make a contribution both by identifying the action needed in specific areas, and by outlining a possible approach to a process which could help advance a consensus in those areas.

The Helleiner Group's recommendations on specific issues were wide-ranging; some of them were commended for immediate implementation, and others for implementation in the near future or over a longer term (see Box 4). Some issues, e.g. developing country debt, attracted more focused consideration in later years. (Debt was to become the subject of a Commonwealth Expert Group in 1984, see Chapter 5.) The major recommendations of the Helleiner Group may be grouped under the following broad areas:

- global management, surveillance and exchange rates,

- international liquidity and the role of SDRs,
- the role of the IMF in adjustment and financing,
- the World Bank and development financing, and
- debt and commercial bank lending.

The Group's recommendations on these issues, and subsequent developments, are discussed on pages 72 to 80. It will be seen that a degree of consensus did emerge in the international community, leading to some policy reforms. In the evolution of this consensus, the Group's suggestions on a process for achieving reforms, and subsequent developments in that regard, were important; the Commonwealth itself took a series of initiatives in advancing the process, helping to underpin the consensus that was emerging through the discussions in the Group of Ten and the Group of Twenty-four and eventually at the Interim and Development Committees' meetings of the IMF and the World Bank (see Box 3).

Reforming the process

The Helleiner Group recognised that securing agreement on the necessary action on such a wide range of issues was hampered by the compartmentalised nature of the global negotiating process; reform in one area was linked to – and often made sense only in the context of – reforms in other areas. At the same time, it was conscious of the danger of the discussions becoming unwieldy. The Group therefore urged:

> Any approach to such negotiations must be rooted in realism. Negotiations exclusively under a UN General Assembly umbrella are not likely either to be acceptable to the industrialised countries or, if acquiesced in under pressure, to win their enthusiastic and constructive participation. This may be regrettable, but it is a reality. Likewise, negotiations strictly under the umbrella of the Fund and the Bank are not likely to be acceptable to the developing countries as a group. In any case, the suggested negotiations necessarily link trading and financial issues and require a broader framework than the Fund and the Bank provide. What is needed is a process which does not pre-determine issues, either expressly or by reasonable implication; which is integrated without being all-encompassing; which is credible in representation without being unwieldly; and which is action oriented while not geared to any single institution.

It thought that the process might, in the first instance, be entrusted to a preparatory group, from not more than twenty broadly representative countries, of persons of ministerial rank plus the heads of relevant international agencies.

The Group stressed that there could be many other approaches towards the holding of an international conference; its was one possible approach. What was important, in its view, was not the acceptance of all the individual components suggested by it, but the adoption of a systematic approach along the lines commended by it.

The Group's recommendations provided the impetus for a series of Commonwealth initiatives (pages 82 - 83).An important outcome of these initiatives was the call, by an intergovernmental Commonwealth Consultative Group established by Heads of Government at their meeting in New Delhi in 1983, for a special meeting of the Development Committee in the spring of 1985 to consider the immediate issues and how to proceed further.

Box 4: Helleiner Report: major recommendations

The Helleiner Group summarised its major recommendations as follows:

(i) **Immediate**, with a view to
   - supporting economic recovery;
   - providing sufficient liquidity from official and private sources to developing countries;
   - alleviating the plight of the poorer countries; and
   - preparing for discussion of international economic reform:
- Increase co-ordination of macro-economic policies.
- Halt protection.
- Maintain flow of private and official credit to countries in debt difficulties.
- Complete current IMF quota increase with unchanged access limits.
- Complete the enlargement of the General Arrangements to Borrow (GAB) and broaden the access.
- Resume issues of special drawing rights.
- Complete IDA VI contributions and agree on IDA VII at an increased real level.
- Authorise increased World Bank lending.
- Begin emergency programme assistance to poorer countries.
- Draw up contingency arrangements against the possibility of an aborted world recovery.
- Start preparatory discussion for an international conference on the financial and trading system.

(ii) **Near future:** The objectives:
   - promoting sustained non-inflationary growth;
   - stabilising the international economy;
   - promoting efficiency in resource use through trade and exchange;
   - ensuring adequate international resource flows for development, and
   - increasing the efficiency of international economic institutions; both individually and collectively:
- Improve exchange rate stability under IMF surveillance.

In the event, agreement was reached at the Bank/Fund annual meetings in 1984 to have extended spring 1985 meetings of the Development and Interim Committees, a development which was influenced by the Commonwealth initiative. These meetings confirmed the value of holding discussions on a range of substantive issues in a small forum, to start with, as recommended by the Helleiner group, but the discussions were not conclusive. Matters were, however, taken further by discussions in the G10 and G24 forums, which

- Regularise SDR issues, with substitution if necessary.
- Improve system for review of IMF quotas.
- Improve the IMF compensatory financing facility.
- Reform IMF conditionality.
- Dismantle trade barriers, restore adherence to GATT undertakings and improve GATT's functioning.
- Renew attempts to seek oil price stabilisation and security of supply.
- Encourage direct investment and other medium - and long-term capital flows to developing countries to reduce the relative role of commercial bank financing.
- Increase lending capacity of World Bank.
- Move towards agreed aid targets, including an increase in the proportion for the poorer countries.
- Protect the poorest countries' import capacity.
- Establish a multilateral forum to discuss trade, money, finance and macroeconomic policies.
- Pursue substantive discussion of long-run improvements to the international financial and trading system.

(iii) **Long-term**: With a view to reforming the system so as to provide a more durable basis for achieving the fundamental aims of economic policy – non-inflationary growth, efficiency, stability and equity in the international system:

- Reduce cyclical instability and the risk of shocks in the system.
- Improve multilateral control of international liquidity and develop SDRs as the principal reserve asset.
- Increase symmetry in balance-of-payments adjustment as between surplus and deficit countries, and between reserve centres and other countries; and strengthen the IMF's role in adjustment processes.
- Stabilise commodity prices.
- Establish regular provision of official development assistance.
- Develop a stronger framework for world trade, production and related activities.

produced reports on the functioning of the international monetary and financial system, from the perspective of the developed and developing countries respectively (see Box 5).

Both reports were intended for preliminary consideration by the Interim Committee. While reiterating the importance of convening an international conference to discuss reform of the global financial and monetary system, the G24 also recognised the strong reservations of some industrial countries on the idea of such a conference and therefore suggested the creation of a representative committee of ministers from developing and industrial countries – possibly in the form of a joint committee of the Interim and Development Committees – which would function on the basis of consensus. To back up discussions by ministers, the G24 also proposed the establishment of a committee of deputies. In these recommendations, there was a strong echo of the Helleiner Group's proposals on the preparatory process.

The belief that the availability of the G10 and G24 reports provided a starting point for a search for consensus led to the establishment of a new Commonwealth Consultative Group by the Commonwealth Heads of Government Meeting at Nassau in October 1985, with a view to assisting the search for consensus at the spring 1986 Interim and Development Committee meetings.

To assist the Group's work, the Secretariat prepared a paper, *International Monetary and Financial Issues: Makings of a Policy Consensus*, suggesting ways towards a convergence between the G10 and G24 positions on the principal issues (see Box 5). The paper noted better possibilities for dialogue than had existed for some time. It said:

> While there remain major differences between developed and developing countries over such basic questions as the need, as seen by the developing countries, for systemic reform in the international monetary and financial system, changes in attitude and policy have taken place which in some important respects can be seen as representing a convergence of approaches. Most developing countries have been adopting far-reaching domestic adjustment and are paying greater attention to efficient resource allocation as a key element of domestic economic policy. Developed countries have recognised the need for a greater degree of co-ordination in the management of the world economy and—as reflected in recent moves by the G5—more active official intervention to improve the functioning of foreign exchange markets. They have also begun to address the problem of deficiencies in financial flows to developing countries, especially to seriously indebted countries, and the need for a higher level of official flows and official support for private flows to assist growth in these countries. These elements of convergence suggests that there exist better possibilities for constructive dialogue than there has been for some time.

The Consultative Group stressed the importance of full consideration being given by the spring 1986 meetings to the appropriate means of achieving and

Box 5 : The G10 and G24 Reports

In response to some support from the industrial countries for reforms in the international monetary and financial system, the Western Economic Summit at Williamsburg in May 1983 'invited Ministers of Finance, in consultation with the Managing Director of the IMF, to define the conditions for improving the international monetary system and to consider the part which might, in due course, be played in this process by a high level international monetary conference. This decision had been followed up in the G10, and resulted in a report by the Deputies of the G10, *The Functioning of the International Monetary System*. The report covered the functioning of floating exchange rates, strengthening multilateral surveillance, management of international liquidity and the role of the IMF. The G10 Deputies Report was considered by the G10 Ministers in June 1985 and received their general endorsement. In the hope that there could be wider discussion, they forwarded the report to the Interim Committee for consideration at its meeting in October 1985.

As a response to the G10 Report, the G24 prepared its own report, *The Functioning and Improvement of the International Monetary System*, dealing with the same issues as the G10 and also the issues of external debt and the transfer of resources to developing countries. The report, which was approved by Deputies in August, was transmitted on behalf of the G24 Ministers to the Interim Committee for discussion at its October 1985 meeting.

The publication of the G10 and G24 reports represented milestones in the process of reform in that they reflected a close consideration of a range of issues of interest to both the industrial and developing countries and were made available for discussion in a small, but representative, forum. This was consistent with the approach commended by the Helleiner Group—and the subsequent Commonwealth Consultative Group, established by the Commonwealth Heads of Government in New Delhi in 1983.

It is not surprising, therefore, that the Commonwealth attached considerable importance to advancing the process further by nudging the world to explore the areas of agreement in the two reports and examine ways of bridging the differences in the other areas—as Commonwealth Heads of Government did at Nassau in October 1985; following Nassau, a new Commonwealth Consultative Group was established to assist such a process. A statement by the Group, together with the Secretariat Report, *The International Monetary and Financial Issues: the Makings of a Policy Consensus*, which noted the areas of agreement and disagreement and the scope for consensus between industrial and developing countries, went before the spring meetings of the Development and Interim Committees in 1986.

implementing the widest possible consensus on the two critical issues: the functioning of the international monetary system and the transfer of real resources to developing countries. A statement by the Group, together with the Secretariat paper, went before the 1986 spring meetings, where a substantial exchange of views took place on the G10 and G24 reports.

Discussions on a number of issues addressed in the Helleiner, the G10 and G24 reports are still continuing in the Interim and Development Committees. While the broad approach of the Helleiner Group towards the preparatory process had received considerable support in the Commonwealth—and the approach adopted by the G24 was congruent—matters have not advanced further. The holding of special sessions of the Interim and Development Committees in the spring of 1985 and the decisions later by the G10 and G24 to forward their reports for discussion in those committees, reflected a movement towards the Helleiner approach to the process; and at points, it seemed as if it would take firm root. However, it remained a promise, to be yet translated into firm development. There has been, however, movement on a number of issues, often in the directions commended by the Helleiner Report. These are reviewed below.

The issues

Global management, surveillance and exchange rates

A major area of concern of the Helleiner Group was global economic management. It noted, as the Arndt Group had earlier done (see Chapter 3), that despite growing interdependence and the increasing international dimensions of macroeconomic problems, industrial countries continued to pursue solutions almost wholly through independent national policies. It stated that the prime objectives in reforming the international system must be improved stabilisation mechanisms and counter-cyclical policies together with improved protection for those most affected when instabilities and shocks nevertheless persist; and provision of adequate liquidity and improved regimes for the flow of capital and trade as automatic stabilising factors. The Group, however, recognised the need to proceed pragmatically, recognising the primacy of national policies.

> It may never be possible to achieve total agreement among governments of varying power, political persuasion and economic interest as to what economic policies are best pursued either within nations or at the international level at any particular time. But it should be possible to reduce the costs to third parties as well as to those directly involved in international disagreements; to increase the mutual consistency of national economic policies; to reduce the degree of arbitrariness and unilateralism in international economic decision-making; and to develop arrangements in which the international implications of domestic

policies are more explicitly and systematically taken into account at the national level.

The Group also saw the need to approach the external adjustment process not in a narrowly conceived framework, but in an integrated manner. The report also stated that apart from the task of smoothing perverse short-term exchange rate volatility, to achieve appropriate exchange rates over the medium term, ''policymakers should work in terms of real effective exchange rate target zones or guidelines'' with a clear role for the IMF on assessing and advocating such guidelines. Noting the steps being taken by the Group of Five (G5) industrial countries to discuss their policies, the Group believed that as the effects of the G5 policies extended well beyond their borders, a more widely representative forum—jointly served by the IMF, World Bank, GATT and UNCTAD—seemed appropriate. It noted that ''Modest amendments to the present operating procedures of the Interim Committee.... expanding its participation and its agenda ...might permit an immediate start in this direction''.

Indeed, the need to improve the decision making procedures in the Bretton Woods institutions with a view to enabling, on the one hand, a more symmetrical treatment of countries and, on the other, a more integrated treatment of monetary, financial and trade issues is an important thrust of the Report.

The Group also considered that efforts to stabilise the prices of primary products could be an important element of contra-cyclical policies. It felt that the implementation of UNCTAD's Common Fund would be useful but not adequate, and called for IMF financing for nationally held buffer stocks of commodities, an effective price stabilising International Grains Arrangement, efforts to secure an oil price stabilisation arrangement and a facility from which countries would be able to obtain compensating external resources when events beyond their control reduced their import capacity.

These themes were later taken up in the G10 and G24 reports, facilitating a measure of policy reform. Subsequent events, e.g. the Plaza Agreement of September 1985 and the Louvre Agreement of February 1987 among the G7 industrial countries, reflected the increasing consensus on the need for co-ordinated exchange rate management.

There has been movement on other issues related to economic policy co-ordination. Industrial countries have steadily moved towards intensified co-ordination, and recognition of the significance of major economies to the rest of the world. At the G7 Summit in Tokyo in June 1986, the need for compatibility of economic policies received substantial attention. At their Venice Summit in June 1987, the G7 leaders committed their countries to using agreed economic indicators in formulating their policies. The IMF was also given a role, enhancing the scope of multilateral surveillance.

However, co-ordination among the major industrial countries and IMF surveillance still have a long way to go to meet the Helleiner Group's objective of improved stabilisation and counter-cyclical mechanisms. There is a need for clearer agreement on the priority and use to be made of various economic indicators. While the application of peer pressure on countries whose policies are out of line is implicit in the present approach of the G7, responsibility for action remains with individual countries and the monitoring of performance is made difficult by the lack of well specified targets. Moreover, while the Fund is represented at the G7 meetings, the discussions are focused on the mutual concerns of the participating countries, with developing-country concerns receiving only muted attention.

On commodity price stabilisation, which the Helleiner Group saw as an important element of contra-cyclical policies, far from reaching agreement on more commodities for stabilisation, the trend has been the reverse, with the handful of commodity agreements in place also falling apart. The Common Fund, however, was ratified in 1989. This issue is considered further in Chapter 7.

International liquidity and SDRs

Another major concern of the Helleiner Group was the need to put in place machinery to ensure an adequate supply of international liquidity. The Group noted:

> The inadequacy of short-term finance can severely damage not only the countries directly experiencing balance-of-payments difficulties but also other countries with which they trade and compete for goods and capital, and thus the entire global economy. Indeed, inadequate liquidity can breed a cumulative process of competitive devaluation, protectionism and beggar-my-neighbour policies, as all struggle to restore national balance in difficult global circumstances.

Pointing to the sharp decline in global reserves in recent years, together with the drying up of commercial bank financing, the Group found that liquidity creation had shown little logic or principle in the post-war years, with the IMF having never fully controlled its supply. According to the Group, if there was to be increased stability and predictability in the provision of international liquidity, the most obvious mechanism to use was the IMF, which had been established, in large part, for that very purpose. Apart from improvements in quotas and access under the Fund's facilities, the report called for the resumption of annual allocations of SDRs and suggested that when from time to time there was excess liquidity, there should be conversion via a substitution account. The Group added that the objective of an SDR-based reserve system remained desirable for the longer term. Apart from promoting the use of the SDR as a unit of account outside the Fund (through private holding of SDRs,

SDR clearing arrangements, etc.), the "merger of the IMF's General Account with its SDR account would greatly simplify IMF lending and have important consequences for the future role of the Fund".

While these themes were also considered later by the G10 and G24, agreement was limited. Considerable discussion of this issue in successive Interim Committee meetings has not led to any change in the position of some of the key industrial countries, despite the call by the IMF's Managing Director at the spring 1988 meetings for a special allocation of SDRs to counter exchange rate instability and the threat to the stability of the international financial system posed by the debt crisis.

IMF role in adjustment and financing

An area which had attracted increasing attention was the role of the Fund in financing the payments deficits of developing countries. The IMF's role was, of course, partly determined by the amount of resources at its disposal, and these were influenced by the level of IMF quotas or subscriptions. The Helleiner Group, recognising this, called for IMF quotas—whose size determines the amount of assistance a country can get from the Fund—to be reviewed every three years and allowed to grow at a pre-agreed rate related to the growth of world trade and payments up to, say, ten years at a time, with additional, selective increases negotiated at shorter intervals. It also suggested improvements in the IMF's Compensatory Financing Facility which compensates for temporary export shortfalls, and the use of SDR allocations to finance the expansion of IMF operations. While increased resources would allow the Fund to provide financing on the scale required, the Group did recognise that economic adjustment by deficit countries—and hence conditionality—was inevitable in certain contexts, though the nature of conditionality required change. Together with enlarged access to finance, it argued, there should be greater reliance in monitoring adjustment programmes, on balance of payments rather than monetary targets and more flexible targets linked in a pre-agreed fashion to external variables; and that, in general, conditionality should be shaped more by the professional judgement of the staff of the Fund and the Bank than by the political influence of their Executive Boards.

A related issue was the relative roles of the Fund and the Bank in the design of adjustment programmes. In the Group's view, "While the design of adjustment policies should evolve through a joint process involving the staff from the Fund and the Bank, a desirable formal step would be for both institutions to assume and declare a joint responsibility for the relevant adjustment programmes". Reflecting on the question further, the Group said:

> The division of labour between the two would correspond to that of their traditional skills. The Fund would also negotiate the conditions for prudent demand management policies while the Bank would deal with questions of

investment priorities over the medium term, and such issues as fiscal reform and institutional development .

A further stage of reform might over the longer-term be implemented in the light of experience gathered with the working out of joint programmes of this sort. This reform would involve the merging of the IMF's EFF [Extended Fund Facility]and World Bank's SAF [Structural Adjustment Lending] facility into a single separate lending entity under the direction of an Executive Board, where representation between developing and industrialised countries would be better balanced and free from weighted voting considerations.

These issues were later also considered by the G10 and G24. The G10 tended to stress the need to maintain effective conditionality to encourage adjustment and restore creditworthiness; the G24, on the other hand, outlined the importance of the role of the IMF in both financing transitory payments problems and in financing and promoting adjustment of persistent imbalances, and the need for conditionality criteria to move from demand deflation to growth-oriented structural adjustment.

Despite these profound differences in the positions of developed and developing countries on the role of the IMF, there was some movement in later years. IMF quotas were increased in 1983 by 50 per cent and the Fund continued its enlarged access policy financed from borrowed resources. Net IMF lending increased sharply to $9.3 billion in 1983 compared to $5.7 billion in the previous year. Moreover several significant steps have been taken to adapt the Fund's role to the changed circumstances facing developing countries:

* Particularly noteworthy was the establishment in the IMF in 1986 of the SDR2.7 billion Structural Adjustment Facility (financed from the Trust Fund reflows), followed in December 1987 by an SDR6 billion Enhanced Structural Adjustment Facility (financed by richer member states) with strong World Bank involvement (the Helleiner Group had recommended joint action) to provide highly concessional balance of payments support to low-income countries.

* The issue of closer collaboration between the Fund and the Bank at operational level has received greater attention in recent years, particularly in the context of the design and implementation of structural adjustment programmes.

* Recognising the fact that their respective areas of responsibility have begun to overlap considerably, the Fund and the Bank, in April 1989, agreed on guidelines which would reduce conflict and maximise co-operation. The G10 also later devoted attention to this issue and endorsed the agreement reached by the Fund and the Bank.

* The IMF's Extended Fund Facility, which provides medium-term balance of payments support to all countries, was revitalised in 1988 and can now offer assistance over four years.

* A contingency financing mechanism to provide additional support if Fund-backed adjustment programmes go off track due to unforeseen external circumstances was also added to the Compensatory Financing Facility to form a new Compensatory and Contingency Finance Facility in August 1988.

Conditionality, however, remains a major area of concern for developing countries. While there is increased acceptance by the IMF of the need for growth-orientation in adjustment programmes, the precise way to accomplish this has yet to be found. There is also some concern that the Fund has emerged in recent years as a net recipient of funds from developing countries (SDR 11.3 billion over 1986-88). There is a growing problem of arrears in repayments to the IMF, leading to several countries being cut off from IMF assistance, and consequently from other sources of finance, which tend to require a country to have a Fund programme in place to make it eligible for credit from them.

World Bank and development finance

Another area of concern for the Helleiner Group was the adequacy of mechanisms for promoting long-term flows of capital to developing countries. In the longer term, in the Group's view, it was desirable to establish a more appropriate and stable pattern of capital flows for development, with a relatively smaller role for commercial bank finance, as market mechanisms do not automatically provide adequate long-term capital. The Group recommended technical exploration of official support for various schemes to improve developing country access to bond markets; establishment of effective codes of conduct, improved insurance arrangements, bilateral treaties and dispute settlement mechanisms to promote foreign direct investment; improved export credit arrangements; and a greater role for the multilateral development banks. It called specifically for an increase in the World Bank's capital, a higher level of IDA resources, increased co-financing with the private sector, greater flexibility in the use of structural adjustment and programme lending determined by the requirements of the time, and examination of the appropriate roles for the World Bank and regional development banks and the division of functions between them. Stressing the importance of concessional aid for low-income countries, it called for the refinement of aid targets and exploration of ways of reaching the target of 0.7 per cent of donor GNP for aid before the end of the 1980s; a renewed commitment to multilateral approaches; more programme aid; simplified and standardised aid procedures; improved arrangements for multilateral discussion of aid issues; and, over the longer term, putting aid on a more predictable and assured basis.

* Since the Helleiner Report, and in the light of subsequent events, the industrialised countries have tended to accept the need to keep IDA resources from falling in real terms. The eighth (1987) and ninth (1990)

replenishments of IDA reflect this approach.

* The World Bank's capital was enlarged in 1988 by roughly 80 per cent, from $95 billion to $171 billion, to enable it to step up lending over the next five years (FY 1989-1993) by around 10 per cent a year (Bank commitments were $11.1 billion in 1983 and $16.4 billion in 1989).

* Following the establishment of its special facility of $1.5 billion to provide additional support to sub-Saharan African countries during the IDA-VII period (FY1985-87), the Bank has helped to put in place an emergency assistance programme of $6.4 billion of bilateral co-financing to be used over 1988-90 for IDA-VIII-supported programmes for low-income sub-Saharan African countries.

* The Bank has also increased its structural and sector adjustment lending (now close to 25 per cent of its total lending).

* The World Bank group has also given greater attention to promoting foreign direct and portfolio investment. The capital of the International Finance Corporation was doubled in 1985 to $1.3 billion so that it could expand lending to the private sector. A Multilateral Investment Guarantee Agency (MIGA) has also been established to insure the non-commercial risks of private foreign investors.

Despite these positive developments, generally on the lines favoured by the Helleiner Group, donor countries have made no progress towards the 0.7 per cent aid target; indeed the proportion has hovered around about half this level. Moreover, since 1985, developing countries have suffered a net negative transfer of resources on debt transactions when interest payments by them are taken into account. From the developing countries' perspective, therefore, the issue of transfer of resources remains a principal area of concern. They have urged continuous consideration of this question at the meetings of the Development Committee, which was originally established for this purpose.

The Secretariat, for its part, has also been looking at ways of assisting Commonwealth developing countries to attract private capital. A report, *Mobilising Capital for Development: The Role of Private Flows*, was prepared for the Commonwealth Finance Ministers meeting in 1988. Ministers' consideration of this report was to result in the Secretariat playing a catalytic role in the establishment of the Commonwealth Equity Fund, designed to promote portfolio investment in Commonwealth developing countries, in 1990 (see Chapter 8).

Debt and bank lending

As noted earlier, the debt crisis was just unfolding as the Helleiner Group sat to deliberate, and it inevitably engaged the Group's attention. The Group emphasised:

> It is crucial for the international financial system that confidence is restored in the creditworthiness of the major debtor developing countries. This can only be achieved by the reduction of their current account deficits and the rebuilding of reserves. This is a politically delicate as well as technically complex requirement the success of which rests in most cases on global economic recovery. Somehow debt servicing capacity must gradually catch up again with debt-service requirements. In the meantime, commercial banks must be persuaded at least to maintain their exposure to developing countries; in particular, they must keep open interbank credit lines, which are vital for foreign trade.

The Group also called on the international and national agencies to prepare contingency plans to be implemented if the debt situation were to deteriorate:

> The simplest plan is for either their own central banks or an international agency such as the IMF to buy the commercial banks' loans (at a substantial discount, to invoke a penalty) which would then be converted, with the debtor's approval, into longer-term debt at a lower rate of interest. Subsequently. the new debt, carrying the guarantee of the central bank or the IMF, could be sold on the market or taken over by another international institution. An emergency issue of SDRs might at the same time bolster confidence.

Noting the particular problems of low-income countries burdened predominantly with official debt, the Group noted:

> The problem is not primarily one of indebtedness; they are too poor to borrow on the market. Instead the recession has lowered the demand for their commodity exports, and reduced their commodity prices, while their import needs and prices have continued to rise. In other words, the industrialised countries' successes in reducing inflation have been achieved partly at the cost of reducing the poorest countries' terms of trade and real incomes earned from exporting. At the same time, aid in real terms has failed to increase significantly. Many of these poor countries are in a state of economic and social collapse. The political dangers are evident.

The Group recommended that contingency plans should be prepared for the major donors to allow rapid expansion of bilateral aid on a case by case basis.

> An appropriate procedure might be for the World Bank and IMF to refer the deserving cases and their recommendations for appropriate structural adjustment policies to an ad hoc group of major donors who would approve allocations on a country-by-country basis. This aid would come from a special contingency fund created by the major aid donors.

As the debt crisis deepened, some of these discussions were carried further in a subsequent (1984) Commonwealth Expert Group (Lever Group) report on debt. Many of the suggestions made by the Helleiner Group were to find reflection in the inititatives undertaken later to tackle commercial and official debts, e.g. the Lawson and the Brady initiatives. (Chapter 5 provides a fuller review of these developments).

Links between trade and finance

Even before the Helleiner Group, the malaise in the international trading system had been studied by another Commonwealth Expert Group—the Cairncross Group (see Chapter 7). The Helleiner Group dealt more explicitly with the relations between the financial and trading systems. It noted that "malfunction in the international trading system and inadequate co-ordination between trade and financial policies had contributed significantly to global economic difficulties", that "GATT in reality does little more than administer contractual arrangements between member states" and that "the gaps in the existing trade machinery are large in spite of the proliferation of institutions involved in some aspects of trade or of finance related to trade." The Group saw policy co-ordination amongst small groups of countries as risking a move away from the multilateral, non-discriminatory approach. It called for "a major effort to strengthen and to rationalise the basic multilateral institutional structure in the field of trade, production and related activities", and suggested that an umbrella institution, incorporating both GATT and UNCTAD together with some of the other trade-related activities within the UN system might eventually emerge. "An effective multilateral policy-making body with a wide ranging mandate would provide the required comprehensive framework to deal with the problems of the trade regime", the Group said.

With the agreement at Punta del Este, Uruguay, to start a new round of multilateral trade negotiations, trade issues are again in the forefront of international attention. However, progress so far has been fraught with difficulty, especially on issues of interest to developing countries. Moreover, while the Interim Committee deals with protectionism in a general way, and GATT's Director-General gives an assessment of trade issues at the meetings of the Development Committee, which also discusses these issues from time to time, there is still no systematic and coherent way for finance and trade issues to be considered together. (Issues relating to the international trading system are dealt with in Chapter 7.)

A long way to go

The Helleiner Group was established at a time when the world was in the throes of economic contraction and when no credible process was in sight to consider the mutuality of interest between developing and industrial countries in significant reform of the world financial and monetary system and in addressing immediate issues with the required urgency. The Group's contribution came at a critical juncture and provided the springboard for further Commonwealth initiatives in the pursuit of a healthier and more stable international economy. Of particular importance is its contribution in nudging the process along, by emphasising the desirability of undertaking preparatory work in a small representative group and in a manner not geared to any single institution.

The subsequent work of the intergovernmental Commonwealth Consultative Groups—and the G10 and G24 Reports—followed this train of thought, enabling a certain amount of debate and a measure of reform in selected areas. This process is continuing. However, while the world has moved away from almost total unilateralism in policy-making—so prevalent at the time of the Helleiner Report—towards greater co-operation amongst major industrial countries as well as towards growing realisation of the acute needs facing developing countries, especially the indebted and the poorest, a monetary and financial system as envisaged in the Helleiner Report is a long way from realisation. The management of global liquidity and the transfer of real resources to developing countries are high among the issues awaiting attention.

The implications of the recent changes and emerging trends in the world economy for economic management and adjustment policies in developing countries continue to engage the attention of the international community. While there is now increased consensus on the principles of sound development, there is recognition that developing countries are faced with grave resource constraints in applying them.

At their meeting in September 1989, Commonwealth Finance Ministers called for the establishment of an Expert Group to examine these issues. There is now a growing belief that the global political and economic climate is much more propitious for dialogue than for many years. Commonwealth Heads of Government, at their meeting in Kuala Lumpur in October 1989, felt that the Commonwealth, within which dialogue had not been interrupted, might have a particular role to play in taking matters forward. They called on the above Expert Group to identify an agenda and make recommendations as to the appropriateness of the Commonwealth taking an initiative in bringing about a meeting of a representative group of the Heads of Government of Commonwealth and non-Commonwealth countries. The Commonwealth thus continues to attach considerable importance to nudging the process of dialogue forward and to keeping itself in a position to influence economic relations between developed and developing countries.

Chronology of events

August 1982   Commonwealth Finance Ministers Meeting in London, noting the vast changes since the establishment of the Bretton Woods institutions, calls for a study of the global financial and trading system as a whole and the role of the international economic institutions.

January 1983 A Commonwealth Expert Group under the chairmanship of Professor G.K. Helleiner begins consideration of issues.

May 1983   Williamsburg Summit asks Finance Ministers of the seven largest industrial countries to define conditions for improving the international monetary system.

July 1983   Helleiner Group submits its report, *Towards a New Bretton Woods: Challenges for the World Financial and Trading System.*

September 1983   Helleiner Report is considered by the Commonwealth Finance Ministers Meeting in Trinidad and Tobago.

November 1983   Commonwealth Heads of Government Meeting in New Delhi takes note of the Helleiner Report and establishes an eight-country Commonwealth Consultative Group comprising of representativs of Britain, Canada, Fiji, India, New Zealand, Tanzania, Trinidad and Tobago and Zimbabwe together with the Secretary-General, to promote a consensus on the issues covered by their *Statement on Economic Action.*

September 1984   Commonwealth Consultative Group submits its report, *International Economic Action,* to the Commonwealth Finance Ministers Meeting, Toronto.

Finance Ministers accept a major recommendation of the Group, viz., that a special meeting of the Development Committee should be held in the spring of 1985 to consider the immediate issues and how to proceed further.

The annual IMF/World Bank meetings agree to have an extended spring meeting of the Development and Interim Committee.

March 1985   Commonwealth Secretary-General submits a memorandum, *Development Prospects, Policy Options and Negotiations,* to the Development Committee meeting, April 1985.

April 1985 Development and Interim Committees meet with extended agendas.

June 1985 The process initiated in May 1983 by the Williamsburg Summit results in a report by the Group of Ten (industrial countries), *Functioning of the International Monetary System.*

September 1985   The Group of Twenty-four (developing countries) produces its own report on all the issues covered by the G10 report as well as on debt and the transfer of resources to developing countries.

Commonwealth Consultative Group set up in 1983 submits Final Report, stating that the reports by G-10 and G-24 provide a starting point for exploring consensus by joint in-depth examination.

Commonwealth Finance Ministers in the Maldives endorse the conclusions of the Consultative Group.

October 1985 Interim and Development Committees agree to give substantive consideration to G10 and G24 reports in April 1986.

Following Commonwealth Heads of Government Meeting in Nassau, a new Commonwealth Consultative Group, comprising representatives of Britain, Canada, Fiji, Grenada, India, Jamaica, Nigeria, Sri Lanka, Tanzania an Zimbabwe, takes up the quest for consensus.

March 1986 The statement of the new Consultative Group along with Secretariat paper, *International and Monetary and Financial Issues: Makings of a Policy Consensus*, is submitted to the Interim and Development Committee meetings.

April 1986 Interim and Development Committee meetings begin substantive consideration of the issues covered in the G-10 and G-24 reports.

Chapter 5
Caught
in a debt trap

The debt issue has been a major problem in international economic relations, and one of direct concern to a large number of Commonwealth countries. While a global financial crisis has so far been averted, there is little sign that the burden of debt servicing faced by many developing countries has become any less onerous; indeed, for many debtor countries the situation has been deteriorating. The severity of the debt problems of many middle-income and low-income developing countries suggests a continuing need both for new approaches at the international level and for improved debt management in national governments.

The Commonwealth has been active in working for improvements at both levels. The debt problem was among the issues that concerned the Helleiner Group of Commonwealth Experts when it addressed the question of reform of the Bretton Woods system in 1982 (see Chapter 4). The deepening gravity of the problem led to its being made the specific focus of examination by another Group of Commonwealth Experts under Lord Lever, a former British Treasury Minister and an acknowledged authority on financial matters; the Lever Group, established on a decision by Heads of Government at their November 1983 meeting in New Delhi, issued its report, *The Debt Crisis and the World Economy*, in 1984.

The debt burden, particularly of low-income countries, has continued to be an important preoccupation of Finance Ministers and of the Secretariat in its economic work. The Secretariat has produced two reports—*Persistent Indebtedness* (1987) and *Debt Distress* (1988)—and made submissions to Select Committees of the British and Canadian Parliaments. The Secretariat has also developed a computer-based debt recording and management package which is now being used by many member governments and has extended its technical assistance to cover policy advice to governments on debt management and renegotiation.

What caused the debt problem?

Not all debtor countries face the same problem. Although there may be common features—the high cost of external borrowing and the adverse external factors which have weakened the borrowers' ability to service debt—there is a recognised distinction between the problems of those mainly middle-income countries that have raised commercial loans from banks and those of low-income borrowers whose loans have come from governments or official agencies, national or multilateral. The debt servicing difficulties of low-income countries have been recognised for rather longer; the practice of 'Retroactive Terms Adjustment' for aid loans from governments has been encouraged, under UNCTAD, since the late 1970s. Recent years have, however, seen acute levels of debt distress especially in low-income African countries, with depressed commodity prices—and lower export earnings—acting as a major aggravating factor.

External debt is not new, nor a problem in itself. Securing loan capital on commercial terms has long been a common practice of countries whose domestic savings are not sufficient to finance the investment needed for rapid growth. Much of the 19th century growth in many countries now regarded as developed was fuelled by capital borrowed in European bond markets. Today the foreign debt to exports ratios of the major debtors—averaging just over 300 per cent—are considered abnormally and unsustainably large. Yet in the period before the First World War, debt-to-exports ratios of 500 per cent were not uncommon (South Africa, Australasia, Russia, Latin America as a whole), and at the top end these ratios reached almost 900 per cent. The instruments were, of course, different from today's. Bonds were then the main form of borrowing. They carried strikingly low nominal interest rates (4 to 5 per cent over much of the late 19th century) and very long maturities (up to a hundred years).

The lending was, however, not trouble free; there was a succession of (usually partial) defaults by governments in Latin America, Eastern and Southern Europe and in individual states of the USA. But, by and large, capital markets were flexible in their operations and able to handle these defaults. Borrowers were able, albeit with strict conditionality in some cases, to draw over a long period on the savings of richer economies like Britain; and investors were able to earn higher returns than on domestic investment. The idea that there is a basic symmetry of interest between commercial lenders and developing country borrowers seemed to have been dealt a severe blow in the Depression of the 1930s when default was widespread and bond lending effectively ceased for a generation. Economic historians have, however, recently cast doubts on the popular view of this period; in fact, much of the debt was serviced satisfactorily and produced reasonable returns for the lenders.

For the first two and a half decades after the Second World War, with capital markets effectively closed to them, developing countries received external finance from three other sources: official aid; direct foreign investment, mainly from multinational companies seeking new supplies of minerals; and trade finance. At the beginning of the 1960s, aid accounted for 60 per cent of the total flows, direct investment 20 per cent and export credits 15 per cent. The last of these, in particular, contributed to debt problems in several countries; seven countries were forced to reschedule, mainly through the Paris Club, between 1956 and 1970 (Argentina, Brazil, Chile, Ghana, Indonesia, Peru and Turkey). Unsatisfactory macroeconomic policies, adverse trends in commodity earnings, excessive short-term borrowing, unsatisfactory investment projects: all these played a part in particular cases. The prominence of the same countries in the debt crisis of the 1980s (except Indonesia which avoided further rescheduling) suggests that lessons were not learnt by creditors or debtors.

Various factors then contributed to a radical change in the pattern of financial flows. Middle-income countries had difficulties mobilising increased official aid; direct investment, especially in mining, came to be regarded with suspicion in the 1970s by countries eager to assert their sovereignty. At the same time the Eurodollar markets, a growing source of credit since the late 1950s to borrowers in industrial countries, became available to those developing countries that banks considered creditworthy. To the borrowers there were distinct advantages in using capital from this source, despite its relatively short-term—five to eight years—character. There were few strings—political or economic; there was no threat to sovereignty; real interest rates, which had been in the 2-3 per cent range in the 1950s and 1960s, became negative in the 1970s. To most developing countries, the issue was one of how to get access to international capital markets rather than a problem of debt. Even before the oil crisis, bank lending had grown from 6 per cent of net flows to developing countries in 1960 to almost 20 per cent in 1973.

The first oil shock—when price increases by members of the Organisation of Petroleum Exporting Countries (OPEC) instantly swelled oil import bills—provided a powerful impetus to this trend since banks were willing, through Eurocurrency lending, to use OPEC surpluses deposited with them to finance the large deficits of oil-importing countries. Official agencies would not provide funds to cover such deficits and project-based direct investment could not. The share of banks in net flows of capital to developing countries rose to 38 per cent in 1980, with a decline in the relative importance of both direct investment (9 per cent in 1980) and aid (36 per cent). There were indications even before 1980 that this new pattern could not continue. The McIntyre Group of Commonwealth Experts (see Chapter 1) warned in 1977 that ''this pattern of financing is naturally giving rise to an escalation of debt servicing and is creating problems for the future development of a number of non oil developing countries. Moreover, doubts are growing about the continued availability of finance to the developing countries on the present scale from private trading sources''.

These fears led to a plea for a stronger official role in providing finance to developing countries. The Secretariat itself launched a programme of seminars on international capital markets in 1978 to help those smaller and low-income countries, in particular, that had difficulty in obtaining access to capital markets. But in inaugurating the first of these seminars, the Secretary-General coupled praise for the positive role of banks in facilitating international adjustment with a warning that the maturities of bank loans ''have resulted in burdensome debt servicing problems and are now an important aspect of the present serious debt problem of developing countries''. Even at that time 8 per cent of bank debt was subject to rescheduling negotiations.

The debt problem reached graver proportions with the moratorium imposed by Mexico in the repayment of its bank debt in 1982. This was followed by a succession of repayment difficulties by major bank debtors mainly in Latin America but including Nigeria. The Commonwealth group headed by Lord Lever considered in detail the causes for the bank debt crisis among Commonwealth countries and the various explanations which had been invoked: large-scale misuse of funds by borrowing countries; reckless lending by the banks; the extraordinary combination of high real interest rates and depressed export markets facing debtor countries which neither borrowers nor lenders could reasonably have envisaged. The Lever Group, while acknowledging the force of the last, conjunctural explanation and the relevance of the others in particular cases, argued that the problem was more fundamental. It pointed out that the large-scale recycling of OPEC funds through the banking system after the first oil shock was inherently unsustainable in the absence of a significantly larger contribution from official capital, guarantees, or other forms of private risk capital to provide both the longer maturities appropriate to development financing and confidence for private financial intermediation.

Consequences of the crisis

The debt crisis created a serious threat both to the world banking system and to the development prospects of debtor countries. At the early stages, concern centred on the vulnerability of the banking system to default by major debtors. The Lever Group starkly warned that the international financial system was ''balanced on a knife edge''. It noted that leading banks had committed sums amounting to twice their capital reserves, and additionally had a high degree of exposure to a small number of developing countries. The nine largest US banks, for example, had a combined exposure of over 200 per cent of their capital, with the four major Latin American countries accounting for 128 per cent of that exposure in December 1983. Thus, the threat of non-payment of debt owed to banks posed a severe threat to the world banking system.

The strategy adopted by creditors and international institutions to deal with the threat to stability involved case-by-case negotiations leading to a rescheduling of repayments of debt principal; adoption by the debtors of an IMF-devised adjustment programme; and—in most cases—some additional 'involuntary' lending by banks. The Lever report argued forcefully that this strategy would not suffice.

However, by 1987, the banks had avoided a serious financial crisis and strengthened their capital base to limit their vulnerability. During that year, they increased their provisions against the possibility of non-repayment of some developing country debt; many US and UK banks increased their reserves to cover 30 per cent of their exposure to developing countries (European banks already had high provisions of 40 to 60 per cent—Japanese banks have much lower provisions for legal reasons but had made provision via an off-shore subsidiary.) In addition, some banks succeeded in disposing of some of their loans on the rapidly growing secondary market. These steps have now somewhat reduced the risks to the banking system, though the big banks still remain heavily exposed to the major debtors.

The threat of default has been contained by the fact that—excepting a temporary moratorium by Brazil and some less important debtors, mainly Peru—debtors have fully kept up their interest payments. Despite the fall in nominal and real interest rates since 1982, interest payments on medium-term and long-term debt by highly indebted countries grew to $30 billion in 1987 ($23.4 billion to banks) from $20.7 billion in 1982 ($17.5 billion to the banks), according to World Bank figures. New net loans and grants covered only around half of this total ($15.4 billion in 1987), of which official and private sources provided roughly equal amounts. New private flows consisted almost entirely of 'involuntary' bank loans (i.e. loans advanced as part of a debt rescheduling package, whereby banks with high exposure express their collective self interest in avoiding default by, in effect, rescheduling some interest payments through the provision of new loans). The burden of maintaining interest payments has, in practice, fallen mainly on debtor countries, which have had to achieve trade surpluses chiefly by holding down imports. The highly indebted countries ran a surplus on trade in goods and non-factor services (i.e. invisibles other than interest, profits and wage remittances) of $25.3 billion in 1987.

The current debt strategy relies heavily on the maintenance of such surpluses until the time—which is not yet in prospect—when private lenders regain sufficient confidence to resume lending on a substantial scale. The IMF in its 1988 *World Economic Outlook* estimated that the trade surpluses of the 15 most heavily indebted countries were around 5 per cent of GDP in 1987 with no fall envisaged before the 1990s. The Lever report, anticipating the strategy that was emerging, was highly critical of its dependence on debtor-country surpluses:

> In our view, it is neither feasible nor desirable for the debtor countries in aggregate, at their present stage of development, to generate the large and sustained trading surpluses which would be required. Such surpluses could be obtained, if at all, in this period only at the cost of frustrating economic advance. Any sustained attempt to achieve what we believe would be a premature transfer of resources from the debtors to their creditors would face continuous political difficulties.

> Moreover, the sustained export surpluses the debtors would require, if present policies are to succeed, would raise new and formidable structural problems for the developed world. Industrial countries have not yet succeeded in reversing the growing protectionist trends which have been prompted by their existing problems of structural adjustment. The obvious connection between export earnings and debt-servicing capacity has so far received insufficient attention.

The Commonwealth Group's apprehensions have been largely vindicated. As a result of the import compression and demand deflation required to achieve trade surpluses to keep up debt interest payments, per capita GDP fell 1.3 per cent per year over the 1980-87 period in highly indebted countries in sharp contrast to growth of 2.9 per cent per year in the 1973-80 period; 1987 was another year of declining per capita income, with little prospect of improvement. Investment has been cut sharply—gross investment fell from 24.5 per cent of GDP in 1981 to 17.6 per cent in 1987—thus undermining future growth. The hope that debt problems would be a transitional concern which debtor countries would be able to grow out of by expanding their exports was based on expectations that brisk growth in industrial countries would allow developing countries to improve their export earnings. In practice, after the recovery year of 1984, industrial country growth has barely reached 3 per cent, commodity earnings in real terms have remained depressed (albeit with some recovery in 1987/88) and protectionist sentiment has grown, especially in the US (see Chapter 7).

The upshot is that after five years of hard striving and stringent austerity the debt position of the major debtors is in some crucial respects worse than at the onset of the crisis. The ratio of debt to exports has increased for the 15 heavily indebted countries from 268 per cent in 1982 to 329 per cent in 1987, reflecting both greater indebtedness from further borrowing (official and 'involuntary' private lending) and weak export earnings. For small low-income countries (mainly African) there has been an increase from 325 per cent in 1982 to 453 per cent in 1987. In terms of the debt service ratio (the share of income from exports of goods and services required for debt service) there has been some improvement for the 15 major debtors—from 49 per cent in 1982 to 36 per cent in 1987, as estimated by the IMF—but a worsening for the small low income countries for whom the ratio rose to 27.5 per cent in 1987 from 22 per cent. Such improvement for major debtors as has occurred is largely due to the rescheduling of principal repayments. Yet even their reduced ratio is way above the 20 to 25 per cent level considered safe for sovereign borrowers raising new loans on a voluntary basis in international markets. The ratio to export earnings of interest payments alone was 22 per cent in 1987 (and the IMF expected it to rise to 27 per cent in 1988).

The seriously indebted countries have therefore little to show for the last five years: they are poorer; their capital stock is older; their debt obligations are still too high to make a voluntary return to capital markets feasible. The prospects for the future depend on growth in the world economy on the one hand, and continued domestic adjustment on the other. The global outlook is clouded by uncertainty generated by the large payments imbalances between the major economies (US, West Germany and Japan), while the political will to continue meeting debt obligations in the debtor countries is being seriously sapped. Even the IMF recognises that "the prolonged period of the debt crisis is now

---

Box 6: Solving the problem of commercial indebtedness

"Any satisfactory solution to the present situation must in our view respect the following criteria:

(a) There should be an equitable distribution of responsibility and costs between debtor countries, creditor country governments and the private banks, having regard to the history of the lending and the contribution it has made to growth of the world economy whatever its defects may have been.

(b) It is a matter of urgency to put an end to the premature outflows of resources from developing countries. Austerity which produces growth is acceptable. But austerity which attempts to secure premature balance of payments adjustments at the expense of investment and growth is not.

(c) Policies to bring about a positive transfer of resources to developing countries must be soundly based—that is, both regulated and designed to produce growth—and of mutual advantage to industrial and developing countries.

(d) Creditor countries must co-operate to assist the debtors, by guarantees or other means, to raise the funds to meet the interest on existing debt obligations and to ensure the flow of new funds referred to in (c) above.

(e) The efficient functioning of the banking system both domestically and internationally must be preserved and insolvencies avoided. The banks must not, however, be bailed out. They must bear an equitable share of the burdens involved and must be given adequate time to make this manageable.

Proper arrangements must therefore be made to keep loans performing and to permit higher levels of growth, and imports, in the debtor countries. This

---

revealing the existence of adjustment fatigue'' (*World Economic Outlook, October 1988*), and the World Bank acknowledges that ''the debt overhang remains an obstacle to growth in the debtor countries and a threat to the world economy'' (*World Development Report, 1988*).

The search for solutions

When it addressed the debt crisis in 1984 the Lever Group set a series of general principles for achieving a more equitable sharing of the burden of adjustment between debtors, banks and governments and in particular to bring an end to ''premature trade surpluses''. It proposed a new approach to policy that would place more emphasis on official or officially guaranteed flows of new finance (see Box 6).

---

requires a level of additional financing sufficient to enable the debtors to pay the interest on their outstanding debt, while removing the pressures for achieving premature trade surpluses. Since the market will not provide this additional amount without guarantee, the industrial countries will have to take steps to ensure the availability of this additional financing. This would come from a combination of:

- commercial bank lending underpinned by a scheme of insurance;
- bilateral official lending, including export credits; and
- multilateral lending via the IMF, the World Bank and the regional development banks.

In parallel with the additional financing, rescheduling arrangements should be enlarged in scope along the following lines to give greater stability to the 'overhang' of debt and to reduce the debt-servicing burden:

- longer maturities and grace periods will be necessary in most cases;
- mechanisms should be established to provide at least temporary relief in respect of interest when it is at exceptionally high levels;
- multi-year rescheduling should be the norm rather than the exception; and
- the possibility should be considered of granting temporary relief by arrangements which would permit debt service in local currency to cover periods of foreign exchange difficulty.

In this way the debtors would be enabled to pay the interest and the banks would be in a position to make realistic write-downs of the debts to sustainable levels over a long period of years. This would bring about that combination of public purpose and private finance that ought always to have been in place.''

From the Lever report.

From Baker to Brady

International recognition that more positive action was required to promote new financial flows to indebted countries was subsequently reflected in the arrangements proposed by US Treasury Secretary James Baker in September 1985. The Baker Plan focused on the 15 major debtors and sought to raise roughly $16 billion in new net lending per year (excluding foreign investment and short-term credit): $6.5-7.0 billion from the multilateral development banks; $6.5 billion of new lending from commercial banks; $3 billion of continued official lending via medium-to-long-term export credits. It laid stress on making available external finance to achieve growth-oriented adjustment and recognised the importance of official finance; this was very much along the lines argued by the Commonwealth Report.

The Brady Plan (March 1989) represented a new approach to the debt problem. It marked a change in emphasis to debt and debt service reduction rather than the creation of additional indebtedness. It offers commercial creditors one of three options: old loans can be swapped for bonds at a discount to face value; old loans can be swapped for par value bonds paying a fixed interest rate of 6.25 per cent; and new money can be provided equivalent to 25 per cent of the medium and long-term debt owed to them. The essence of the proposals are as follows:

- Voluntary market based reduction of debt and debt service burdens of countries demonstrating a commitment to structural adjustment, and the repatriation of flight capital.
- Commercial banks are encouraged to reduce their claims for principal or interest in return for greater security on their reduced assets.
- The greater security on reduced assets is to be provided by the IMF and the World Bank. These institutions are to use their resources to improve incentives to debt reduction. Funding from these institutions and the Government of Japan will amount to US$25-30 billion over three years. Furthermore, delays in implementing the necessary programmes in the debtor countries will be reduced by the Fund and the Bank not insisting on an "assured critical mass" of financing for anticipated balance of payments shortfalls before their funds are provided.
- In order to speed up the negotiations between debtors and lead banks, there would be a waiver of the "sharing and negative pledge" conditions which figure in all securitised/multi-bank loans. The conditions ensure that any losses of debt service will be shared among all lenders, and therefore, that no debtor will engage in debt reduction mechanisms without agreement by all the banks involved.

While the explicit role given to voluntary debt reduction measures under the

Brady Plan has been broadly welcomed, some concerns have been expressed from several quarters. Debtors are concerned that the scale of debt/debt service reduction might not be substantial enough; bankers fear, that arrears and default might be encouraged; creditor governments are concerned that private sector risk might be transferred to the public sector; and developing countries outside 'the Brady net' are worried that the initiative might pre-empt IMF and World Bank resources to the detriment of those countries that are not major debtors. It has been clear for some time that the debt reduction issue had to be addressed and it was given some prominence in the Secretariat's report, *Persistent Indebtedness*, in April 1987. The response of creditors, in practice, has been the introduction of various mechanisms of further debt restructuring, or relief, which work through market mechanisms and are known as the 'menu approach'. The most important of these, designed to contribute to a reduction in the debt 'overhang', are:

Debt-equity swaps, whereby foreign currency debts are converted into domestic currency equity investments. There is now sufficient experience of such schemes for debtor countries to be able to design new schemes which maximise the benefits and minimise the costs. The experience to date was reviewed in the Secretariat's 1988 report, *Mobilising Private Flows for Development*. Jamaica is one Commonwealth country with a scheme specifically designed to boost increased foreign investment, while Nigeria and Zambia, on a smaller scale, are also seeking to promote debt equity swaps.

Debt-security conversions, whereby debt is converted into a tradeable security at a discount (the discount being set by the secondary market in debt and representing the amount of debt reduction). The Nigerian conversion of trade credit into medium-term rates set a precedent in this type of conversion. The Mexican scheme of December 1987 was the most ambitious attempt so far to convert bank debt to securities—the securities were 'collateralised' against US treasury bonds—but the amount converted was much less than hoped. This was because the banks saw no advantage in bidding for securities at a large discount, close to the discount they could obtain—for cash sale of debt —in the secondary market, while the Mexicans saw no advantage in the scheme unless the discount was sufficiently deep to achieve a significant debt reduction. 'Exit bonds' employing the same principle were tried, unsuccessfully, in the case of Argentina. But for Brazil in the latest—1988—debt restructuring agreement a more ambitious scheme has been launched.

Debt buy-backs, with which a debtor country buys back its own debt at the discount offered in the secondary market, and so retires the debt. To do this, however, the debtor country requires substantial reserves, beyond its immediate liquidity requirements, or else a donor country must be willing to finance it as has occurred with Bolivia's programme of buy backs.

Numerous other techniques are available which involve converting foreign debt into some other claim (e.g. debt converted into goods; foreign debt into local currency debt). So far, however, the total volume of conversions is small – rather less than 1 per cent of the long-term developing country debt of $1,200 billion at the end of 1987. And the volume of market conversions is limited by the size of the secondary debt market. A substantial increase in demand for debt for conversion purposes would significantly raise the price, i.e. lower the discount, of the debt. Thus, while these schemes are playing a useful and expanding role, it has been, except for a few countries such as Chile, marginal so far.

The Baker and Brady Plans still represent the basic framework for dealing with the problems of major debtors. They must be credited with helping to avert more serious confrontation between debtors and creditors, and outright financial collapse. But the financial flows generated have been insufficient to reverse negative net financial transfers (i.e. transfers from developing countries); new bank lending in particular has been lower than expected; and there has been little experience of 'growth oriented' adjustment. In part, dissatisfaction in debtor countries with the Baker Plan has been due to factors external to the Plan itself: the disappointingly slow growth of industrial countries' economies in particular. But it was also underfinanced to meet its objectives and the co-financing of private by public funds has proved an insufficiently strong linkage to generate new private flows from commercial banks on the required scale. It is not yet clear whether the Brady Plan will overcome these problems satisfactorily.

Time for debt forgiveness

The question now at the centre of the debate about bank debt is whether, in view of the growing evidence of 'fatigue' by debtor countries, the time is ripe for a more ambitious, far-reaching 'concessional' approach to debt relief—in effect, for banks to write off some of their debt. Numerous schemes, involving varying degrees of involvement by international public agencies, have been canvassed. Many of them were summarised in the Lever Report. So far, there have been several basic objections. One is the damage such relief could inflict on the banks, though their recent provisions could cushion the losses. Another is the cost to taxpayers in industrial countries—though there is no reason why relief of bank debt should involve explicit or implicit public subsidy. A third is that such involuntary debt relief would encourage future defaulters and reward countries that do not service their debt as against those which do. This 'moral hazard' issue has, however, already been faced in relation to debt relief for low income countries, reviewed below. A firm commitment to an adjustment programme by the debtor is the most obvious way of dealing with that problem.

Finally, and perhaps most seriously, it has always been argued that forgiveness of debt (and, even more, unilateral renunciation of debt) could have severe consequences for the debtor by cutting it off from future long-term credit. The example of the interwar defaults on bonds is often cited in aid of this argument. However, as noted above and as the Commonwealth Secretary-General has argued (*Sovereign Default: A Backward Glance —Third World Quarterly, April 1989*), the historical record is very mixed. There are particular cases where debt forgiveness has enhanced creditworthiness. These include Indonesia where under the Abs Plan, in 1969-70, \$82.2 billion of official debt was rescheduled over 30 years with provisions for deferring interest obligations and repayment, and the forgiveness of Second World War debts. The experience of the 1930s and the 19th century also does not warrant a pessimistic view of the consequences. If the world economic situation were to deteriorate the issue would surely be put to the test. As it is, the present situation is fragile and the strategy for debt does not look sustainable without steps to achieve a better balance of responsibilities and costs between debtors, creditors and creditor country governments.

The poorest debtors

A major theme of the Lever report—followed up in more recent Secretariat work such as the report *Debt Distress*—was the importance and severity of the debt problems of low-income countries, especially in Africa. This problem differs from that of most middle-income countries whose debt is primarily owed to commercial banks (though there are some exceptions, like Jamaica); the debt of most of the low-income countries originates in past official lending, officially guaranteed export credits, ODA loans, and multilateral loans from the IMF, World Bank and regional development banks.

The Lever report explained this problem in the following terms:

> The combination of declining ODA in real terms and rising debt-service obligations has sharply reduced net transfers to low-income countries, particularly in sub-Saharan Africa. This contraction occurred during a period in which the prices of primary commodities collapsed to the lowest levels since the 1930s and market access has been reduced. The drought in Africa has aggravated the difficulties of a decade of declining living standards. Even countries pursuing appropriate adjustment policies have been forced, in these circumstances, to renegotiate their debt. ... The terms of official finance—IMF and World Bank loans and officially guaranteed export credits—have hardened in response to increases in interest rates.

Since the onset of the debt crisis, this particular problem has seriously deteriorated. The ratio of external debt to exports of goods and services rose every year between 1982 and 1987 for small low-income countries, moving up from 325 to 453 per cent, and for sub-Saharan Africa, excluding Nigeria, from 218 to 323 per cent. Despite the virtual cessation or rescheduling of principal repayment by a large number of debt-affected countries in these two categories, and the accumulation or rescheduling of interest arrears, actual payments on debt service including IMF charges and repurchases rose from 25.8 per cent of export earnings in 1982 to 35 per cent in 1987 for small low-income countries and from 25.2 to 29.3 per cent over the same period for sub-Saharan Africa less Nigeria. If account is taken of debt service due but not paid, some of the worst affected countries like Madagascar, Sudan, Tanzania and Somalia would have to pay all they earn from exports to honour their obligations in full. Projections do not suggest any alleviation of the problem in the short or medium term; even if adjustment efforts are made, debt servicing obligations relative to exports are set to rise further in the face of weak export earnings - though some countries like Zambia have benefited from improved commodity prices recently—and rising debt service. Giving priority to debt service would further reduce imports; in the 15 most seriously indebted countries in Africa imports per head are now barely half the level of the mid-1960s and per capita incomes have fallen to two thirds of what they were in the mid-1960s.

Recognising the problem's severity, its deterioration and its special character, creditor/donor countries have recently launched a variety of initiatives for what are now called the 'low-income debt-distressed countries' (low-income African countries whose debt service obligations exceed 25 per cent of their exports earnings):

- Based on the 'Lawson Initiative' and subsequent suggestions from France, the terms of rescheduling official debt have been improved in Paris Club debt renegotiations. Longer repayment periods (20 years) and grace periods (10 years) are now available. There has been more controversy over the granting of interest relief (interest is at present being capitalised and commercial rates are applied to rescheduled debt). It now appears, following the Toronto Western Economic Summit of 1988, that a way has been found to ensure that creditor countries do grant some interest relief or offer equivalent measures.

- Some donors—Britain, Canada, France, the Netherlands, the Nordic countries— have made a commitment to writing off further 'aid debt' under the Retroactive Terms Adjustment (RTA) provisions of UNCTAD Resolution 165 and to doing so with additional aid finance (previous RTA, worth S6 billion in total, seems to have been financed from existing aid budgets). But some major 'aid creditors' (Japan, US, USSR, Saudi Arabia) are not part of the current round of debt relief and others want to link RTA to policy conditionality for the first time.

- The establishment of the IMF's Enhanced Structural Adjustment Facility (of SDR6 billion), has reduced negative net transfers to the IMF from low-income beneficiaries.
- At a meeting in Paris in December 1987, an additional $1 billion a year in bilateral ODA over three years was pledged to the low-income 'debt distressed' countries.
- The World Bank is channelling more resources to low-income debt distressed countries as a result of a larger, $12.4 billion eighth replenishment of the International Development Association (IDA) and a bigger share of its funds (50 per cent as against 35 per cent under IDA VII) going to Africa; the Bank's Special Programme of Assistance for Africa has also mobilised commitments of $6.4 billion. The Bank has also made available $100 million to a special facility of IDA for support of commercial bank debt reduction.
- Replenishment of the African Development Bank's concessional African Development Fund.

Taken together, these measures have made, or will make, a substantial contribution to the external financing problem of low-income debtors in Africa. However, the total additional concessional finance involved does not seem adequate to meet the World Bank's modest target of restoring per capita imports to 1980 levels and the debt relief measures do not yet extend to several IDA-eligible African countries (Kenya, Malawi, Ethiopia, for example). The UN (Wass) Report estimates that over and above existing commitments, $2 billion a year is needed for a minimal recovery programme for sub-Saharan Africa less Nigeria. This would have to come from additional bilateral aid, plus generous implementation of the Lawson Initiative on interest relief. These estimates also exclude non-African 'debt distressed' low-income countries (Guyana, the Yemens, Burma) and other low-income and middle-income African countries. There is a particular danger of 'new' aid money being switched from low income Asia. There is, moreover, a view in Africa that the current measures for debt are of a stopgap kind and that a much more radical approach to debt relief, together with new finance, is required.

The IMF and the World Bank

A continuous thread in Commonwealth work in recent years has been a recognition of the crucial role of the main international financial institutions —the IMF and the World Bank—and the need for both of them to have increased resources as well as reformed mandates. Their role was most comprehensively analysed in the Helleiner Group's report, *Towards a New Bretton Woods* (Chapter 4), but was also given considerable attention in the Lever report (see Box 7) and in subsequent Secretariat work on debt and financial flows, e.g. in *Mobilising Capital for Development.*

The role of the IMF in relation to the debt problem has been crucial in several respects: providing direct financial assistance from its own resources; designing the adjustment programmes to which almost all debt rescheduling agreements, both for bank and official loans, have been anchored; acting as a catalyst for new bank lending; and providing or encouraging contingency financing when adjustment programmes are thrown off track by external events. In each of these respects, the Fund's role has been criticised, and it has evolved considerably since the debt crisis began.

The revolving fund nature of the IMF's resources has meant that it cannot sustain a continuous net flow to recipients of its loans and this has created increasing difficulties in recent years. The Fund responded to the initial phase of the debt crisis promptly. It made net loans to developing countries of S6.9 billion in 1982 (S2.2 billion to the 15 heavily indebted, S0.7 billion to sub-Saharan Africa less Nigeria) and S11.4 billion in 1983 ($6.3 billion and S1.3 billion respectively). But by 1986 net flows had turned negative and money was flowing to the IMF from developing countries. In 1987 there were negative net flows of S6.1 billion of which $1.3 billion was from the 15 heavily indebted countries and S0.5 billion from sub-Saharan Africa. Over and above the repayments ('repurchases') are loan charges which, being at commercial rates, are particularly onerous for low income countries. IMF loan charges and repurchases accounted for no less than 7.5 per cent of the exports of goods and services of small low income countries in 1987, and 3.7 per cent for the 15 most highly indebted countries. This has led to problems of arrears to the Fund in the case of a growing number of countries. The Lever Group argued forcefully for concessional—lower interest, longer maturity—Fund lending to low income countries. This call has been met in large part by the creation of the Fund's SAF, and later the Enhanced Structural Adjustment Facility, which promise to end negative net flows, at least to low-income countries.

The content of the adjustment programmes devised for debtor countries by the IMF has been even more controversial and it has been widely blamed for imposing deflationary policies that have resulted in reduced growth, investment and employment. A central demand in debtor countries—echoed in the Lever report—is that the Fund's programmes should be both more 'growth oriented' and have a longer perspective than its traditional 12-month standby agreements for balance of payments emergencies. The Fund has moved some way to accommodate these concerns: it espouses 'growth orientation' (and now recognises the need also for considering the human impact of its programmes); multi-year rescheduling has enabled some countries to formulate medium term programmes (but only a few so far); and the structural adjustment programmes designed jointly with the World Bank for low-income countries are intended to introduce a longer-term, developmental perspective.

Box 7: Lever Report recommendations in relation to the international financial institutions

The IMF
• Reactivation of the IMF Trust Fund and interest subsidy account to promote medium-term, low-interest balance of payments finance for low-income countries which have great difficulty in using high-conditionality short-term IMF finance at normal interest rates.
• Ajustment programmes should be designed with an emphasis on investment and growth.
• Longer periods should be granted for adjustment, particularly in the case of low-income countries. This would entail a consistent joint approach by the Fund, the World Bank and the debtor countries' governments to financing structural adjustment, along the lines envisaged by the report of the Commonwealth Study Group, *Towards a New Bretton Woods*.
• The present facilities with regard nto compensatory financing should be enlarged.
• The IMF should have substantial increases in resources mainly through an increase in quotas. A further allocation of SDRs is also necessary.

The World Bank and regional development banks
• Recognition that while IMF lending of an appropriate kind is desirable, the essentially long-term, structural nature of adjustment required in most low-income countries calls for the central role in external financing for adjustment to be played by the World Bank, in conjunction with regional banks.
• A significantly higher fraction of World Bank loans should be in the form of programme lending to countries with balance of payments financing difficulties; in particular, the proportion of programme lending should be raised to cover 30 per cent.
• The World Bank's lending resources should be increased by a further substantial general capital increase and by relaxing the gearing ratio.
• Lending by IDA, which under present policies would decline even in nominal terms, should at least be maintained.
• The World Bank and regional banks should undertake a larger role in supporting private lending (for example, via co-financing) and equity investment.
• The World Bank and regional banks should play a more central role in drawing up adjustment programmes, especially for low-income countries.
• The regional banks have a useful role in development financing in addition to that played by the World Bank; to perform this they need greater resources and more flexibility to respond to the need for programme loans.

The IMF's own position as a net recipient of flows from indebted countries has prevented it from playing a catalytic role in respect of commercial flows. That is reflected in the growing reluctance of banks to make new money available. The Fund could play a larger role—both directly and as a catalyst —if it was given substantially more resources through a quota increase.

The Fund's role has also been cramped by the serious limitation on the size of—and access to—its Compensatory Financing Facility. Nonetheless, in the case of the 1986 Mexican programme it has acted as intermediary to private contingency financing, and it has formally established an external contingency mechanism as part of the new Compensatory and Contingency Financing Facility; this will cover fluctuations in interest payments as well as in export earnings. This was an innovation which the Lever Group specifically sought (but without the conditionality associated with the new arrangement.)

The World Bank, somewhat peripheral in its influence at the earlier stages of the debt crisis, has now become more important in its role, following the urgings of the Lever report, among others. Its ability to respond quickly was —and still is to some degree—restricted by its financing capacity and by the practice that a substantial majority of its loans should be in traditional project form, usually with long lead times and complex appraisal procedures. Also the terms of World Bank loans—at around market rates—are unattractive to some borrowers, while servicing them led to net transfers of funds to the Bank in 1987/88.

In relation to the major middle-income debtor countries, the Bank built up its annual net lending from \$2.2 billion, out of a net financing requirement of \$27.8 billion, in the 1980-84 period (with another \$0.9 billion from other multilateral development banks) to \$2.8 billion out of \$10.9 billion in the 1985-87 period (and another \$1.4 billion from other multilateral development banks). The Agreement on a new General Capital Increase will enable such expansion to be maintained. Increased involvement has been facilitated by a switch to lending to finance structural adjustment—and, even more, sectoral adjustment—and fast disbursing programmes generally. With the new emphasis on programme —as against project—lending has also come an increased role in formulating medium-term, 'growth oriented' adjustment strategies.

The World Bank's increased lending to the major debtors is in line with the Baker and Brady Plans, and it has become the largest single source of finance for these countries. But net flows are still small in aggregate and the Bank's future success will hinge largely on the extent to which it can create a 'multiplier effect' through catalysing private lending. The Bank has endeavoured to do this through cofinancing but this has so far failed to generate substantial additional commercial lending. The Bank is now considering how to play a much more vigorous catalytic role through 'credit enhancement' in relation to debtor countries. Specifically, new financing instruments—new money bonds, convertible bonds, interest capitalisation, interest swaps and options, conditionality linked bonds—could be helped by means of World Bank guarantees or technical assistance. A problem which has not yet been confronted is the mounting arrears on World Bank loans to indebted countries. Some relief has been extended by the decision that countries which now borrow only from IDA but had borrowed from IBRD are eligible for supplememtaty IDA credits equivalent to about 60 per cent of interest payments due to the IBRD.

World Bank assistance to low-income countries was seriously curtailed by the reduced resources available to IDA under its seventh replenishment. Net flows from IDA to low-income Africa more than doubled between 1982 and 1986 ($610 million to $1.3 billion) but this was achieved in large part by holding net lending to low-income Asia around the $1.5 billion level. Nonetheless, the World Bank has recently played an important role in orchestrating the international community's response to the problems of 'the low-income debt distressed' in Africa both at an aggregate level, by mobilising additional resources from bilateral donors, and, at a country level, by formulating adjustment programmes alongside the IMF. The Bank's ability to back its programmes with concessional finance will be enhanced by the agreement to replenish IDA IX at $15.5 billion. A key issue for the future however will be whether the partnership between the Fund and the Bank leads to a long term approach to adjustment or results in Bank programme objectives being subordinated to the shorter perspectives of the Fund. In any event developing countries have already signalled their concern at growing 'cross-conditionality' between the two institutions and in 1986 the Secretariat prepared a report reflecting that concern (*Co-operation Without Cross-conditionality : An Issue in International Lending*).

Whither the debt problem?

In its work on debt, the Secretariat has been very conscious of the fact that the debt problem is not simply a financial issue. At one level within developing countries, it is an integral part of the wider question of development and policy reform designed to achieve maximum sustainable growth. On another level, it is bound up with the functioning of the world economy. In that respect, solutions are likely to be found less in innovative debt restructuring schemes than in economic policies in leading industrial countries that lead to more rapid growth, lower interest rates and reduced protectionism.

In relation to the major debtors, a situation has arisen in which there is still little confidence among creditors and debtors in the ability of the existing debt strategy to restore indebted countries to 'creditworthiness' and 'normal' relationships with capital markets. Debt 'fatigue' has become endemic At the same time, there is little immediate prospect of generalised solutions involving one or other of the various comprehensive reform proposals. The emerging trend is more towards complex solutions—including more use of market instruments—which reflect the particular needs of individual creditors and debtors. The Brady Plan has been implemented for only a few countries so far. As at the end of March 1990, the IMF had provided assistance to Mexico, Philippines, Costa Rica and Venezuela, while the World Bank had arrangements with Mexico, Philippines and Venezuela. Only Mexico and Philippines had reached agreements with their commercial bank creditors under the initiative, although Costa Rica is close to doing so. A deterioration in the international economic environment could well precipitate a renewed crisis in which demands for more far-reaching debt relief became irresistible.

For low-income debtors, mainly in Africa, there is no real conceptual disagreement between creditors and debtors on the need for special measures. One unresolved question concerns interest relief on official loans, but following the Toronto Summit in 1988, agreement on a rather limited programme has been set in train. The issue for the future is essentially one of political will in donor countries to make available substantially more ODA to debt-distressed countries in support of long-term adjustment without diverting aid from other low-income countries which (like India) could face debt problems in turn.

For all groups of developing countries, however, there is a need to look at ways of facilitating substantially increased net flows of private as well as official capital in terms that do not aggravate the debt problem. For creditworthy countries, there is a variety of financing instruments available (foreign and domestic bonds in a growing number of markets; notes and commercial paper; swaps and options) which can provide cheaper or longer term finance for new borrowing or refinancing old debt. Countries such as India and Malaysia are making wide use of these opportunities. Seriously indebted countries have fewer options and there is an urgent need for restoring short-term credit where this has been disrupted and opportunities to make use of new project financing techniques. Equity finance is now recognised to be potentially of considerable value to development—as well as less subject to external servicing problems —not only as direct investment but as portfolio investment in emerging stock markets, through country funds in particular. In the fields of foreign investment and capital markets, the Secretariat is seeking to help member countries maximise opportunities for new flows.

Underlying this work—and reflecting the prescriptions of the Lever report and other analyses—is a stress on the need for a judicious balance among, as well as larger volumes of, capital flows to developing countries: private and official; commercial and concessional; equity and debt, reflecting the very varied needs of member countries.

Chapter 6
Malfunctioning commodity markets and the Common Fund

Concern over the instability of commodity markets has a long history. The very disturbed international economic environment of the first half of the 1970s heightened this concern as it had serious consequences for many developing countries whose foreign exchange receipts, government revenue and indeed national income and employment depended in large measure on the export of commodities. Their problems as producers of commodities were articulated at various international fora during that period and led at UNCTAD IV in Nairobi in 1976 to the adoption of a resolution for an Integrated Programme for Commodities (IPC). The Programme's main objectives were to achieve stable conditions in commodity trade and to improve and sustain the real income of developing countries from exports of commodities. But although there was a consensus on the objectives, there were substantive differences on how they might be achieved, in particular on the role, scope and functions of a Common Fund for Commodities proposed as the integrating mechanism of the IPC.

Commonwealth countries, as leading producers as well as consumers of commodities, have been much affected by the fluctuations and trends in international prices and traded quantities of these primary products. They are responsible for more than half the world's exports of such important commodities as wool, palm oil, jute, tea, palm kernels, rubber, cocoa, certain spices, bauxite, tin and copper, and for more than one-third of the sisal, tropical timber and groundnuts. Moreover, many Commonwealth members, including developed countries such as Australia and New Zealand, are dependent on commodity exports for a large part of their export earnings (see Table 1).

It was natural, therefore, that Commonwealth Heads of Government should devote considerable attention to commodity issues when they met in London in June 1977. At the conclusion of their discussions they agreed to work towards the early establishment of the Common Fund. To this end, they asked the Commonwealth Secretary-General to establish a technical working group drawn from Commonwealth countries to examine the issues which needed to be addressed in further work on the subject in UNCTAD. The Group was expected in its report to inform Commonwealth leaders on ''the range of objectives and purposes for which the Common Fund might be used, its methods of operation and the measures to be adopted to help developing countries which are net importers of the commodities concerned'', with a view to facilitating progress at the UNCTAD conference due to be held in November 1977.

This chapter considers the contribution of the Commonwealth Technical Group (see Annex), under the chairmanship of Lord Campbell, in resolving issues related to the Common Fund. It first examines the problems which the Fund was expected to solve, and sets out the evolution of the concept. The major negotiating issues and recommendations of the Commonwealth Group are then indicated, and the chapter concludes with a brief consideration of subsequent developments.

The commodity problem

The commodity problem has two major strands: a secular decline in the terms of trade; and price and earnings instability. On the first, there is much controversy on both theoretical and empirical grounds concerning the long-run comparative behaviour of the export prices of commodities and manufactures. The evidence, on balance, indicates that in many cases the commodity or net barter terms of trade tend to decline in the long-term or at least for long periods. There is thus a falling trend in the unit values of primary commodities as measured in 'real terms' (i.e. deflated by the unit value index of exports of manufactures from the developed market economy countries) over the period 1950-89 (see Table 2).

The instability of commodity prices and of export earnings from commodities has been studied extensively and a consensus seems to have emerged that, largely because of the importance of commodities in their exports, the foreign exchange earnings of developing countries tend to be less stable than those of developed countries. Moreover, for agricultural products, which form the bulk of exports from most developing countries, price and earnings instability appears to have been increasing. The main causal factors (none of which has of itself been of overriding importance) include: low price elasticity of demand and supply; low income elasticity of demand; sudden variations in supply as a result of natural disasters like droughts and floods, to which agricultural producers are particularly vulnerable; variations in industrial countries' demand for raw materials in line with their business cycles; and concentration of a country's exports in one or a few commodities or in one or a few markets. In calling for the establishment of price stabilisation mechanisms, developing countries have emphasized the adverse impact these characteristics have had on their economies.

A related issue is the structure of commodity markets. Some of these are characterised by many sellers (usually from developing countries) who are financially weak and have limited staying power in the market, and a few financially strong buyers. Although this description may not be valid in the long term for all commodities, it is credible for a large number of them. It can lead to sales of surpluses at 'distress' prices and to losses that will not normally be compensated by gains in rising markets. It can also lead to substantial differences in export unit values between 'arms-length' and 'related-party' transactions for the same product from the same country. The main implication is that, normally, prices are not competitively determined; and developing countries have suggested that the 'excess' profits involved present an opportunity for beneficial redistribution.

Some commodity-exporting countries have been able to raise export volumes to such an extent that the increase in exports more than compensates for the adverse trends in relative prices. As a result their export values have risen (see Table 3) and there has been some, albeit inadequate, growth in their capacity to import. Nevertheless, the more countries individually and collectively expand their export volumes, the lower will be the price for each of them, given the price elasticities for most commodities. This erosion or lack of satisfactory growth in the purchasing power of primary commodities has made urgent the need for diversification, principally into manufactures, by developing countries. Estimating the foreign exchange losses caused by adverse terms of trade is extremely difficult, though an UNCTAD study has calculated that 48 developing countries lost around $38 billion during 1980-84, equivalent to about 28 per cent of their accumulated debt during that period.

To resolve the twin problem of secular decline and instability, developing countries called for the establishment of a mechanism to ensure that commodity prices are remunerative to producers and take into account, inter alia, world inflation and the prices of imported manufactures (i.e. the practice of indexation). Prices and earnings were sought to be stabilised and where possible raised through supply control by setting up international commodity agreements (ICAs) (see Box 8), whose establishment could also be seen as an attempt to mobilize countervailing power to minimise the adverse effects for producers of oligopsonistic structures, typical of certain commodity markets. This approach was embodied in the UNCTAD Secretariat's proposal for an IPC, adopted as a framework for international commodity policy at UNCTAD IV in 1976. A strong 'central source of finance' was proposed for funding buffer stocking operations envisaged under the ICAs.

The concept of a Common Fund

Proposals to stabilise commodity prices go back to the early years of the century and supply control schemes were set up for tin, rubber and coffee in the 1920s. A committee set up by the League of Nations to study the problem of raw materials in 1937 came out in favour of such arrangements (see pages 124-127). In 1942, the eminent economist, Maynard Keynes, advocated an integrated system of ''commodity organisations supervised by a General Council for Commodity Controls and financed by an International Clearing Union''. But it was not until the second half of the 1960s, after the United Nations Conference on Trade and Development (1964) and its permanent Secretariat had provided an impetus for expanding the number of ICAs and changing their role, that an IPC began formally to be considered. The developing countries (which in the meantime had banded together in the Group of 77) began to inject a political dimension into this process in the early 1970s.

In response, the UNCTAD Secretariat in 1974 proposed an overall programme which attempted to deal, comprehensively and in an integrated way, with the major commodity problems of developing countries. The programme was based on a common set of principles, objectives, techniques and guidelines, and provided for action to be taken on groups of commodities through measures such as multi-commodity buffer stocks. Its authors saw a system of international buffer stocks as playing a key role. They noted that past attempts to establish buffer stocks had floundered because developed countries had been unwilling to contribute to their financing and the developing countries had been unable to finance such stocks themselves. (The IMF Buffer Stock Financing Facility, established in 1969 and designed to assist developing countries in this regard, was small in size.) It was proposed that the funds required for setting up buffer stocks in the context of an integrated programme should be investigated together with the feasibility of establishing a 'central pool of finance' which could minimize the capital costs involved and obtain loans more easily than each separate buffer stock could.

Later the same year (at the request of the UNCTAD Trade and Development Board), the UNCTAD Secretariat elaborated proposals for the major elements of an IPC. International buffer stocks were viewed as the cornerstone for stabilising commodity prices and earnings. This would benefit producers, but consumers would also enjoy stabilised prices and security of supplies. The stocking operations could also yield profits, and thus provide the flexibility to adjust to extraordinary situations, and to stimulate resource shifts for diversification to resolve problems of persistent overproduction. A solution to the problem of acquiring sufficient funds for the stocking operations, at that stage estimated at $10.7 billion for 18 commodities* was a key element in the IPC.

---

* The ten 'core' commodities of the 18 in the IPC are: cocoa, coffee, tea, sugar, jute, hardfibres, cotton, rubber (natural), copper and tin. The other eight commodities in the original Programme are: bananas, bauxite, iron ore, manganese, meat, phosphates, tropical timber, and vegetable oils and oilseeds.

The establishment of a central facility—a Common Fund—was therefore deemed essential.

The Common Fund was seen as an institution constituted for the specific purpose of financing internationally held stocks for a number of commodities. It would be supported by the governments of both exporting and importing

---

Box 8: International Commodity Agreements

Traditionally the main rationale for international commodity agreements (ICAs) has been to stabilise prices. The chief instruments employed have been export controls (e.g. for the ICAs on coffee and sugar) and buffer stocks (e.g. for those on cocoa and natural rubber). Some ICAs (e.g. on tin) have used both. In addition, ICAs have had several long-term objectives including product diversification and increased competitiveness through research and development. However, they have not normally been provided with adequate resources to achieve these objectives. This was a major reason for the incorporation of a Second Window in the Common Fund for Commodities.

Assessing the past effectiveness of ICAs in stabilising prices is extremely complex. Their degree of success has varied from one agreement to another, but at present only one of them—on natural rubber—operates the market intervention mechanisms necessary to help stabilise prices. As to the past, three major lessons can be drawn from studies of agreements on cocoa, coffee, natural rubber, sugar and tin. First, ICAs have only been successful when they have commanded a wide measure of support from major producers and consumers. This has been particularly important in ICAs based on export controls and thus on quota allocations (e.g. for coffee and sugar). In agreements based on buffer stocks, an absence of consensus has nullified their effectiveness through its impact on financial contributions (e.g. on cocoa). Second, certain agreements have not been robust enough to withstand marked fluctuations in the exchange rates in which their operative clauses have been denominated - this was considered a major contributory factor to the collapse of the sixth International Tin Agreement. Third, some agreements seem to have been inadequately drafted. This was demonstrated by the controversy over the role of the tin buffer stock manager and was also apparent in the lack of specificity in clauses on revising the price range in certain agreements.

Various policy measures are required to resolve these issues, but the entry into operation of the Common Fund can at least help in solving the financing problem.

---

countries; and able to seek funds from sources other than governments on terms comparable with those at which official international financial institutions can borrow. Among the reasons advanced for its establishment were the increased effectiveness and lower financial outlays of stocking activities when undertaken on an integrated basis for several commodities and with government co-operation; the greater incentive to conclude ICAs if a funding instrument already existed; and the contribution to the stability of national economies and external payments made possible by such an instrument. The proponents of the Fund saw it as a central source of finance, able to borrow from the market as well as from governments and international financial institutions, and to lend to international commodity organisations (ICOs) supervising those ICAs based on stocking.

The IPC Resolution (93(IV)) adopted by consensus by UNCTAD in Nairobi in 1976 called on the UNCTAD Secretary-General to convene a negotiating conference on the Common Fund in order to elaborate its objectives, financing needs, sources, structure, mode of operations and decision-making processes. An important development of the concept at that stage was an implicit acceptance that its functions could include the financing of commodity development measures in addition to buffer stocking. This had been called for by the Group of 77 in the Programme of Action it had adopted at Manila in 1976 in preparation for UNCTAD IV. At Nairobi the IPC Resolution listed various other measures, such as financing for diversification projects and other programmes. This raised two issues. First, whether the Common Fund should charge varying rates of interest according to the type of operations or borrowers being financed. Second, what interest rate would be required. A number of approaches were discussed, but the UNCTAD Secretariat concluded that it would seem advisable to separate the financing operations into two accounts: the first for buffer stocking, and the second for other measures. It was felt that given the financial structure of the Common Fund and the likely average interest rate, the net income from the operations of its 'First Account' would be unlikely to allow for substantial transfers to the 'Second Account'. This would therefore have to rely mainly on contributions from member countries. The UNCTAD Secretariat estimated the funding requirement at $6 billion (1976 prices) for ten core commodities: $4.5-5.0 billion for stocking operations and $1.0-1.5 billion for other measures. This was much lower than the OECD's estimate of $8.3 billion.

In March 1977, the Conference to negotiate the Common Fund was duly convened. But the debate, at times ill-tempered, reached a stalemate almost at the outset, and during most of the four weeks of the Conference the scheduled plenary and committee meetings were adjourned indefinitely while delegations met in country groups. Some delegations among the developed market economy countries (Group B) were not prepared to accept the need for a Common Fund without considering alternatives. Group B supported a commodity-by-commodity approach and was not prepared to endorse a central financing facility as the principal or only source of funds for commodity buffer stocks. Rather it saw members of individual ICAs as continuing to be responsible for providing the finances required for these agreements. If a sufficient number of ICAs deposited their surplus funds with the Common Fund, the facility could be used as a clearing house or pooling facility, on-lending the funds to ICOs in need. To that extent the Common Fund might save on total cash requirements. But these Group B countries did not contemplate any direct capital contributions to the Fund. In their view the individual ICAs, and not the Common Fund, would remain the axis of price stabilisation measures.

In contrast, the developing countries (Group of 77) saw a far more active role for the Common Fund. They sought to remove the financial constraints on the negotiation of ICAs by establishing a strong central source of funding which would relieve the financial burden on member countries of the ICAs. The financial viability of the Common Fund had to be guaranteed, so that it could raise money in the capital markets and provide funds to ICOs on attractive terms. Potential lenders would place much more weight on the Common Fund if it had its own capital base; a demonstrated commitment from member governments through contributions to the capital would improve its credit rating.

Tasks for the Commonwealth Group

It was against that background that Commonwealth Heads of Government, meeting in June 1977, asked the Secretary-General to establish the Commonwealth Technical Group. They requested the Group, which was chaired by Lord Campbell, to clarify a whole range of issues relating to the Common Fund. These included its role in buffer stocking and other measures, the type of fund, its level of capitalisation, decision-making and management, and the treatment of least developed countries and of developing countries which are net importers of commodities. And they sought a report which would help facilitate progress when the UN Conference was reconvened later that year.

Role of the Common Fund

Regarding buffer stocking, the Campbell Group noted in its report, *The Common Fund*, that in those ICAs that had been negotiated, the financing of such stocks had been mainly the responsibility of exporting countries, and that importing countries had been reluctant to contribute. But it pointed out that the stabilisation of commodity prices about their long-term trend was in the interest of both producers and consumers. The establishment of the Common

Fund would increase the availability of finance and greatly help in negotiating new ICAs with buffer stock provisions.

Developed market economy countries felt that the Common Fund's role would not be restricted to stabilising prices but that the Fund would be used to try to raise prices (indexation). They argued that this would diminish consumption and raise production. These, in turn, could necessitate long-term controls on production and a freezing of the market structure, and could thus lead to a restriction of investment, especially in low-cost production. The problem would be exacerbated for commodities where there was a downward secular trend in prices and where there were natural or synthetic substitutes. The developing countries' call for indexation arose from their belief that commodity prices were subject to a secular decline. The Campbell Group pointed out that within individual ICAs, prices could not be forced against long-term market trends, and that buffer stocking on its own might not suffice to achieve one of the IPC's stated aims: an improvement in the terms of trade of developing countries. That objective would depend mainly on other elements in the Programme.

The Group's report also discussed the size of stocks required to achieve the stabilistion objective, and the other benefits associated with buffer stock operations - the 'hidden' gains caused by the indirect repercussions of market operations by the buffer stock manager. On the scope for buffer stocking, the report noted that a central financing facility could assist more than the 10 core commodities originally proposed if it was allowed to finance national stocks held under internationally agreed arrangements. In addition to stocks held under ICAs, it was considered that those under agreements being negotiated should be eligible for financing by the Common Fund, as should stocks in developing countries of commodities for which there was no ICA but where the main exporters were developed countries.

The second of the proposed activities of the Common Fund concerned measures other than stocking to improve the position of commodity-exporting countries. While recognising the need for the IPC to include such activities, the developed countries argued that they should be financed through established institutions such as the World Bank. They claimed that the Second Window (or Account) of the Common Fund, which it was proposed should finance these activities, might replicate the history of the International Fund for Agricultural Development (IFAD) established in 1976. Intended to act as a catalyst in financing food production projects, IFAD was already attempting to become an important source of finance for them.

The Campbell Group considered that past piecemeal efforts at improving the conditions of world commodity markets had produced results that could hardly be deemed acceptable; it was against that background that the IPC's broad-based approach to international action in the commodities field had been developed. The Group felt that the Common Fund should be in a position to take an overall view of the various aspects of commodity trade problems and to act as a catalyst in finding solutions.

The developing countries remained firm in demanding that the Fund should contribute to achieving the wider objectives of the IPC by financing measures such as commodity diversification, research and development, productivity improvement, market promotion and the encouragement of processing activities. They argued that duplication did not necessarily mean waste, any more than a multiplicity of banks meant a waste of economic resources. Besides, the crucial point was how to achieve the central objectives of the IPC. Other measures could be supportive of buffer stocking in achieving the pricing and other objectives of the ICAs. Moreover, buffer stocking was not a suitable mechanism for certain commodities, like bananas, of great importance to some developing countries. A commodity financing facility needed a balance of objectives and functions, taking into account the varied requirements and interests of different developing countries (including the least developed countries) as exporters of a variety of commodities as well as the interests of developing countries which were net importers of commodities. The proposal for supportive measures in addition to buffer stocking was therefore a vital element in seeking to achieve the goals of the IPC, of which the Common Fund was the lynchpin.

The Campbell Group strongly supported the concept of a Second Window for 'other measures', arguing that the Fund could not play its designated key role unless it could be active in a wide range of measures in addition to buffer stocking. It would need to have the financial and technical capability to catalyse action in appropriate cases but without interfering with the autonomy of the individual ICOs. The Group considered, however, that Second Window operations should be kept distinct from stock financing. It envisaged a programme of activities financed by the Second Window based on an initial capital of $250 million, and expected non-recoverable expenditure (which would have to be replenished by voluntary donations from governments and other agencies) to amount to some $100 million per year.

The type of activities the Group had in mind for priority action under the Second Window included the provision of finance (on World Bank terms) for building storage facilities; undertaking feasibility studies and other technical assistance; the provision of catalytic funds for projects concerned with commodity diversification, processing, marketing and distribution; the support of R&D to improve commodity productivity and develop new uses; the support of export market development; and the encouragement of international risk pooling arrangements against natural hazards.

Type of Fund

The Campbell Group discussed the two main funding proposals then under discussion on the structure of buffer stock financing. It considered that the 'pool model', under which ICAs would deposit their cash balances with the Common Fund, did not offer any particular advantage to existing ICOs as the Common Fund would be simply a banking facility, unable to play a catalytic role in concluding new ICAs. The Group viewed this method as an unreliable basis on which to structure a Common Fund intended to play a key role in the IPC. Instead, it acknowledged the special attractions of the 'source model', favoured by developing countries, under which the Common Fund would be the principal or only source of finance for buffer stocking arrangements, and would derive its resources from capital subscriptions from governments, together with some loans from governments, international financial institutions and private capital markets. However, the Group acknowledged the concerns expressed on the pure 'source model' and felt that modifications were both necessary and feasible.

Its conclusion was that the time had come to move away from the polarised 'source' and 'pool' concepts in favour of a Common Fund designed to make maximum use of the funds available from governments, international financial institutions, ICOs and the private sector. The Group recommended a type of Fund "which would have independent financial capability to provide support to ICOs and commodity producers, whether or not individual ICOs initially participate, and to play a catalytic role". It noted that "to the extent that ICOs contribute their own deposits to the Fund it may be described as a 'source'/'pool' combination".

Capitalisation and sources of finance

The Campbell Group noted the difficulties in estimating the capital requirements for stocking operations, and thought a logical procedure would be to specify a maximum figure within which a financial plan for the Common Fund could be devised, pointing out that the capital contributions would be called only over a fairly long period of time. It agreed that the upper limit of the UNCTAD Secretariat's estimates of $5 billion for buffer stocks and $1 billion for other measures provided a realistic base for devising a financial plan. Emphasising the need to phase in capital subscriptions according to the requirements of the operation, the Group said that it might be possible to start with equity subscriptions of only $500 million on the basis of $1 billion equity being issued and 50 per cent paid-up. Regarding the initial paid-up capital, it suggested that $130 million should come from the developing countries, $305 million from the developed countries, $50 million from the centrally planned economy countries, and $15 million from China.

After consulting bankers, the Campbell Group thought it unlikely that the

Common Fund would attract medium and long-term loans from private capital markets, at least until its operations had proved viable. Initially, therefore, funds would have to come from governments and possibly from international financial institutions. The Group believed that the World Bank and the IMF should play a role in providing support for the Fund and, in particular, that the IMF should be enabled to assist member countries in meeting their own capital contributions. While recognising the problems involved in direct IMF assistance to the Common Fund, the Group felt that the opportunity should be grasped, especially because commodity stocking provided scope for international counter-cyclical operations. At times when the world economy needed stimulation, the issue of SDRs to provide financing for buffer stocking should be considered.

Decision-making and management
The developing countries took the view that the voting structure of the Common Fund should reflect the thrust of the UNCTAD Resolution on the IPC; it had called for efforts by the international community in favour of developing countries. The distribution of voting rights should therefore be related to factors other than the size of countries' capital subscriptions and should give developing countries a decisive role in the Fund's management. The developed countries were opposed to a structure which gave a decisive role to one of the country groups. The Campbell Group agreed that the Fund's structure should allow substantial and effective participation of developing countries in its decision-making and management. It proposed that voting rights should be based partly on equality of membership status and partly on the size of capital subscriptions so as to provide at least 50 per cent of the votes to developing countries.

Least developed countries and net importers of commodities
The draft IPC presented at UNCTAD IV included a wide array of special measures to assist countries designated as least developed. But it was also thought necessary to add two special 'safeguard' clauses. First, the interests of developing countries that are net importers of commodities, particularly the least developed among them, should be protected by appropriate differential and remedial measures within the Programme. Second, special action, including exemption from financial contributions, should be taken to accommodate the needs of the least developed countries in the IPC.

The Campbell Group took the position that the least developed countries were substantially more important as exporters than as importers of commodities, and that in any case, all countries would be expected to gain from the IPC, either directly or indirectly. It recommended measures by which the least developed countries could schedule their payments of subscriptions to the

Common Fund without lowering their total contribution. To meet any specific difficulties facing countries which are net importers of commodities (most of whom are petroleum-exporting and middle-income developing countries), it was recommended that the Common Fund should support their commodity sectors through action under its Second Window.

Towards a consensus

The Campbell Group's report was favourably received by Commonwealth Governments. Finance Ministers, meeting in September 1977, considered it an important document, and requested the Secretary-General, beside giving it wide international circulation, to arrange for Commonwealth ministerial consultations in the context of the UNCTAD negotiations. The report was also commended by many countries represented at UNCTAD. By indicating possible ways of accommodating the position of both main country groups, it was felt to be contributing to the process of consensus building so necessary to facilitate progress in the negotiations.

A better prospect for agreement had emerged in the preceding months as a result of the endorsement of the concept of the Common Fund by the summit meeting of leading industrial countries (Group of Seven) in May 1977, and from the agreement at the Conference on International Economic Co-operation (CIEC) in Paris in June 1977 that it should be established to play a key role in achieving the agreed objectives of the IPC. However, these decisions did not identify any particular form of Fund or specify its purposes and objectives.

The Campbell Group's report was submitted to the second session of the UN negotiating conference on the Common Fund, held in November 1977. This session also ran into difficulties, however, and was suspended without advancing beyond the statement of differences. Its only positive outcome was that the developed countries did generally acknowledge the acceptability to them of the Common Fund concept. The major stumbling-blocks were two: whether the Fund should have a 'Second Window' to finance measures other than stocking, and whether direct government contributions should be an essential component of the Fund's capital structure.

The developing countries' view remained close to the UNCTAD Secretariat's concept of the Common Fund as the central source of funding for both buffer stock operations and other measures. They felt it was imperative for the Fund to have independent resources based on government contributions. In contrast, the developed countries reiterated their support for a pooling arrangement, in which ICOs would deposit with the Common Fund up to 75 per cent of their maximum financial resources, where these were not needed for stock purchases, in return for guaranteed drawing rights. Any additional funds required by the Fund would be borrowed. These countries did not envisage a direct role for the Fund in 'other measures', while recognising that such measures had an important role in commodity policy. They insisted that the scope of existing international arrangements for supporting such measures should be first examined to see if any deficiencies could be remedied - before considering any role for the Common Fund in this area.

With the lull in negotiations, UNCTAD's Secretary-General undertook a series of informal consultations during the following year (1978) with a view to assessing prospects for agreement on the fundamental issues. In February a meeting of Commonwealth Heads of Government of the Asian and Pacific region welcomed the Campbell Group's report as a constructive contribution and ''agreed to promote action in relevant international forums to secure greater progress in the negotiations on the implementation of the resolutions of the Fourth Session of UNCTAD and of CIEC on the Integrated Programme for Commodities, in which the establishment of a Common Fund is a key instrument''. They undertook to do all they could to facilitate an early resumption of the negotiations and ''indicated their willingness to participate actively and constructively in them to achieve an early successful outcome''.

In April 1978, a special meeting of Commonwealth Ministers concerned with commodity policy was held in London—as suggested by Finance Ministers in September 1977—to review the state of negotiations on the Common Fund, to consider the Campbell Group's report, and to seek an acceptable basis for the resumption of negotiations. Ministers saw the Group's analysis as helpful to efforts aimed at reaching an accord on the essential elements of the Common Fund, and ''expressed their determination to work for an early resumption of the negotiating conference on the Common Fund and its successful conclusion''. In particular—and in line with the report—Ministers ''considered that the time had come when the international community should move away from the polarised 'source' and 'pool' concepts and work towards establishing a Common Fund designed to make the fullest use of all available funds''. They ''recognised that there was now greater international willingness to consider favourably ... proposals both for direct government contributions to the Fund's capital and also deposits by ICOs and borrowing as possible sources of finance''.

The meeting agreed that, in addition to buffer stocking, other measures had an essential part in the implementation of the IPC; it accepted the possibility of a financial role for the Fund in this area, though it would need to be precisely defined, taking account of existing international activity and appropriately reflecting the collective interests of commodity producers and consumers. It was the view of Ministers that the negotiations should take particular account of the interests and problems of the least developed countries and the most seriously affected net commodity importing countries, including island and landlocked economies and those lacking in natural resources. Finally it was agreed that it would be beneficial for discussions among Commonwealth Ministers to be held again when the second session of the UN negotiating conference was resumed. The Commonwealth meeting thus proved to be particularly fruitful in indicating possibilities for compromise, and is now widely recognised as having helped to improve the climate for the subsequent informal consultations.

The resumed second session of the UN negotiating conference was held in November 1978. By that time it had become apparent to the developed countries that agreement on the Common Fund would be impossible without a Second Window; they would, however, want contributions to that Window to be on a voluntary basis and its activities to be clearly defined and limited. They also accepted that there could be a role for direct government contributions to the Fund's capital, together with deposits by ICOs and borrowing. The developing countries, for their part, accepted that the Fund was initially likely to have much smaller resources than the S6 billion proposed by the UNCTAD Secretariat, and that the possibility of using deposits from ICOs should not be excluded, although they continued to insist that government subscriptions should be the main source of capital. And they did not raise the contentious issue of indexation.

At the third session of the conference, in March 1979, agreement was reached on the fundamental elements of the Common Fund. The Articles of Agreement were later drafted by a committee, and in June 1980, at the fourth session of the negotiating conference, 101 governments approved the Agreement establishing the Common Fund.

In many respects, the final settlement was much closer to the Campbell Group's recommendations than to the original positions of either the developing or the developed countries. On the type of Fund, for example, what eventually emerged was a source-cum-pool model, with a mixture of direct government contributions and deposits from participating ICOs as the Group had recommended. In terms of capitalisation, the directly contributed capital (DCC) was set at $470 million, of which $370 million would be in the form of paid-in shares (cf. the Commonwealth Report's $1 billion and $500 million). The payable shares ($100 million) would be subject to call only if needed to meet the Fund's liabilities arising from borrowings for the First Account ($400 million). The remaining $70 million could be allocated to the Second Account's activities. A target of $280 million was set for initial voluntary contributions to this Account, with provision for periodic replenishment on a voluntary basis. The Campbell Group had recommended $250 million, with annual replenishments of $100 million.

While the UNCTAD Secretariat's original proposal saw the entire resources for buffer stock operations as being provided by the Common Fund, the final package involved the Fund in providing two-thirds of the resources and the

ICOs the remainder. Acceptance of the principle of joint financing by producing and consuming countries, called for by the developing countries, should help to relieve the financial burden on the former.

The developed countries' acceptance of a Second Window, through which measures (other than stocking) which met agreed criteria would be jointly sponsored and monitored by producers and consumers within the framework of ICAs, widened the Common Fund's scope and increased its relevance to the large number of developing countries that might not have benefited from the 'Stock Window' (a point emphasised in the Campbell report). While the developing countries would probably have wished to see the activities of the Second Window somewhat wider than those actually agreed, the potential for evolution remained.

Discussions on the allocation of votes in the Governing Council were dogged by conflict between the developing countries' objective of equality of treatment for all members and the developed countries' view that votes should be allocated in accordance with the members' financial contributions. In the event it was agreed that 47 per cent of the votes would go to the developing countries, 3 per cent to China (the Campbell Group had suggested 50 per cent of the votes for developing countries), 42 per cent to the developed market economy countries and 8 per cent to the centrally planned economy countries. These can be compared with their shares in the DCC of about 10 per cent, 5 per cent, 68 per cent and 17 per cent respectively.

The Agreement was set to enter into force by end-March 1982 provided that by then at least 90 member states comprising not less than two-thirds of the DCC had deposited their instruments of ratification, acceptance or approval, and that pledges of voluntary contributions to the Second Window had equalled at least 50 per cent of the target. But from the outset, support for the Common Fund was hesitant. By the March 1982 deadline, although the Second Window condition had been fulfilled, only 26 countries had ratified the Agreement. These countries agreed to extend the qualifying period by 18 months, but by September 1983 the number was still far short of the qualifying criterion. Since the deadline could only be extended once more, a third deadline was not set, for fear of precipitating a collapse of the Agreement. By January 1986, 90 countries had ratified the Agreement but they only accounted for 58 per cent of the DCC. A breakthrough occurred towards the end of 1987 with ratification by the Soviet Union (accounting for 6.2 per cent of the DCC). In July 1988, 12 years after its conception, the Agreement completed its entry-into-force requirements when ratification by Maldives (the 102nd country to do so) took the contributions to 66.68 per cent. (The US, though a signatory, showed no sign of ratifying the Agreement.)

The long delay in bringing the Common Fund into force reflected a combination of influences. Perhaps the major constraint on ratifications was the disillusionment felt by many developing countries over the eventual compromise package. The truncated nature of the Fund caused many of them to be sceptical of its usefulness. The Fund did not appear to have the makings of a powerful financial institution able to respond to critical market developments. It could not intervene directly in commodity markets nor finance national stocks held outside the framework of ICAs. There was also growing frustration in many of these countries about negotiations on the ICAs which were to be an essential part of the Fund's operations. It had been hoped that by providing funds for buffer stocking, the Fund would ease the financial constraints on ICAs. But progress in concluding new Agreements has been very slow despite the large number of preparatory meetings held and expert groups and task forces formed; even the renegotiation of existing pacts has proved arduous and protracted, and most of them have been shorn of their price stabilisation provisions.

The Fund is established

The Common Fund entered into force on 19 June 1989, at which time it had 104 member countries and total resources of about $545 million ($315 million for its First Account and $230 million pledged voluntarily by governments and allocated to its Second Account—to which an additional $70 million might be allocated from its DCC). At the first annual meeting of the Governing Council (July 1989), 26 Executive Directors and their Alternates were elected for the 28-member Executive Board. (The other two Directors and their Alternates will be elected at the second annual meeting.) The Council elected an Indonesian as the first Managing Director of the Fund, for a four-year term, and accepted an invitation from the Netherlands to locate the headquarters in Amsterdam. The Fund was expected to become fully operational by mid-1990.

At the Governing Council's first meeting the spokesman for the developing countries emphasised the catalytic role the First Account could play in the conclusion of ICAs with price stabilisation provisions. In contrast, the spokesman for the developed countries suggested that the Fund should focus its attention on Second Account measures—rather ironic in that it was these countries that had opposed such a concept earlier.

How much of a contribution the Common Fund can make is still to be seen. The commodity problems discussed earlier in this chapter remain unresolved. The revival of prices in 1988 was neither strong enough nor sufficiently sustained to reverse the secular trend of deterioration in the terms of trade of commodity producing developing countries. And the outlook is for continued weakness in commodity prices well into the 1990s. In the meantime, the performance of ICAs in stabilising prices has been disappointing. All but one of them (natural rubber) have been, in effect, shorn of their operative mechanisms for market intervention, as a result either of inadequate funds to support buffer stocking arrangements of the necessary size (tin and cocoa) or of member countries' failure to agree on quotas (sugar and coffee). The entry into operation of the Common Fund provides a practical opportunity both for making existing ICAs more effective and for negotiating new ones. However, to improve the role of ICAs, much greater attention will have to be given to reducing supply through product and market diversification. In this regard, the Second Account of the Fund could make a vital contribution.

The Commonwealth contribution

The Commonwealth Technical Group on the Common Fund and the Commonwealth Ministerial Meeting held to discuss the Group's report enabled the Commonwealth to make both technical and political contributions to the fruitful outcome of the negotitions. Of even greater significance to the outcome, however, was the timeliness and good management of the Commonwealth's involvement in what became very protracted and difficult negotiations.

Table 1: Commodity share of merchandise exports[a] for Commonwealth countries, MRE

Country	Commodity Share (%)	Share in Merchandise Exports (%)
Australia	54	Wool 14, Beef 5
Britain	11	*
Canada	28	Wood 4, Wheat 2
New Zealand	69	Wool 14, Beef 8
Antigua & Barbuda	1	*
Bahamas	2	*
Bangladesh	25	Jute 14, Tea 7
Barbados	27	Sugar 16
Belize	72	Sugar 29, Citrus fruit 15
Botswana	20 (98)	(Diamonds 77), Copper 14
Brunei	1	*
Cyprus	36	Potatoes 7, Citrus fruit 6
Dominica	59	n.a.
Gambia	51	Groundnuts 27
Ghana	95	Cocoa 54, Timber 7
Grenada	92	Nutmeg 47, Cocoa 13
Guyana	100	Bauxite 36, Sugar 38
India	39	Tea 5, Iron ore 5
Jamaica	72	Alumina 32, Bauxite 14
Kenya	72	Coffee 26, Tea 19
Kiribati	73	n.a.
Lesotho	88	Mohair 30, Wool 14
Malawi	91	Tobacco 62, Tea 11
Malaysia	39	Rubber 9, Palm oil 8
Maldives	72	Fish 67
Malta	6	n.a.
Mauritius	44	Sugar 40
Nauru	33	n.a.
Nigeria	4	Cocoa 3
Pakistan	26	Cotton 16, Rice 7
Papua New Guinea	84	Copper 39, Coffee 9
St. Kitts-Nevis	n.a.	Sugar 62
St. Lucia	96	Bananas 67
St. Vincent & Gren.	99	Bananas 30
Seychelles	30	Copra 2
Sierra Leone	55 (78)	(Diamonds 23), Cocoa 14
Singapore	10	Rubber 3
Solomon Islands	74	Fish 39, Timber 23
Sri Lanka	50	Tea 26, Rubber 8
Swaziland	80	Sugar 35, Timber 21

Country	Commodity Share (%)	Share in Merchandise Exports (%)
Tanzania	99	Coffee 26, Cotton 24
Tonga	67	Coffee 49, Cotton 9
Trinidad & Tobago	5	Sugar 2
Tuvalu	81	Copra 81
Uganda	98	Coffee 92
Vanuatu	65	Copra 37, Cocoa 11
Western Samoa	78	Coconut oil 37, Cocoa 4
Zambia	96	Copper 85
Zimbabwe	57	Tobacco 17, Cotton 5

Notes to Table 1

*none exceeds 1 per cent, the lowest unit used in column 2.
MRE   Most Recent Estimate, generally 1988.
[a]   Thirty-three major commodities (excluding fuel) of interest to developing countries have been included in estimating commodity shares; the figures given in parentheses include items not covered by the 33 but which are important to the countries concerned.

Sources: Compiled mainly from IMF, *International Financial Statistics*, December 1989; and UNCTAD, *Commodity Yearbook*, 1989.

Table 2: Prices of non-fuel primary commodities (1979-81 = 100)

Year	33 Commodities [a] Current US$	Constant [b] US$	Agricultural Products Current US$	Constant [b] US$	Beverages Current US$	Constant [b] US$	Cereals Current US$	Constant[b] US$	Metals & Minerals Current US$	Constant[b] US$
1950	34.8	149.3	39.0	167.4	34.1	146.2	41.2	176.7	28.4	122.1
1951	41.9	155.8	46.2	171.7	37.7	140.3	44.5	165.4	35.6	132.4
1952	38.7	137.1	39.4	139.6	36.0	127.7	44.1	156.5	41.6	147.6
1953	36.1	131.6	37.2	135.7	36.7	134.0	44.2	161.3	37.7	137.4
1954	38.7	144.3	41.4	154.3	52.1	194.3	41.1	153.2	36.0	134.3
1955	38.3	140.4	38.7	141.7	41.3	151.5	36.3	132.9	42.1	154.1
1956	38.9	137.6	38.9	137.3	43.4	153.4	36.7	129.8	43.9	155.2
1957	37.0	127.9	37.8	130.9	39.7	137.3	35.0	121.0	39.4	136.3
1958	34.5	117.2	35.1	119.3	36.2	123.0	35.4	120.6	37.1	126.1
1959	33.9	117.1	34.6	119.3	31.8	109.7	33.7	116.3	35.9	123.9
1960	34.1	115.3	34.4	116.3	30.9	104.2	32.1	108.5	36.7	124.1
1961	32.7	108.7	32.5	108.0	29.2	97.1	34.5	114.6	36.2	120.3
1962	32.6	106.1	32.6	106.1	27.8	90.7	38.1	124.2	35.2	114.6
1963	33.2	110.1	33.8	112.2	27.5	91.4	38.1	126.6	34.4	114.4
1964	35.8	117.1	34.9	114.0	31.6	103.2	37.9	124.0	42.0	137.4
1965	36.8	118.9	33.7	109.0	30.3	98.2	37.2	120.4	48.0	155.2
1966	38.0	119.2	34.1	106.8	29.6	92.7	41.9	131.5	51.5	161.5
1967	35.7	110.5	33.7	104.4	28.8	89.3	44.2	136.8	43.5	134.7
1968	35.9	112.1	33.5	104.8	28.5	89.1	43.0	134.4	44.5	139.1
1969	37.9	112.5	35.0	103.7	29.6	87.8	42.6	126.5	48.8	144.7
1970	39.8	111.2	36.7	102.5	34.4	96.0	39.0	108.9	51.1	142.8
1971	37.0	97.8	35.2	93.2	30.0	79.3	37.7	99.8	44.2	117.0
1972	38.7	93.9	37.9	92.1	33.0	80.0	39.7	96.5	43.8	106.4
1973	59.2	124.0	59.1	123.9	41.9	87.9	81.2	170.2	63.5	133.0
1974	78.1	134.4	78.2	134.7	48.3	83.1	117.6	202.4	84.1	144.8
1975	65.2	100.9	64.5	99.8	45.8	71.0	92.0	142.4	73.1	113.1
1976	73.3	111.9	75.9	115.9	87.7	134.0	75.2	114.8	72.2	110.2
1977	88.4	122.9	96.4	134.1	147.8	205.6	69.1	96.1	75.0	104.4
1978	84.0	101.5	89.3	107.9	109.5	132.3	82.8	100.1	76.2	92.1
1979	98.3	104.8	98.9	105.5	113.5	121.0	86.5	92.2	96.7	103.1
1980	107.8	104.9	107.3	104.4	101.8	99.1	103.3	100.5	108.1	105.2
1981	93.9	90.8	93.7	90.7	84.7	81.9	110.2	106.6	95.2	92.1
1982	84.0	82.4	82.7	81.1	86.5	84.8	80.3	78.7	86.1	84.4
1983	88.6	89.2	88.8	89.4	87.5	88.1	86.8	87.4	88.9	89.5
1984	90.0	92.2	91.9	94.2	101.2	103.7	82.9	85.0	83.9	85.9
1985	79.8	80.9	80.1	81.2	93.3	94.6	72.6	73.6	79.4	80.5
1986	80.2	69.4	82.5	71.3	114.0	98.5	63.4	54.8	73.2	63.2
1987	80.3	63.3	75.1	59.2	74.9	59.0	59.9	47.2	84.1	66.3
1988	96.6	70.5	86.0	62.8	83.6	61.1	80.9	59.0	115.6	84.4
1989[c]	95.7	67.9	84.6	60.0	78.4	55.6	83.3	59.1	116.8	82.8
2000[c]	147.7	61.2	138.2	57.3	140.1	58.1	122.7	50.8	155.3	64.4

[a]   The 33 commodities included are: coffee, cocoa, tea, maize, rice, wheat, sorghum, palm oil, coconut oil, groundnut oil, soybeans, copra, groundnut eal, soybean meal, sugar, beef, bananas, oranges, cotton, jute, natural rubber, tobacco, logs, sawnwood, aluminium, bauxite, copper, iron ore, lead, nickel, tin, zinc and phosphate rock.

[b]   Deflated by an index of unit values of exports of manufactures from the five largest developed market economy countries (G5).

[c]   Estimated.

Source: The World Bank, Commodity Price Forecasts, June 1989.

Table 3: Developing countries' export earnings from selected commodities

Commodity	1985	1986	1987	1988
			(SDR billions)	
Cocoa	2.7	2.5	2.2	1.6
	(1.3)	(1.4)	(1.4)	(1.5)
Coffee	10.4	11.8	7.1	7.1
	(4.2)	(3.8)	(4.2)	(3.9)
Cotton	3.1	2.6	2.6	2.2
	(2.3)	(3.0)	(3.1)	(2.9)
Hardwood logs	1.8	1.5	1.9	1.8
	(26.9)*	(25.6)*	(29.2)*	(27.3)*
Natural Rubber	2.7	2.5	2.8	3.1
	(3.6)	(3.7)	(3.9)	(4.0)
Sugar	6.9	6.0	5.8	5.8
	(19.2)	(17.9)	(18.3)	(17.4)
Tea	2.0	1.5	1.4	1.5
	(1.0)	(1.0)	(1.0)	(1.0)
Bauxite (including aluminium)	2.6	2.6	3.1	4.6
	(1.6)	(1.7)	(1.8)	(1.9)
Copper (including refined)	3.9	3.5	3.7	4.6
	(2.9)	(2.9)	(3.0)	(3.0)
Iron ore	3.0	2.7	2.4	2.3
	(175)	(175)	(180)	(186)
Tin (including metal)	1.9	0.8	0.9	0.9
	(180)**	(176)**	(196)**	(205)**

Notes:
    Figures given in parentheses are export volumes in million tonnes (except
    where otherwise shown).
     * million cubic meters.
     ** thousand tonnes.
Source: Compiled from IMF, *Primary Commodities, Market Developments and Outlook*,
    July 1989.

Chronology of events

1927 World Economic Conference under the auspices of the League of Nations recommends that international commodity agreements should be established to permit a more rational organisation of production. It expresses the hope that negotiations of such agreements would prevent artificial rises in prices regarded as detrimental to the interests of consumers and producers alike.

1932-33 A League of Nations Monetary and Economic Conference appoints a sub-committee to consider issues relating to commodity price instability. Its report, subsequently accepted by the League, proposes that the main purpose of international commodity agreements should be to increase the purchasing power of raw material producers by raising export prices to 'reasonable', 'fair' and 'remunerative' levels.

1937 Council of League of Nations appoints Committee for the Study of the Problem of Raw Materials, and discusses international supply regulations.

1942 Maynard Keynes proposes an International Trade Organisation as a part of the Bretton Woods system; among its objectives would be the stabilisation of commodity prices.

1943 United Nations Conference on Food and Agriculture recommends establishment of international organisation to supervise negotiation and functioning of international commodity agreements.

1948 United Nations Conference on Trade and Employment agrees (in Havana Charter) on objectives of commodity price stabilisation around long-term trend and appropriate and stable incomes for primary producers; also on the creation of an International Trade Organisation to achieve these objectives. (Due to the failure of the US Congress to ratify the charter, the International Trade Organisation was never established. Instead, its commercial policy provisions have been applied 'provisionally' by contracting parties to the GATT.)

1950 United Nations issues report on 'Instability in Export Markets of Underdeveloped Countries in Relation to the Ability to Obtain Foreign Exchange from Exports of Primary Commodities'.

1953 United Nations issues report on 'Commodity Trade and Economic Development'.

1956 GATT attempts to negotiate Special Agreement on Commodity Arrangements.

1958 GATT report 'Trends in International Trade' (Haberler Report) recommends measures to stabilise commodity markets through buffer stocking and consideration of co-ordinated action.

1961 UN General Assembly adopts resolution on trade and development.

1964 UN Conference on Trade and Development (UNCTAD I, Geneva) brings renewed emphasis to international commodity policy (Prebisch report *Towards a New Trade Policy for Development* proposes international commodity agreements as a means of raising commodity prices).

1967 Charter of Algiers (Group of 77 Ministerial Meeting) lists 18 commodities for international action.

1968 UNCTAD Secretariat issues study on Development of an International Commodity Policy, in which it suggests the setting up of a central commodity stabilisation fund.

1968 UNCTAD II (New Delhi) recommends action programme (buffer stocking, market access, pricing policy) for each of the 18 commodities.

1969 IMF establishes Buffer Stocking Financing Facility.

1971 Lima Declaration on trade and development (Group of 77).

1972 UNCTAD III (Santiago) Resolution 83(III) sets up intergovernmental consultations on 14 commodities.

1973 Organisation of Petroleum Exporting Countries raises prices and sets example to other commodity producers.

1974 UN General Assembly Sixth Special Session (on raw materials and development) adopts Declaration and Programme of Action on the Establishment of a New International Economic Order, including the establishment of an integrated programme for commodities, designed to stabilise and raise commodity prices and to increase the export earnings of developing countries.

1974 UNCTAD Secretariat releases paper ''A Common Fund for the Financing of Commodity Stocks''.

1975 Dakar Conference of Developing Countries on Raw Materials recommends the establishment of international stocks and market intervention arrangements for commodities.

1975 UNCTAD Committee on Commodities (Eighth Session) considers a Secretariat paper on 'An Integrated Programme for Commodities' which foresaw a comprehensive set of commodity negotiations based on a series of buffer stocks financed by a common fund and complemented by multilateral trade commitments.

1975 UN General Assembly Seventh Special Session proposes that UNCTAD IV reaches decisions with respect to an integrated programme for commodities and the applicability of the programme's various elements.

1976 Manila Declaration and Programme of Action endorses integrated programme for commodities and recommends establishment of common fund for financing international commodity stocks, harmonisation of stock policy, indexation of commodity prices to prices of imported manufactures, and promotion and support of diversification in developing countries (February).

1976 UNCTAD IV (Nairobi) adopts Resolution 93(iv) on the Integrated Programme for Commodities covering ten core products and eight others, with a series of agreements on buffer stocking and other operations including pricing arrangements, export quotas and commodity development measures, financed through a Common Fund (May).

1976 Two preparatory meetings on Common Fund (November and December).

1977 Third preparatory meeting on Common Fund (March).

1977 First session of UN Negotiating Conference on the establishment of a Common Fund fails to reach agreement and is suspended (March-April).

1977 Western Economic Summit (London) indicates support in principle for Common Fund (May).

1977 Conference on International Economic Cooperation agrees that a Common Fund should be established as a key instrument in attaining the agreed objectives of the Integrated Programme for Commodities (May).

1977 Commonwealth Heads of Government agree to work towards early establishment of Common Fund and ask Commonwealth Secretary-General to set up a technical working group to examine the issues and make proposals with a view to facilitating progress (June).

1977 Report of Commonwealth Technical Group on Common Fund (September).

1977 Second session of UN Negotiating Conference on the establishment of a Common Fund fails to reach agreement on modalities (November).

1978 Informal consultations held among participants with the aim of seeking to bridge differences.

1978 Commonwealth Heads of Government of Asia and Pacific, meeting in Sydney, agree to work towards early resumption of negotiations on Common Fund (February).

1978 Commonwealth Ministers, meeting in London, reiterate their determination to work for successful conclusion of negotiating conference; express view that international community should move away from polarised 'source' and 'pool' concepts and that measures in addition to buffer stocking should play an essential role (April).

1978 Resumed second sesion of UN Negotiating Conference on Common Fund (November).

1979 Third session of UN Negotiating Conference reaches agreement on basic elements of Common Fund and agrees on interim committee to draft Articles of Agreement (March).

1979-80 Interim Committee on Common Fund meets five times.

1980 Fourth session of UN Negotiating Conference on Common Fund reaches consensus (Agreement to enter into force when ratified by 90 countries accounting for two-thirds of Directly Contributed Capital (DCC) of $470 million; total fund of $750 million, of which $400 million for price stabilisation and $350 million for commodity development measures (the Second Window); target date for entry into force set as 31 March 1982) (June).

1982 Only 26 countries ratify Agreement by 31 March, deadline extended by 18 months.

1983 Ratifications still below required number on 30 September.

1986 Number of countries ratifying reaches 90 (January) but does not account for two-thirds of DCC.

1988 Ratification by Maldives (the 102nd country to do so) brings proportion of DCC to 66.68 per cent and triggers procedure for entry into force (July).

1989 Agreement enters into force (June).

1989 First meeting of Governing Council (July).

1990 Possible start of operations (June?).

Chapter 7

Increasing protectionism and its impact on developing countries

A persistent threat to the international economy is that the post-war system of generally liberal trade could be undermined by protectionism. International economic disorder—the oil price 'shock' of the late 1970s, the recession that followed, and prolonged macroeconomic imbalances between leading industrial countries—has created an environment within which the rules underlying the trading system's stability have been brought into question. One feature of this period has been a weakening of respect for the disciplines evolved under the General Agreement on Tariffs and Trade (GATT) (see Box 9). Developing countries face particular problems in respect of access to developed-country markets. Whilst successive rounds of multilateral trade negotiations (MTNs) under GATT have progressively reduced tariffs, non-tariff measures (NTMs) have been more widely used, are a less transparent instrument of protection and have particularly affected developing-country exports to developed-country markets.

A Commonwealth Expert Group which was set up to consider protectionism issued its report, *Protectionism : Threat to International Order*, in 1982; the report provided a framework for formulating proposals to strengthen the international trading system. Its recommendations and conclusions have also provided a basis for Secretariat activities in the trade policy field, especially its work in support of governments participating in the current—Uruguay Round—of MTNs. In the Vancouver Declaration (1987) on international trade policy, Commonwealth Heads of Government signalled their concern over intensified protectionist pressures, many directed against developing countries, and stressed the need for early action in the Uruguay Round to resolve these difficulties.

Barriers of many kinds

Protectionism, especially as experienced by developing-country exporters in major developed-country markets, is not new. The traditional areas of export specialisation for these countries, at least in manufacturing and raw material processing, were subject to various degrees and forms of protection well before the 1970s. However, NTMs have since proliferated. While quantification may be difficult, it is generally accepted that protectionism has expanded considerably since the mid-1970s. A 1985 OECD study indicated that, between 1963 and 1983, the number of NTMs had quadrupled and that the proportion of trade affected within protected sectors had increased (e.g. in iron and steel the proportion rose from 37 to 73 per cent).

Protectionism has become generally more discriminatory in recent years, with a move towards more bilateral measures involving voluntary export restraints (VERs) and orderly marketing arrangements (OMAs). In 1979,

---

Box 9: The General Agreement on Tariffs and Trade

The General Agreement on Tariffs and Trade entered into force in 1948 and now has 96 member governments as contracting parties. GATT rules for the conduct of international trade are based on the following principles:

1. Trade without discrimination: according to the 'most-favoured-nation' (mfn) clause, all contracting parties grant each other treatment as favourable as they give to any country in the application and administration of import/export duties and charges.

2. Protection through tariffs: where protection is given to domestic producers it should be through customs tariffs and not through other commercial measures. Among other things the aim of this rule is to make the extent and degree of protection clear.

3. A stable basis for trade: to be provided by the binding of all tariff reductions negotiated among the contracting parties. The renegotiation of tariffs at higher rates is discouraged by the requirement that compensation should be paid for any increase.

4. Consultation, conciliation and settlement of disputes : this should be sought through the GATT machinery established for the purpose.

5. 'Waiver' procedures: these allow a country to seek a derogation from particular GATT obligations when its economic or trade circumstances so warrant.

6. A general prohibition of quantitative restrictions: except when a contracting party is in balance of payments difficulties.

7. Regional trading arrangements: these are permitted as an exception to the general rule of mfn treatment, provided barriers to trade with third parties are not raised.

---

nearly one-third of manufactures imported by OECD countries from developing countries were controlled by NTMs compared to only one-tenth of those imported from other OECD members. In the 1980s, although these figures have not changed significantly, the severity of restriction has increased. Further, there has been a shift away from direct subsidies for manufacturing towards protection by voluntary restraint or import controls, especially in those manufacturing sectors (e.g. steel) in which developing countries had a growing export interest. This has made protection less transparent. A substantial majority of textile and clothing imports from developing countries is now regulated—between 70 and 80 per cent in the European Community (EC), the US and Canada. More than half the steel imported into developed countries from developing countries is also now tightly controlled.

It appears that the spread and intensification of NTMs has now largely offset the reduction of tariffs on imports into the developed countries. A World Bank study in 1988 indicated that the economy-wide tariff equivalent of US NTMs on textiles, steel and automobiles, for example, was about 25 per cent, bringing protection back to its level of the early post-war years. Such barriers affected nearly one-quarter of the value of all non-oil imports into 18 developed countries in 1987, a 21 per cent increase over the coverage of 1981.

A significant factor in this increase has been the expanding use of VERs. To the extent they can be quantified, their number has grown from about 50 in 1978 to 135 in late 1987 and, based on preliminary information, to 253 by April 1988, with much of the latter increase attributable to the European Community. In April 1988, the exports of developing countries were restrained by at least 120 VERs, with an estimated 89 VERs in place on exports of OECD countries.

There is also evidence of increasing resort to anti-dumping and countervailing actions. UNCTAD reported that there were 557 anti-dumping investigations in 1985 and an average of 160 in the previous four years. In 1984-85 70 of the 193 new cases were against developing countries (i.e. over one-third). A similar pattern is apparent in countervailing duty investigations, with a quadrupling in the same period of cases against developing countries, largely by the US.

These non-tariff actions, onerous enough in their effects on developing country exporters, occur against a background of relatively high tariffs. These have only been partially liberalised through preference schemes - they still average around 20 per cent for garment items - and also demonstrate significant escalation in the tariff structure, leading to high effective rates of protection and discrimination (see Table 4).

Table 4: Escalation in tariff structure of industrial countries

Level of processing [a]	Average ad valorem tariff (post Tokyo Round)	
	Nominal (on total values)	Effective (on value added)
Stage 1	3	3
Stage 2	8	23
Stage 3	9	20
Stage 4	9	15

[a] Based on processing "chains" for 21 agricultural and mineral products.
For example, the chain for cotton and products is (1) raw cotton,
(2) cotton yarn, (3) cotton fabrics, (4) clothing.
Source: World Bank

There is also a long-term problem of protectionist measures. While they have grown in intensity, they stem from a long-standing determination by major industrial countries to protect farm incomes by a combination of price support, import restriction and export subsidies. Agricultural protection is not especially directed against developing countries but it happens to bear upon them hard in some sectors, such as sugar, vegetable oils, fruit and fruit juices, vegetables, and tobacco, where they have major export interests (see Table 5). Some attempt has been made in the Tokyo and Uruguay Rounds to isolate, for more liberal treatment, the tropical products which developing countries export. But in practice, tropical products liberalisation in a GATT context has so far been confined largely to nominal tariffs and to non-competing items. Even there, barriers remain in the form of high consumption taxes on tropical beverages, for example, in some countries such as Germany.

The Commonwealth intervenes

In 1981, when the Commonwealth Expert Group was established, it was becoming clear that the various GATT bodies were unable to stem the growing protectionist tide. This further undermined the credibility of the international trading system in the eyes of many developing countries which had already been disappointed by the results of the Tokyo Round which had ended two years earlier. Despite the progress this Round had made in reducing tariffs, and the fact that it represented the first substantive effort by GATT to address NTMs, the result left considerable barriers in place, including tariff peaks and tariff escalation, notably on the products of export interest to developing countries. It also failed to reach substantive agreements on some major issues (e.g. safeguards) or to achieve needed reforms in some key sectors (particularly agriculture).

The safeguards issue was particularly serious for developing countries which were seeking to strengthen the multilateral and non-discriminatory elements in the safeguards arrangements (GATT's Article XIX) under which countries can take emergency measures to protect their industries against damage caused by a sudden surge in imports. They were doing so in the face of opposition in particular from the EC which was seeking to incorporate discrimination through 'selectivity' in GATT, along the lines already conceded in the Multi-Fibre Arrangement (MFA), under which developing-country exports of textiles and clothing are extensively controlled. The Tokyo Round also introduced several new causes for concern in other areas of negotiation, mainly the use of a conditional most favoured nation (mfn) approach. This use, which further weakened the consensual multilateral basis assumed to underlie the trading system, occurred through the adoption of codes which were negotiated to achieve liberalisation of NTMs, only those countries which participated in the codes and accepted their obligations benefited from liberalisation in practice. Developing countries felt that they had been sidelined in the MTNs.

Already by 1981, there were pressures from both developed and developing countries for further trade negotiations (although at that stage not necessarily another round of MTNs) to complete the unfinished business. The growth of 'new protectionism' and the erosion of the GATT system were being aggravated by the global recession of the early 1980s, and the subsequent slow and partial recovery. Many governments, responding to sluggish world export demand and depressed commodity prices and to unemployment at home, were resorting both to export subsidies and to import restrictions. There were particular problems in agriculture. But those industries where serious excess capacity emerged in the period of recession—steel, cars, petrochemicals, electronic goods, machine tools, man-made fibres, etc.—also generated protectionist pressures and trade frictions.

A further element in the situation was that the severe external adjustment problems facing many developing countries in the early 1980s were leading more of them to follow outward-looking, export-oriented policies. Hitherto, manufactured exports had largely been the preserve of a small number of newly industrialising countries (NICs) mainly in Eastern Asia. Indeed, by 1986 the four East Asian NICs accounted for 8 per cent of the manufactures imported by developed countries, compared with 4 per cent in 1973. The evident success of these countries despite protectionist barriers and the need for export diversification by other developing countries into products whose income and price elasticities are higher than that of traditional commodities, created a wider constituency in developing countries seeking a reduction in

Table 5: Some non-tariff measures on food products

Product group	Principal NTMs applied by		
	EC	Japan	United States
Meat	VL, NAL,TQ,QC,RS	GQ, SM, IA	MON
Fish (fresh, chilled or frozen)	RP, ST, TQ	GQ, IA	TQ
Dairy products	VL, NAL, TQ	GQ, SM, TQ	GQ, QC, TQ, ST
Vegetables	RP, VL, NAL ST, Q, TQ	GQ	ST
Fruits and nuts	RP, NAL, ST, VER	ST, GQ	ST, GQ
Cereals	VL, NAL	GQ, SM, TQ	
Sugar and syrups	VL, VC, NAL		Q, FF
Cocoa and preparations	VC	GQ, CT	QC,GQ
Animal oils	NAL, VL	IA	QC
Spirits	RP, NAL, RS	SM,TQ	ET
Fruit juices	RP, NAL, VL	GQ	ET
Tobacco	FT, SM	SIA	ET

Note: The above list is for illustrative purposes only. In some cases, a particular measure affects only certain products within a product group.

CT = Commodity tax; ET = Specific taxes; FF = Flexible import fee; GQ = Global quota; IA = Import authorisation; Q = Quota; QC = Quota by country; MON = Monitoring; NAL = Non-automatic licensing; RP = References prices; RS = Restrospective surveillance; SIA = Sole import agency; SM = State monopoly; ST = Seasonal tariff; TQ = Tariff quota; VC = Variable component; VET = Voluntary export restraing; VL = Variable levy

Source: UNCTAD Data Base on Trade Measures.

barriers to the main export markets.

These pressures resulted in proposals to hold a GATT Ministerial meeting to examine the functioning of the trading system. The first such meeting for nine years, it was to be preceded by an intensive series of preparatory negotiations in GATT in late 1981 and most of 1982.

These circumstances provided the background to the decision of Commonwealth Heads of Government, at their meeting in Melbourne in October 1981, to pay particular attention to trade policy. They requested the Secretary-General to bring together an independent group of Commonwealth experts with the following terms of reference:

to investigate the impact of protection on developing country trade and to report back in time to assist governments in their preparations for the proposed GATT Ministerial Meeting. They agreed the group would examine the effects of protection on developing countries, including the impact of tariff and non-tariff barriers on industrial and agricultural products. In this respect the group should consider, *inter alia*, the question of emergency safeguards, and non-conventional measures which, among other things, include such matters as voluntary export restraints and orderly marketing arrangements, structural adjustment, the escalation of tariffs and trade barriers that constrain the expansion of trade in processed commodities, and the adequacy of existing arrangements for the settlement of disputes.

Highlights of the Group's report

Sir Alec Cairncross, who had been Chief Economic Adviser to the British Government, was the chairman of the 11 member group set up by the Secretary-General. The Group's report based its arguments on an underlying belief in the strongly positive role which trade can play in development: "There have generally been strong links between the growth of developing countries' exports and that of their economies, and few would doubt that restricting exports inhibits growth. Whatever development strategies are adopted, access to external markets is important to the great majority of developing countries and vital to those with small populations."

The need for removing trade barriers was not however solely one for developing countries. Indeed, the report argued that "trade provides a bond between developing and developed countries. In spite of all barriers, trade has continued to grow. It is in the interests of both groups of countries to encourage this growth. For the developed countries, it brings a welcome expansion in export markets when production is flagging and for the developing countries it is an indispensable element in their development".

The report treated the problem of protectionism against the background of global economic turbulence and slow-down in economic growth of the late 1970s and early 1980s. These represented a particular challenge for developing countries which had, in the main, successfully weathered the first oil-price shock in the early 1970s and some of which had begun to make serious progress in world markets for manufactures. They were, however, now faced with slow-growing overseas markets and market access barriers on top of adverse terms of trade for traditional commodities and increased debt servicing difficulties. Many faced the need for far-reaching adjustment measures, but the prevailing pessimism about export prospects was not conducive to their adoption. While the growth of trade in the late 1980s improved the position to some degree, doubts remain about the capacity and willingness of industrial countries to absorb manufactured imports from developing countries on a scale necessary for successful adjustment.

The report went on to deal with the malfunctioning of the trade regime as a whole. Because of the traditional preoccupation with manufactures—and tariffs—there were major areas where the rules of GATT did not apply:

agriculture, services, restrictive business practices and trade aspects of foreign investment. Intra-firm trade, particularly by transnational corporations, was another area not covered by GATT rules. While it did not necessarily follow that GATT was the appropriate forum to create rules in all these areas, the report argued that generally accepted, transparent, multilateral disciplines were needed. It was also among the first to recognise the importance of the role of trade in services, in terms both of the potential benefits of liberalisation and of the need to undertake adequate preparatory studies as a prerequisite to any substantive multilateral negotiations.

In addition to the omissions within the GATT treatment of trade, the Cairncross Group identified an adverse trend in those areas where GATT rules were supposed to apply. One was a tendency to drift away from the concept of multilateralism towards bilateral approaches to trade conflicts. Bilateralism favoured stronger trading nations relative to weaker, smaller countries (particularly in the Third World) and undermined the credibility of the system as a whole. A second source of deterioration in the system was the increasing recourse to NTMs either outside GATT, through VERs and OMAs, or within it, through derogations in GATT rules and disciplines, as exemplified by the MFA. The Group also highlighted the spread of protectionism, mainly in the form of VERs and OMAs, into other sectors such as steel, motor vehicles and consumer electronics. Much of this protectionism was discriminatory— against developing country interests—despite the nominal commitment to 'positive' discrimination in favour of these countries in the GATT (Part IV). The levels of protection, and the accompanying discrimination, in traditional areas of export interest to developing countries have continued to grow. The World Bank estimated in 1988 that the costs of this protection to developing countries was almost twice as great as the concessional aid flows to them.

There is an extensive empirical literature which demonstrates that, except in rare instances, protection also imposes economic costs on the countries that impose it. The Expert Group reported work underway in both academic and international organisations on the costs of protection. These suggested, for example, that the cost to consumers of protecting each job in the US—in footwear, steel, television sets, meat, sugar—was over $50,000 a year on average, considerably more than the wages paid per worker. Subsequent research has underlined the extent of these costs. For example in 1984 a study for the UK Government estimated that average retail prices of textiles and clothing in Britain would be 5-10 per cent lower in the absence of protection. A study for the Washington-based Institute for International Economics estimated that for 1984, the annual cost per job saved in the US textiles and clothing industries as a result of protection amounted to $50,000 and $39,000 respectively, as compared with the then annual average textile and clothing wages of $13,400 and $10,500. An OECD study in 1985 showed that each job protected under a restraint agreement on exports of colour television sets to the United States cost about S60,000 per year. These examples relate to manufacturing; the costs of agricultural protection are far higher. The report cited a figure of $40 billion as the global cost ten years ago; since then there has been a considerable increase, and in 1990 OECD put the loss in income from farm subsidies and protection at over S70 billion.

Such is the degree of protection now afforded by NTMs in some areas, that liberalisation, were it to occur, would generate substantial economic gains, including extra export earnings for developing countries. In 1987 UNCTAD estimated that removal by industrialised countries of all barriers on imports from developing countries would increase the latter's exports of textiles and clothing by some 125 per cent, of steel by about 62 per cent, and of footwear by approximately 85 per cent. These estimates are based on static effects only. Those including dynamic effects would be higher as they would include the increased opportunities for economies of scale, product differentiation and specialisation. The benefits would accrue mainly to those developing countries, such as Brazil and South Korea, that already have well-established manufacturing sectors, though others would also gain, especially in such areas as clothing where many developing countries now export competitively.

The extent of potential benefits for developing countries from liberalised market access raises the issue of whether developing countries can—or should —achieve this through multilateral negotiations or preferential and other special arrangements. The report recognised that, for some of the more advanced developing countries, preferences were of little value. For instance, under most schemes within the Generalised System of Preferences (GSP), 'sensitive' items such as textiles, clothing and footwear are excluded from preferences, while others, such as certain petrochemicals, receive limited coverage. For example, in the EC some 140 'sensitive' products are subject either to GSP ceilings, where the mfn tariff can be reintroduced at the request of the domestic industry once the ceilings are reached, or to GSP tariff quotas where the mfn tariff is automatically reintroduced when the quota level is reached. According to an IMF study published in 1985, the textiles and clothing sectors, whose products represent about 17 per cent of all industrial tariff lines, accounted for about half the industrial products excluded from GSP schemes when these are taken together. (Tariffs are not, in any case, the major barrier to access for most textile and clothing products.) Overall, preferential tariff treatment under the GSP was accorded to about one-quarter of all OECD dutiable imports from developing countries, according to an UNCTAD study in 1985. These may be affected in the future by provisions in the schemes of some countries for graduation of products of more developed suppliers, when sufficient competitiveness has been demonstrated or per capita income levels have been reached. But the Experts argued that graduation had to be handled carefully on the basis of multilaterally agreed rules.

The Cairncross Group's recommendations (see Box 10 for summary) were guided by several overriding concerns. One was that the short-term problems of the moment should not lead to the neglect of the "long-term requirements for efficient growth, international order and future welfare". Thus, priority had to be given to strengthening such basic underpinnings of the GATT trading system as multilateralism, non-discrimination (except for what is agreed multilaterally), transparency and predictability. A second was the need for developing countries to have a "fair and equitable place" in the system. Such a place would recognise the need for "special and differential" treatment and would involve high priority being given to such developing country concerns as textiles, tropical products, tariff escalation and the need for non-discriminatory, multilaterally supervised use of safeguard action.

The recommendations were naturally tailored to topical concerns at the time of the report: to make a success of the GATT ministerial meeting of 1982 and to influence the ensuing work programmes for the decade ahead. The Experts saw the first step as addressing the unfinished business of the Tokyo Round, particularly agriculture, safeguards, and mechanisms for dispute settlement. Nonetheless the recommendations have a long-term, enduring, relevance.

Developments after the report

The general economic context of slow growth and continued economic instability, which had fostered protectionist tendencies in the period before the Group's report, has since changed in several respects. The first has been the emergence of serious macroeconomic imbalances between leading industrial countries, in particular the large current account deficit of the US and corresponding surpluses elsewhere, notably of Japan. The US deficit has provided a fertile ground for protectionist sentiment in US manufacturing and farming and the US Congress has been exercising sustained pressure—in the name of 'fair trade'—to tighten import restrictions in sensitive sectors, including textiles. There has been no corresponding movement to unilateral liberalisation in the 'surplus' countries, suggesting a kind of 'ratchet' effect is at work whereby protectionism is strong in periods of balance of payments difficulty (and/or high unemployment) but is not reversed when these difficulties are eased.

A second development has been the debt crisis. Some debtor countries have been required, in the absence of large net capital inflows, to run substantial trade surpluses to cover service payments on past debts; this has given a strong impetus to the growth of their exports, particularly of non-traditional manufactures, which has in turn led to some protectionist resistance in major markets. On the import side, indebted countries have been pushed in two different

Box 10: Main recommendations of the Cairncross report

Rules and procedures

• The principles of multilateralism, non-discrimination (except for what is agreed multilaterally), transparency and predictability, consistent with special and differential treatment accorded to the developing countries, should be upheld and supported.

• The growing volume of officially and unoffically administered trade should be brought under international surveillance and submitted to internationally agreed rules and procedures.

• Joint machinery should be established linking GATT and UNCTAD to monitor and assess protectionism and structural adjustment in both agriculture and industry, with special attention directed to non-tariff measures.

Safeguards and codes

• Article XIX of the GATT should be revised to ensure that resort to quotas, VERs and OMAs are subject to greater multilateral discipline; the code should be explicit as to the permissible scope and duration of action; all such action should be time-bound.

• Provision should be made for phasing out arrangements such as VERs and OMAs.

• The burden of proof in respect of 'market disruption', 'injury' etc. should lie with the importing, not the exporting, country. There should be precise and multilaterally agreed means, based on economic concepts, of determining the link between imports and 'market disruption', or 'injury', and the extent of appropriate redress.

• Stricter disciplines are required under the Code on Subsidies and Countervailing Duties with respect to subsidies employed by the developed countries which adversely affect developing countries.

• The drift towards reciprocity and conditional mfn in negotiations on non-tariff codes should be reversed.

• A 'legal aid' service should be established for small countries to help them to pursue legitimate grievances under the GATT.

Multifibre Arrangement for textiles and clothing

• The Multifibre Arrangement should be brought within the rules and procedures of an improved Article XIX. Developed countries should undertake a phased liberalisation.

Transparency

• Any country maintaining protective barriers or imposing new ones inconsistent with international rules and procedures must justify its action in an open, multilateral forum.

• The GATT panel system for dealing with complaints and settlement of disputes

should be strengthened and opened to public scrutiny.
- Transparency and surveillance activities should be assisted within each developed country by a public forum at which those seeking protective barriers should justify them.

Preferential arrangements
- Preferential schemes should be improved in terms of simplicity, predictability and harmonisation of operation, extended in coverage, freed of limitations damaging to developing countries, especially the least developed among them, and if possible, extend to non-tariff measures.
- Eventual phasing out of preferences for the more advanced developing countries should be subject to multilaterally agreed rules; and, compensatory concessions should be negotiated.
- The rules of origin under the Lomé Convention should be relaxed for African, Caribbean and Pacific member countries.

Agriculture, raw materials and processing
- The immediate objectives should include: (i) a standstill on current protection levels; (ii) the development of codes of principles on agricultural support; (iii) gradual improvement in access and reduction of surpluses; and (iv) agreements on limits to export subsidies.
- Trade liberalisation for tropical products should be completed by removing remaining tariff and non-tariff restrictions.

Manufacturing and services
- Tariffs on manufactures of interest to developing countries should be cut more heavily than those on other manufactures.
- Comprehensive and co-ordinated effort should be made between GATT, UNCTAD and other agencies to assist governments to define possible options for any future negotiations.

Structural adjustment
- Assistance to individuals and enterprises should not be given in forms that encourage the retention of resources in activities in developed countries that are more suited to developing countries.

General
- Markets in the centrally planned economies should be more open to trade with developing countries.
- The newly industrialising and other economically more advanced developing countries should reduce trade barriers, especially for the products of other developing countries.

directions. On one hand, the need to secure surpluses has required import compression. This has greatly limited the scope for any form of reciprocal liberalisation. On the other hand, debtor, and other, developing countries are being called upon, as part of structural adjustment programmes with international financial institutions, to undertake trade policy reforms with the objectives of liberalising quota and tariff regimes; some are doing so, though this is being undertaken unilaterally rather than as part of the multilateral negotiating process.

The negotiating process

The 1982 GATT Ministerial Meeting was a disappointment, in particular failing to reach consensus on a declaration committing all parties to an immediate standstill and gradual rollback of protectionism. All governments did, however, reaffirm their commitment to GATT's basic principles and rules. The contribution of the Cairncross Group's report was recognised at the meeting and in the ensuing discussions in GATT and other fora. By the time Commonwealth Heads of Government met in Nassau in 1985, a preparatory process on the proposed new Round had already been started. This process ended in September 1986 with the declaration from the Special Ministerial Session of GATT at Punta del Este launching the Uruguay Round.

The first two years' work on the new Round were reviewed, with the initial intention of producing an 'early harvest' of agreements, at a mid-term review meeting in Montreal in December 1988. The failure of this meeting to reach agreement on the main issues presented to it, even to the extent of not agreeing a future work programme for four areas, cast a shadow over the negotiating process. It revealed fundamental divergences of interest. The US Government is under strong Congressional pressure to take action against imports in sensitive industries and to obtain a firm commitment to phasing out trade-related agricultural supports. The EC is ambivalent about its trade policy stance after 1992, has shown a firm disposition to uphold the Common Agricultural Policy, and taken a strong line on 'reciprocity' and on using its tough new anti-dumping rules. Japan has a continuing large export surplus and is reluctant to open its market to imports of rice. These have all combined to undermine confidence in the commitment of the main trading powers to the maintenance of a liberal trading system. And many of the concerns of developing countries on both traditional and new issues are still far from being met—as reviewed in more detail below.

Commonwealth action

The Uruguay Round has served as a focus for Commonwealth activities at both a political and a technical level. Commonwealth Heads of Government at their

1987 meeting issued the Vancouver Declaration on World Trade, demonstrating a strong commitment to multilateral liberalisation (see Box 11).

The Commonwealth Secretariat has been closely involved, both through its Trade Adviser's office in Geneva, and through publications and seminars, in providing technical assistance and in increasing awareness of trade policy issues of concern to Commonwealth countries. It prepared a report at the outset of the Round detailing Commonwealth interests and opportunities, and suggesting a phased negotiating approach. Subsequently it has published a regular bulletin on developments in the negotiations. In addition, the Secretariat has responded to specific government requests in producing more detailed technical studies on tropical products, agriculture, trade-related investment measures (TRIMS), trade-related aspects of intellectual property rights (TRIPS), the functioning of the GATT system, professional services, textiles and clothing, and safeguards. It has organised a series of regional and Pan-Commonwealth seminars at which senior trade policy officials from member countries have explored their interests in the Round.

An assessment of progress

Although the Uruguay Round is now more than three-quarters of the way to its scheduled completion in December 1990 it is not yet possible fully to evaluate progress in implementing the recommendations of the Cairncross report. These were linked to the prolonged programme of work that was envisaged with the launching a new round of negotiations and which is incomplete. The differences that dominated the mid-term review in December 1988 were resolved—in certain cases somewhat cosmetically—at a meeting in April, and the negotiations put back on track. But the positions of the main protagonists on these issues remain far apart and it will not be clear until the middle of 1990 whether these differences are transitional or herald a fundamental breakdown in the negotiations, with far-reaching implications for the trading system. Progress can perhaps best be evaluated by looking at the main area where the report made specific recommendations related to current negotiations.

In relation to GATT rules and procedures, and transparancy, the importance of which the report stressed, progress was made in negotiating a new procedure for dispute settlement (this has been applied on a trial basis since 1 May 1989). Firm guidelines have been established for the conduct of consultations, mediation and for the various phases of the dispute settlement process involving the use of the panel system in an expeditious way. In negotiations on the functioning of the GATT system, agreement was reached on the establishment of a trade policy review mechanism to enhance the surveillance by GATT of its members' trade policies. This would involve preparation of regular reports by the GATT Secretariat on the trade policies of its member countries, and an appraisal of the general thrust of national trade policy which would be both discussed in the GATT Council and published. This publicity could act as a check on protectionist tendencies, making it harder for member countries to adopt 'grey area' measures inconsistent with GATT rules. While all countries with weak bargaining power should benefit from such rules, little explicit attention is given in the agreements to the particular problems of developing countries. Nor is there any evidence that individual countries have followed Australia's example in opening up trade policy instruments to public examination—a reform which the Cairncross report judged to be of special importance.

The issue of safeguard action under Article XIX of the GATT has been highly contentious for many years. The negotiating dilemma – for developing countries and all those seeking a more liberal system—is that a clause that is too onerous in the demands on the countries imposing safeguard action will lead to a proliferation of illegal 'grey area' actions outside the GATT, while a clause that is too lax will legitimise protectionism—and discrimination—within GATT. Despite the priority which the Cairncross Group urged contracting parties to give to the matter, there has been little progress in over a decade in reconciling the demands of certain developed countries, on the one hand, that Article XIX should be made easier to use and allow discriminatory, selective action, and those of developing countries, on the other, that the principle of non-discrimination should not be undermined and that there should be strict 'safeguards on safeguards'. This impasse also prevents agreement on the related issue of dealing with VERs and OMAs and providing alternative arrangements within GATT principles for textiles and clothing.

The Cairncross Group argued for a carefully controlled and temporary concession on 'selectivity'; provided that this led to an open and effective safeguards system in GATT in which both the MFA and the multiplicity of other safeguard actions would eventually be incorporated. The Commonwealth Secretariat argued along the same lines in its 1986 report, *The Uruguay Round of Multilateral Trade Negotiations: Commonwealth Interests and Opportunities.* This analysed the negotiating options on issues in the Round. Negotiations are now in progress on a draft text which states that safeguard measures should be applied on an mfn basis, but also suggests that consideration should be given to establishing strict guidelines and procedures under which measures might be applied on a selective basis when injury results from actions of a few suppliers. In relation to the other major contentious codes, the negotiators have agreed a framework for discussing subsidies and countervailing duties but not yet reached a substantive agreement.

The Commonwealth Secretariat report attached considerable importance to liberalisation of the MFA which represents a major derogation from GATT

Box 11: The Vancouver Declaration on World Trade

The Commonwealth leaders representing a wide range of both developed and developing countries note with grave concern rising global protectionist pressures. Continuing implementation of protectionist measures would be counter-productive, would increase the risk of further exchange rate instability and would exacerbate the problems of development and indebtedness. Trade restrictions affect particularly the exports and growth prospects of developing countries and their ability to service debt, all of which in turn impact adversely on the economies of the industrial countries.

We welcome the progress of negotiations in the Uruguay Round covering a range of important subjects. We will work for a balanced outcome to develop a more open, viable and durable multilateral trading system to promote growth and development. We recognise the growing importance and the asymmetrical position of developing countries in the trading system. This underlines the need to give special consideration to their interests within the agreed framework of the Uruguay Round. It is essential that the Punta del Este commitments on ''standstill'' and ''rollback'' be fully respected and implemented.

We agree on the crucial need for reform of all trade distorting agricultural policies, both domestic and international. We urge early action on agriculture in the Uruguay Round so as to reduce the uncertainty, imbalances and instability in world markets. This will benefit both developed and developing countries.

A strong, credible working GATT is essential to the well-being of all trading countries and is the best bulwark against mounting protectionist pressures. The functioning of the GATT should be improved through enhancing its role in maintaining an open multilateral system and its capacity in the area of dispute settlement. We hope that the negotiations will make sufficient progress on agriculture and other key subjects to enable a mid-term ministerial review of the Uruguay Round as allowed for in the Punta del Este Declaration.

We welcome the assistance which the Commonwealth Secretariat is providing to member governments in the trade field, including the re-establishment of a Trade Adviser's Office in Geneva and increased levels of technical support, and we request the Secretary-General to continue to give priority to work in this field. In addition, the larger states of the Commonwealth undertake to assist developing countries, including smaller states, through regular consultations and trade policy training programmes.

Issued by Commonwealth Heads of Government,
Vancouver, Canada. 15 October 1987

principles. The report suggested a phased process of liberalisation. But the controls have since been generally tightened, albeit with some relaxation, by the EC for example, for least developed countries and small suppliers. An opportunity to make a fresh attempt at liberalisation will come with the need to agree a set of procedures to replace the current MFA when it expires in July 1991. With this in view, participants in the Uruguay Round are mandated to negotiate "modalities that would permit the eventual integration of this sector into GATT, on the basis of strengthened GATT rules and disciplines, thereby also contributing to the objective of further liberalisation of trade".

However, progress on this issue has proved difficult. A procedural agreement in April 1989 established that the modalities for integrating trade in this sector into GATT over an agreed time span should cover the phasing out of restrictions under the MFA, as well as those outside it. The time-span discussed has been sufficiently flexible to allow for the continuation of MFA types of restriction for several years after the expiry of the current MFA. The hard question that still has to be answered is how long or short that time-span should be and how many restrictions should remain during it. Significant progress on this issue will remain central to developing countries' negotiating concerns. This is both because of the substantial export interests involved and because of the issue's symbolic importance: whether developing countries are allowed to expand exports freely in a sector where their market efficiency has established a competitive advantage. Some developed countries—notably Sweden—have indicated that they will liberalise unilaterally if multilateral agreement cannot be reached.

The Cairncross report correctly anticipated an important preoccupation of the Uruguay Round when it judged that "a decisive move towards bringing agricultural trade more fully within the purview of GATT would signify a serious attempt by governments to come to grips with the general problem of protectionism". The Round has seen the first serious attempt for 40 years to tackle the issue. However, at the mid-term review there was deadlock between the EC and the US, essentially over the US demand that trade-distorting subsidies and market access barriers should be completely eliminated over a specified period. Developing countries have supported moves towards global liberalisation (though some net importers of food would face higher, non-subsidised prices as a result, at least in the short term). And they have achieved a large measure of acceptance for the principle of a clause recognising that support for the sector has a special role in development. Agreement was reached in April 1989 that until the end of the Round the current levels of protection and domestic support would not be exceeded, and that substantial and progressive reductions in them would be brought about in the long run. However, a year later the positions of the EC and the US remain far apart.

Trade in tropical products is of greatest interest to the large number of developing countries that are not yet significant exporters of manufactures. The Cairncross report envisaged the removal of remaining tariffs and NTMs on tropical products. That is still some way off. The negotiating objective of the Uruguay Round is to give special attention to trade in this sector and aim at its fullest liberalisation. At the mid-term review meeting, most developed countries and some developing countries agreed to cut tariffs on some tropical products. While the offers were not insigificant in their totality, substantial barriers to tropical product exports remain. The concessions made so far by the EC, Japan and smaller developed countries still have important exclusions (tobacco and rice, for example), make only limited movement on the main NTMs (such as excise duties on beverages) and, in the case of the EC, are tailored to preserve some element of preference for African, Caribbean and Pacific countries associated with it under the Lomé Convention. Tariff escalation has scarcely been addressed*. Concessions have also been linked to demands for various forms of reciprocity by developing countries, contrary to previous understandings of the nature of these negotiations.

The Cairncross Group envisaged the MTNs being extended to services and some other new issues. One of the achievements of the negotiating process so far has been to find a way of dealing with services that has eased the considerable anxiety of developing countries. Negotiations on defining the principles and rules for trade in services have not yet reached a critical stage, but if the interests of developing countries are to be safeguarded, it is clear that any agreed rules must cover labour and labour-intensive services on a par with technology-intensive services, and recognise that developing countries face severe constraints in building their service industries to internationally competitive levels.

---

* Even where tariffs are generally low, they can still be a considerable barrier to processed exports by producers of primary products. For example, jute enters most industrial countries duty free, but Austria's 3 per cent duty on jute fabrics provides 7 per cent effective protection for the Austrian processing of jute fabrics. Likewise, Australia imports hides and skins duty free but its 20 per cent duty on leather manufactures provides 36 per cent effective protection for leather manufacturing. Effective rates of protection for the processing of oilseeds into vegetable oils exceed 50 per cent in the EC and in Japan. Furthermore, escalation often protects very simple processes. For example, the US tariff on pineapples in bulk is 0.64c per kilogram. Based on 1984 import-unit values, this comes to 8.4 per cent ad valorem. If packaging increases by 20 per cent the value of a shipment of pineapples, then the effective rate of protection these nominal rates provide for packaging is 5.2 times higher than the rate of protection provided to pineapple growers. The EC duty is 9 per cent ad valorem on pineapples, 20 per cent on unsugared pineapple juice. Its GSP rate on unsugared pineapple juice is 17 per cent, and on sugared juice, 19 to 42 per cent, depending on density, plus an additional charge on the sugar content. Again, the effective protection provided to the juicing process is proportionally higher.

What the report did not envisage was the introduction into future MTNs of contentious issues in relation to TRIPs and TRIMs. Negotiations on the former in particular have been characterised by wide differences of view between developed and developing countries. Major issues on which consensus has not been so far possible include whether the protection of intellectual property rights is the responsibility of GATT or of other agencies such as the World Intellectual Property Organization; and how to achieve a balance between the need to protect creative ideas and the need to ensure access to such ideas. While there is a fair degree of consensus that GATT rules should cover such measures as counterfeiting, developing countries feel it necessary to resist more far-reaching GATT provisions that would give strong protection to holders of intellectual property rights at the expense of the development—and wider public—interest in rapid technological diffusion, and which also seemed to cut across attempts to reach agreements in other multilateral fora.

In the face of such a range of interlocking difficulties and disagreements, much importance attaches to standstill and rollback commitments, reiterated while launching the Round, which act as a—rather fragile—device for keeping protectionism at bay. Recent trends clearly suggest that the standstill provision has been subject to a good deal of erosion and rollback has not seriously been attempted.

There has in addition been a lack of substantive progress so far in the multilateral negotiations in the areas of textiles, safeguards and TRIPs; only limited, qualified progress in tropical products; and difficulties of having a development dimension fully integrated in the negotiating proposals in agriculture and services. All of these have combined to lead developing countries to question the strength of the commitment of developed countries to giving them special treatment. They suggest, furthermore, a lack of appreciation of the role that trade plays in the development process— especially in the current difficult environment where debt-service burdens have reduced net financial inflows and depressed commodity prices have increased the importance of developing countries expanding the range and volume of exports.

Although many years have passed since the Cairncross report was completed, its conclusions and recommendations remain highly pertinent to the current problems facing the international trading system. Little progress has been made in securing adoption of those recommendations, and on present indications of progress in the Uruguay Round, it would seem that the report will remain highly relevant even after the negotiations are concluded.

Chapter 8
Co-operation to assist
industrial development

The action taken to advance a New International Economic Order following the resolutions adopted at the Sixth Special Session of the UN General Assembly in 1974-75 included attempts to devise new forms of international co-operation in industry. The second General Conference of the United Nations Industrial Development Organisation (UNIDO), held in Lima, Peru, in March 1975, adopted a Declaration and Plan of Action on Industrial Co-operation and Development. This set out a broad strategy for accelerating industrial development in Third World countries. It called for an energetic drive to increase the share of developing countries in world industrial production, with the aim of raising it to at least 25 per cent by the year 2000.

Meeting in Kingston, Jamaica, one month after the Lima Conference, Commonwealth Heads of Government agreed that the time was ripe for action to promote industrial activity in developing member countries. They stressed the need to accelerate the development of industry and endorsed the expansion of industrial co-operation, particularly between Commonwealth countries. The leaders also considered the wider issue of a new international economic order and decided to set up a Commonwealth Group of Experts to draw up a comprehensive and interrelated programme of practical measures to close the gap between the rich and the poor countries (see Chapter 1). In doing so, they proposed, inter alia, that the Group should review existing organisations for industrial co-operation and development and pay particular attention to programmes for industrial development involving new and expanded forms of industrial co-operation. Over the following 15 years there have been a series of Commonwealth initiatives in pursuit of this goal.

The Lima strategy

In 1975 some 90 per cent of world industrial production was located in the developed countries and only 10 per cent in the Third World. The Lima strategy sought as a minimum target to alter this ratio to 75:25 by the year 2000. In addition to this global quantitative production target, the Lima Declaration stressed the qualitative aspects of industrialisation. It called for policy measures to achieve greater social justice through a more equitable income distribution within countries and the optimum development and utilisation of human resources (including women), sustained self-reliance and participatory development, and an integrated, multisectoral approach to industrial development, with the technological and socio-economic implications fully taken into account in both planning and implementation. A series of actions at global, regional, country and sectoral levels were recommended and it was envisaged that, through a special system of consultations, the dialogue between industrialised and developing countries on ways to achieve a more equitable distribution of industrial resources would be strengthened.

To help achieve these objectives, a number of initiatives were pursued by UNIDO after the Lima Conference. These included the introduction of a system of consultations, a proposal to establish a United Nations Industrial Development Fund, and the pilot-stage operation of an Industrial and Technological Information Bank. UNIDO's technical co-operation activities and its representation in countries and regions were strengthened. It set up a network of investment promotion offices, made a series of studies of industrial redeployment and launched programmes to encourage co-operation among developing countries.

The success of the Lima strategy was seen to depend principally on the UNIDO system of consultations and the effectiveness of international co-operation on the redeployment of industrial capacity from the developed to the developing countries. The system of consultations was designed to promote the sharing of world industrial capacity and the transfer of know-how, management skills and capital to bring about a significant rise in industrial output in developing countries. Consultative meetings were to be convened in the various industrial sectors to provide a forum in which all concerned parties —labour, industry, government and consumers—would be able to exchange views on its future global development. UNIDO attached great importance to these meetings, envisaging that they would not only identify the areas in which increased international co-operation was needed but also generate proposals to put such co-operation into effect.

Central to the objectives of the Lima strategy was the redeployment of industrial capacity from the developed to the developing countries, pursued on the basis of mutual self-interest in order to realise the benefits of a more rational international division of labour. Redeployment was defined as a process by which new or existing production capacities are transferred, because of cost, market and other factors, from one country to another, with the encouragement of official policies in both. It was acknowledged that, in industrial market economy countries, it was private enterprises that owned most industrial capacity and would therefore make the final decision on its location. It was envisaged, however, that in making such decisions, private enterprises would take due account of government policies, and that governments would play, therefore, an important, if largely indirect, role. Governments in industrial countries were called upon to consider designing programmes to facilitate the long-term restructuring of those of their industries more suited to the economic conditions of developing countries.

The Commonwealth report

The McIntyre Group of Experts set up at the Kingston meeting of Heads of Government devoted a chapter of its interim report, *Towards a New International Economic Order* (July 1975), to industrial co-operation, as it did in its further report of March 1976. But it did not have the time or resources to cover the subject of industrial co-operation in depth. The Commonwealth Secretary-General, after consulting the Group's members, proposed to a meeting of Commonwealth Senior Officials in May 1976 that a team of industrial specialists should be invited to recommend specific measures that governments and industry could take, bilaterally or multilaterally, to expand industrial activities and deepen their impact in the developing countries.

The reaction was positive and a Commonwealth Team of Industrial Specialists was set up in November 1976 to identify specific forms of co-operation that would enable developing countries to enlarge their industrial base. The Team was chaired by Mr.L.K. Jha, an eminent Indian administrator and economist (see Annex for list of members).

Following the suggestion of the McIntyre Group, the Jha Team set about its work by seeking from the governments of Commonwealth developing countries information on the obstacles and difficulties they had met in pursuing industrial development, the kind of support they required and the ways in which they could assist other Commonwealth developing countries. Developed member countries were asked for their views on new forms of bilateral and multilateral co-operation to promote industrial progress in developing Commonwealth countries. Four regional consultations were held with governments, international and regional institutions, trade unions and employers, and some field studies were undertaken.

The Team concluded that in most developing countries the chief deficiencies were underdeveloped entrepreneurship, inadequate capacity to identify feasible and viable industrial projects, shortages of trained manpower, difficulties in relation to the acquisition and use of industrial technologies, shortages of financial resources, and market limitations. At the international level, it found that small countries and small industries were generally neglected in multilateral and bilateral co-operation arrangements; that different bodies had often to be approached for assistance on the same project; and that it was difficult to mobilise resources, especially equity capital, from international agencies and similar bodies.

The Jha Team's report, *Co-operation for Accelerating Industrialisation*, issued in May 1978, made a series of suggestions to the international community, and recommendations to Commonwealth governments, in relation to promoting industrial development and training, improving technologies, mobilising finance, and developing markets.

On industrial promotion, it suggested that national and international agencies should provide funds on appropriate terms for financing pre-investment studies on a contingent recovery basis. Agencies should also set up more effective programmes to help developing countries establish and strengthen their facilities to collect and disseminate the types of information needed to start industrial enterprises. Those conducting programmes of industrial training were asked to lay greater emphasis on supervisory and operative skills, to provide for more on-the-job training and, in training outside the trainees' own country, to give special attention to the environment in which the trainees would work.

The Team suggested that the relevant international agencies should help developing countries to evaluate and select industrial technologies. It asked the industrialised countries and the more industrially advanced developing countries to publish directories listing the types and sources of technology available from their countries, and to examine the concept of shared financing and joint ownership of technologies developed specifically to suit the needs of developing countries. Another suggestion was that developing countries should consult one another on the terms and conditions on which they acquire technologies, with a view to improving their capabilities in negotiating with technology suppliers, and formulating their own 'guidelines' for the transfer of technology.

In dealing with finance, the Jha Team suggested that development banks should consider financing pilot plants; that industrialised and developing countries should examine ways in which their state corporations and private enterprises could help bring about mutually beneficial collaborative arrangements; and that industrialised countries should devise ways to mobilise the capabilities of medium- and small-scale manufacturing enterprises in their countries to assist the industrialisation of developing countries.

On market development, the report criticised industrialised countries' use of tariff and non-tariff measures to discriminate against imports of manufactures and semi-manufactures from developing countries. It argued that they should devise programmes to facilitate the long-term restructuring of those industries that were more suited to the economic conditions of developing countries. Developed countries were also asked to establish or expand agencies to promote imports from developing countries which, for their part, were urged to increase the use of 'buyer/seller meets', store displays and other export promotion devices.

The Team also recommended that donor countries should untie aid to facilitate procurement in developing countries and that international agencies should provide funds to export financing institutions in developing countries. The International Standards Organisation and national standards institutes in the industrialised and the industrially more advanced developing countries should help the less developed of the developing countries to formulate suitable standards and should test at nominal cost their manufactures and semi-manufactures.

Lastly, the Jha Team suggested that advantage should be taken of countries' differing strengths in technology, manpower, finance and other resources to develop industrial projects in developing countries through co-operation among three or more industrialised and developing countries.

The report's recommendations for action by the Commonwealth were informed by the request by Commonwealth Heads of Government, at their meeting in London in June 1977, that the Team should :

> identify a programme of Commonwealth action in the field of industry, including in particular and if necessary, the establishment of new mechanisms for financing industrial development, the transfer, development and diffusion of appropriate technology and measures to promote the development of specific industries, where the developing countries have developed or will develop a comparative advantage, in Commonwealth developing countries.

The actions recommended for the Commonwealth Secretariat are summarised in Box 12, page 152.

The Team expressed the belief that acceptance of these recommendations would be the most effective way of achieving the objectives which lay behind the further request, remitted by Commonwealth Heads of Government, for it to study the establishment of a Commonwealth Fund for Industrial Co-operation and Development. It also considered that the proposals it had made for stimulating the development and flow of appropriate technologies in Commonwealth developing countries, by supporting the development of technological institutions, with external assistance as necessary, would be the best means of attaining the aims underlying the proposal, made at the same meeting, for a Commonwealth Centre for the Development and Diffusion of Appropriate Technology.

Finally, the Jha Team proposed the establishment of a Commonwealth venture capital company that would primarily provide equity capital to relatively small enterprises not served by existing financial institutions. It would normally operate through the industry promotion agencies or local investment companies of the host countries but, in the absence of such bodies, other institutions (including banks) could be used or the company could make direct investments. Raising funds on capital markets, it would be able take a (usually minority) stake in, or underwrite, selected industrial projects, mainly

Box 12: Actions recommended for the Commonwealth Secretariat by the Team of Industrial Specialists

The Secretariat should:

- sponsor programmes of bilateral co-operation between industry promotion agencies in developing member countries, so as to facilitate project identification, pre-investment studies and implementation
- start a programme to stimulate entrepreneurship by arranging exposure visits by small-scale entrepreneurs to other developing member countries
- institute a programme to encourage the establishment of industrial extension services in developing member countries through bilateral co-operation and 'twinning' arrangements between research and development institutions
- support a programme to promote bilateral co-operation between developing member countries for the development of small-scale industries and the establishment and development of related institutional support measures
- establish, within the Commonwealth Fund for Technical Co-operation (CFTC), an Industrial Pre-Investment Unit to undertake project identification and pre-feasibility studies; advise on appropriate technologies and industrial know-how; and provide guidance on sources of finance
- establish a Commonwealth Industrial Consultative Group to assist in mobilising relevant expertise in member countries to solve industrial problems experienced by developing members; promote co-operation between developed and developing countries and among developing countries in establishing industrial enterprises; operate as a forum for exchanging experiences between countries; advise and assist other Commonwealth institutions in the field of industrial development; encourage and support Commonwealth programmes to strengthen the capability of developing member countries to industrialise and to facilitate the external pre-conditions for industrialisation; advise on issues related to industrialisation that may be tabled for consideration at international fora; and monitor and guide the work of the Industrial Pre-Investment Unit
- make a determined effort to help developing member countries implement some industrial projects.

To finance the work of the Pre-Investment Unit and other activities proposed for the Secretariat in the industrial sphere, the Team recommended an initial fund of £5 million. In the case of successful projects, it felt that some of the costs would be recoverable.

to encourage the participation of other parties, both domestic and foreign. The company would divest itself of its investment as soon as possible after the success of the project had been demonstrated.

Action on the report

The Jha Team's report was considered at a specially convened meeting of Commonwealth Ministers of Industry, held in Bangalore, India, in March 1979. Ministers also reviewed a Secretariat elaboration of the Team's recommendations. This included a proposal for the establishment of an Industrial Development Unit (IDU) which would incorporate the operational functions proposed by the Team for the Pre-Investment Unit and the Consultative Group. Ministers agreed to put forward to Heads of Government the framework of a Commonwealth Action Programme on Industrial Co-operation (see Box 13). The Programme was approved by Commonwealth leaders when they met in

---

Box 13: The Commonwealth action programme on industrial co-operation

The establishment within the Commonwealth Fund for Technical Co-operation of an Industrial Development Unit to help solve specific industrial problems in developing member countries and provide continuing assistance to them in their industrialisation efforts. This would include pre-investment services as well as the expansion of training opportunities in the promotion, establishment, management and operation of industrial enterprises, and assistance to improve the effectiveness of industrial promotion and extension services.

The introduction by the Commonwealth Secretariat of a programme to enable small-scale entrepreneurs from Commonwealth developing countries to undertake exposure visits to other developing and developed member countries.

The undertaking by the Secretariat of a catalytic role in industrial development by promoting, supplementing and linking bilateral and multilateral programmes of co-operation in the industrial sector.

The provision of additional resources to enable the Action Programme to be implemented for an initial three-year period at a cost of £5 million.

The convening by the Commonwealth Secretary-General of a working group to examine all issues relevant to the establishment of a Commonwealth venture capital company, with a view to facilitating an early decision on this matter.

Lusaka, Zambia, in August 1979. Its implementation was seen as part of the worldwide effort to fulfil the global objectives of the Lima Declaration, with the experience gained being applicable to a wider international context.

Industrial Development Unit

The Lusaka meeting approved the establishment of an IDU in the CFTC with additional financial resources of £5 million for an initial three-year period. The Unit's functions were, in the words of the Secretary-General, to help developing Commonwealth countries to ''strengthen their indigenous industrial capabilities and thus to increase their self-reliance.'' It would ''aim to fill current gaps in industrial assistance.... In its work the IDU will give priority to those industrial projects and programmes which will most accelerate national economic development, taking into account such factors as employment generation, the processing of indigenous raw materials, rural development, foreign exchange savings/earnings, and the more rational location of industries.''

The development of small-scale industry, the establishment of business and technology information centres, and the rehabilitation and expansion of production of established enterprises have been the main categories of IDU activity since it was established in March 1980. The Unit has given attention largely to small and disadvantaged countries (e.g. islands and those in the least developed category) and has drawn on expertise in technology, engineering and finance from individuals in the private and public sectors from both developed and developing member countries. This approach was endorsed by Commonwealth Industry Ministers in August 1984.

The IDU has done much to raise output in a large number of industrial enterprises and to resuscitate several which had fallen on hard times. In the two years 1987-89, it assisted more than 200 enterprises, over 70 per cent of them small-scale concerns, and many outside the main centres of population and involved with the processing of indigenous raw materials.

Industrial Training and Experience Programme

The IDU has not been the only outcome of the Action Programme. A Commonwealth Industrial Training and Experience Programme (CITEP) was set up within the Secretariat's Fellowships and Training Programme in November 1986 to help developing member countries improve industrial performance by providing practical training in industry, and opportunities for familiarisation with advanced technologies and new manufacturing processes. CITEP has been of increasing importance and during the two years to mid-1989 it arranged over 200 training projects covering a wide range of industrial sectors and benefiting trainees from almost all developing member countries.

A venture capital company

There have also been significant developments concerning the Team's recommendation for the establishment of a Commonwealth venture capital company. A Working Group* set up in 1979 to examine the proposal felt that a conventional type of venture capital company would not adequately meet the risk capital needs of small enterprises. It saw the need for a more specialised institution to facilitate the flow of risk capital in all its forms: not just equity but also convertible and/or subordinated loans and long-term credits with flexible amortisation schemes. The Group proposed the establishment of a Commonwealth risk capital facility. To avoid duplication and minimise administrative costs, the facility would promote small- and medium-scale enterprises indirectly, by strengthening the capabilities of national agencies to provide them with risk capital. Its main functions would be to make these funds available in a form and on a scale and terms that would enable the intermediaries to provide financing to such enterprises. It would also help to set up national institutions where these did not already exist.

The Group proposed that the facility should be funded by subscriptions from all Commonwealth governments which, given the risk-bearing functions involved, should be on concessional terms. A commitment of at least £10 million was recommended, of which £3-4 million would need to be subscribed to make the facility operative.

Governments showed appreciable interest in the Working Group's proposals when they were presented to the September 1980 meeting of Commonwealth Finance Ministers. But in the more stringent financial climate later in the decade it did not prove possible to implement them in the form proposed.

A Commonwealth Equity Fund

The 1980s were marked by increasing disquiet at the contraction in net financial flows to developing countries and by a trend in the main aid-giving countries in favour of the private sector. At the 1987 meeting of Commonwealth Finance Ministers the Secretariat suggested that Ministers might wish to consider the feasibility of setting up a Commonwealth Equity Fund which could tap sources of portfolio and possibly venture capital investment. Ministers asked the Secretary-General to put in hand an examination of the possibilities of facilitating increased private flows, including venture capital, to Commonwealth developing countries.

The design of the Fund was refined over the following two years. In 1989 the Heads of Government meeting warmly welcomed the Secretariat's initiative and looked forward to the early launch of the Fund, with its first capital

---

* Members were M.F. Strong (Chairman), R.H. Grierson, J. Millett, A.M.A. Muhith, G.O. Onosode, F.B. Rampersad, T.T. Thanahe and Thong Yaw Hong.

issue named "the Hibiscus Issue" after the symbol of their meeting in Malaysia. It commended the Secretariat's catalytic role in paving the way for the Fund's establishment, while noting that the executive responsibility would be carried entirely by commercial interests. It was envisaged that Commonwealth governments would review sympathetically any national legislation which could affect the operations of the Fund in their countries.

The Commonwealth Equity Fund launched in May 1990 has an initial capital of at least US$ 100 million and the possibility of further tranches. It is able to invest in equities (or related instruments such as convertible debentures) in any Commonwealth developing country. The Fund will build up a diversified portfolio reflecting the availability of suitable listed stocks and market size. It will invest up to 30 per cent of its funds in unlisted securities. The Fund will raise capital initially by privately placing shares with institutional investors inside and outside the Commonwealth, while subsequent issues of shares may be public and underwritten. It is a closed-end investment company (with a London listing) controlled by a Board of Directors predominantly reflecting the stake of investors. The Fund is incorporated in Guernsey.

Diffusion of technology

Although the idea of a Commonwealth Centre for the Development and Diffusion of Appropriate Technology, floated at the 1977 Heads of Government meeting, was not supported by the Jha Team and has not been pursued further in that form,* there have been several significant developments concerning the diffusion of technology through Commonwealth institutions. Diffusion depends on the provision of advice and the dissemination of information. The Commonwealth Science Council has introduced several programmes for this purpose. One is the Programme on Awareness of Rapid Advances in Science and Technology (ARAST) under which meetings are held to enable member countries to identify areas of scientific and technological interest and economic importance to them. Another is the Commonwealth Project on Strategic Management and Planning of Science and Technology (COMMANSAT), which provides an advisory service on aspects of technological change through a network arrangement drawing on the expertise of senior science and technology managers with diverse experience and skills. The latter has been the model for the proposed Commonwealth Consultative

---

* The proposal was not re-examined by the Commonwealth Working Group whose report, *Technological Change : Enhancing the Benefits*, was considered by Heads of Government at Nassau in 1985. (This Group was concerned mainly with the effects of 'new technology' rather than solely with technologies 'appropriate' to developing countries—see Chapter 9 for details.)

Group for Technology Management, endorsed by Heads of Government at their 1989 Meeting, and intended to enable the Secretariat to provide a technology advisory service to governments.*

International developments

Progress in achieving the central target of the Lima Declaration has been disappointing. The expansion of the developing countries' share in world industrial production is of course determined by the relative growth of the industrial sector in the developed and developing countries. The UNIDO Secretariat calculated that, assuming 5 per cent annual growth of manufacturing value-added (MVA) in the developed countries during 1975-2000, the rate of growth required in the developing countries to achieve the Lima target of 25 per cent would be of the order of 10-11 per cent a year. This would require substantially greater domestic investment and foreign capital flows, an acceleration of international trade, increased regional and interregional production arrangements, and a considerable improvement in the technological capacity of developing countries.

But economic growth since 1975 has been markedly slower than in the previous 15 years. The obstacles to industrial redeployment have been intensified as a result of the crisis in the world's monetary and financial system, the rise of unemployment, the acceleration of technological innovations, and the growth of protectionism and especially the emergence of new forms of restraint to trade.

MVA growth at the required rate could not be achieved in such global economic conditions. In contrast to a gradual, but fairly steady, upward trend in the developing countries' share in the world's MVA during the period 1960-75, the gains in later years were erratic, with little improvement during much of the 1980s. From 10.3 per cent in 1975, the share of developing countries in global MVA rose to 11.9 per cent in 1985 (see Table 6) and registered 13.8 per cent in 1989.

In the early 1980s, the decision by the governments of major industrial countries to fight inflation by monetary means drove up interest rates to very high levels and caused borrowing to become very costly. At the same time there was the deepest global recession since the 1930s. The consequence was that Third World countries had to pay much more to service the debt they had built up during the previous decade, just at the time when their foreign exchange earnings from exports to industrial countries were being severely constrained. The resultant debt crisis and the challenges to the world's

* This Group has certain similarities with the Commonwealth Industrial Consultative Group proposed by the Team of Industrial Specialists (see also Chapter 9).

Table 6: Regional share of world MVA and regional MVA growth rates
(percentages)

Item	1975	1980	1985	Annual average growth rates		
				1975-80	1980-5	1975-85
TOTAL MVA	2,219,670[a]	2,701,001[a]	3,016,497[a]	4.01	2.23	3.12
Developing countries						
Caribbean and Latin America	5.70	6.00	5.37	5.07	0.01	2.51
Tropical Africa	0.44	0.42	0.40	2.81	1.18	1.99
North Africa and Western Asia	1.29	1.20	1.58	2.26	8.04	5.29
Indian Subcontinent	1.23	1.13	1.27	2.36	4.68	3.52
East and South-East Asia	1.67	2.43	3.26	12.14	8.38	10.24
Total	*10.33*	*11.18*	*11.89*	*5.68*	*3.49*	*4.58*
Developed countries						
North America	22.10	22.38	22.53	4.28	2.36	3.31
Western Europe	36.33	34.05	31.34	2.67	0.54	1.60
Eastern Europe	19.75	20.03	21.26	4.31	3.45	3.88
Japan	9.47	10.55	11.36	6.28	3.74	5.00
Other Developed	2.03	1.80	1.63	1.54	0.24	0.89
Total	*89.67*	*88.82*	*88.11*	*3.81*	*2.06*	*2.93*

Source: UNIDO, *Industry and Development 1988/89*, Vienna, 1988, page 104.
[a] Millions of 1980 constant dollars.

monetary and financial system are dealt with elsewhere in this volume (see Chapters 4 and 5).

The severe recession experienced by the industrial countries during the early 1980s led to a steep increase in their unemployment, which remained high almost throughout the decade. Its effects were transmitted to the developing countries through the international trade and payments mechanisms. A decline in the demand for raw materials and other goods and services imported from the Third World led to diminishing employment in these countries' export sectors. The collapse of bank lending to them, with no increase in official development assistance to offset it, led to widespread problems, so much so that the 1980s have been dubbed as a decade 'lost to development'. Both unemployment and underemployment rose in the Third World, with specially harmful effects on vulnerable groups such as women and young people (see Chapters 11 and 12).

Higher unemployment in the industrialised countries came at a time of rapid technological change (see Chapter 9). Major innovations in information technology were already causing dramatic worldwide changes in the patterns of producing goods and services. For instance, the introduction of new systems of automation to formerly labour-intensive assembly activities or to small-batch production techniques have had considerable effects on employment. They have often been the cause of redundancy for particular groups of workers. The short-term, sector-specific effects of new technologies have usually been negative in terms of numbers employed, even though the longer-term, economy-wide and indirect repercussions are almost certainly positive.

The combination of slower economic growth, rapid technological innovation and rising unemployment in the industrial countries led to progressively more intense pressure for trade protectionism. This was especially marked in such sectors as textiles, clothing, footwear, steel, consumer electronics (notably radios and televisions), and some metal goods (e.g. cutlery), where non-tariff measures such as 'voluntary restraint agreements' were increasingly accepted by developing country exporters under pressure from the industrial countries (see Chapter 7).

In such periods the perceived social and personal costs of adjustment were high. Workers in industrial countries became increasingly resistant to change, and especially to industrial restructuring on an international basis. Largely for electoral reasons, their governments yielded to these pressures.

Hence, the redeployment of industrial capacities from developed to developing countries, necessary to achieve the Lima target, has taken place much more slowly and fragmentally than most attending the UNIDO Conference would have hoped. What has been achieved has occurred predominantly through market forces rather than by means of the UNIDO system of sectoral consultations intended to spearhead the process. A Code of Conduct for the Transfer of Technology—considered by many to be vital in enabling developing countries to obtain from developed countries the types of technology they require on terms appropriate to their circumstances—remains stalled in UNCTAD. UNIDO's Industrial Development Fund has still to achieve its $50 million annual target. Protectionism—and protectionist pressure—in developed countries against imports of manufactures from developing countries has generally got worse rather than better. The UN Code of Conduct on Transnational Corporations has yet to be agreed, while the multilaterally agreed set of principles and rules for the control of restrictive business practices continues to disappoint many countries which judge it to be ineffective.

On the other hand there have been some positive developments. Several agencies, UNIDO and the World Bank among them, are giving increasing attention to industrial development in Africa, which lags far behind other continents. The World Bank has set up a Multilateral Investment Guarantee Agency which would help to insure foreign investment against political risks. Several networks have been established to spread technological information among developing countries. The International Labour Organisation and other agencies are equipping progressively greater numbers of people with the vocational skills needed for industrialisation. A new round of multilateral trade negotiations in the GATT brings some hope—if not yet the promise—of greater access for developing-country manufactures, not only in the developed-country markets but in other developing countries as well.

Conclusion

The overall picture of industrial development leaves much to be desired. Although the direct impact of the Commonwealth report in furthering industrial co-operation internationally may have been small, the objectives which lay behind the Jha Team's recommendations are as valid now as when they were espoused more than ten years ago. It is still vital to adopt measures that: strengthen developing countries' indigenous capabilities in such areas as entrepreneurship, management, technology, financing and marketing; foster co-operation among developing countries by, say, providing more access to markets or through joint funding arrangements; increase industrial countries' support, e.g. by opening markets further and untying more aid; and enable international agencies to improve the quality and quantity of their assistance. Many of the weaknesses in industrial co-operation identified in the report remain. If small countries and small industries are not quite so neglected by international agencies and in bilateral arrangements as they were, it is still true that the compartmentalisation of functions means that different bodies often have to be approached for assistance and that there are still problems in mobilising resources, particularly equity capital, to implement viable projects. Much remains to be achieved.

Within the Commonwealth however, the response to the Jha Team's recommendations for action has been quite positive. Though the Commonwealth Secretariat has not been able to undertake all that the Team might have hoped, the Industrial Development Unit and the Industrial Training and Experience Programme have significant achievements to their name. Various developments in the provision of technology advice and information through the Commonwealth Science Council have also proved helpful. Although the idea of a Commonwealth Equity Fund did not originate from the work of the Jha Team, the Fund will help to advance the Team's objectives by providing finance for industrial enterprises.

Chapter 9
The management
of technological change

Technological change is a wider and more complex issue than most of those addressed by Commonwealth Expert Groups. It is also fundamental to development and, indeed, to economic growth and living standards in all countries.

The origins of the Commonwealth Expert Group which examined technological change were in the discussions of Commonwealth Employment and Labour Ministers in 1983. There the paradox was highlighted that new technologies were hailed as a great boon to humanity but were almost everywhere treated with extreme suspicion and reserve. Examples were cited of tea plucking robots that could raise yields and exports—but also lower employment in tea plantations in East Africa and South Asia; of computerised airline booking systems that could boost tourism but decimate employment in the travel trade in the Caribbean; and of new materials, including synthetic substances, that have great potential for human betterment but which threaten the market for textile fibres, sugar and other commodities.

Commonwealth Heads of Government, meeting later the same year, acted on a recommendation of Labour Ministers to set up an Expert Group to look at the whole issue of the management of technological change, recognising its impact on employment in particular. Professor M. G. K. Menon, then Chief Scientific Adviser to the Government of India, was invited to chair the Group (see Annex for list of members).

The Group's Report,*Technological Change: Enhancing the Benefits*, was discussed at the Heads of Government Meeting in 1985 and led to a series of regional seminars for policy-makers. From these evolved a programme of work on policy development and advisory services. This programme is being substantially enlarged with the establishment of a Commonwealth Consultative Group for Technology Management (CCGTM), following discussions at the Kuala Lumpur summit of Commonwealth leaders in 1989.

Approach of the Group

The Menon Group approached the issue by emphasising that technological change had a large measure of inevitability, and that it was not possible to avoid upheaval and uncertainty by avoiding new technologies. "The extent of interdependence through trade, investment, telecommunications and travel is such that knowledge of new technologies is being spread everywhere", it said in its report. It went on to point out that in most applications, new technologies could confer positive benefits and were the main long-term influence on economic growth.

Nevertheless, the Group acknowledged that there could be unfavourable impacts in the form of displacement of labour from employment and traditional skills, on environmental systems and patterns of social relations. The objective of public policy should be to try to mitigate these negative consequences while encouraging beneficial change. The Group urged all governments to have a positive outlook, develop their capacity for forecasting, assessing and monitoring the impact of new technologies and evolve a strategy with clear priorities to achieve the greatest benefits and minimise adjustment costs. It is this approach which the Group envisaged in the term 'management of technological change'.

The experts emphasised three concepts—a differential approach as between countries, a systems approach to new technologies, and the importance of technology which could assist the poorest people. The rationale for *differentiation* was the enormous range of technological capabilities and needs between countries because of variations in size, living standards, availability of scientific and technically trained manpower and resource endowments (see Table 7 on pp. 178-9). The report pointed out that "27 out of 49 countries each have under one million population—but India alone has almost three million scientists and engineers. Britain has a GNP of over 1000 times the size of the ten smallest Commonwealth countries' economies combined". There must inevitably be implications for policy: in large developing Commonwealth countries, like India, there was considerable technological capacity that could be developed; in small states the policy orientation must inevitably be towards importing and adapting new technologies.

A *systems* approach to technologies emphasised the need to look at technologies not in isolation but in the context of the organisational structure—of society or enterprises—in which they were introduced. In microelectronics the most important applications were occurring in factories and offices where systems can be devised to utilise more effectively the properties of new technologies—miniaturisation, increased flexibility and precision. In biotechnology the productive potential of both crops and animal husbandry was only likely to be realised within a system which furnishes appropriate economic incentives and support services. The Group argued that "societies which are deficient in creating a 'systems capability' for new technologies will be retarded in employing them... and equipment will be inefficiently used".

The concept of *technology for the people* emphasises the difficulties—but also the importance—of establishing a linkage between the needs of low income and other vulnerable groups and the potential of new technologies. Typically, "governments and large companies in major developed countries provide the 'push' for developing new technologies; the consumers in these societies and government departments, including the military, provide the 'pull'... ", the report said. Most of the world's population—75 per cent— lived in poor countries. But most of the world's R&D—95 per cent—took place in rich countries and an even higher proportion for emerging technologies. Such an imbalance was not merely inequitable but dangerous. The report said: "One danger is that technologies which originate in developed countries are likely to incorporate a labour-saving bias... Another is that most new products... will reflect the tastes of relatively high income consumers...". An important task of technology management was seen by the Group as the development of products and services specifically geared to meeting the urgent needs of the poor and to creating conditions for blending traditional with emerging technologies.

The Group approached technology change by focusing on new, or 'frontier' technologies—microelectronics, biotechnology, and new materials technology, in particular—"which are distinguished from other modern technologies by the speed at which their application is proceeding and by their wide scope, which transcends narrow sectoral boundaries" (see Box 14, pp164-5).

The impact of new technologies

The report noted that the new technologies would affect the Commonwealth in many ways, both positive and negative. The net impact would vary according not only to the country in question but also to the time period and social groups. This range of possibilities could best be understood by considering the potential effects on economic growth, employment, working conditions, international trade and society.

Economic growth

Historically the major impact of new technologies had been in stimulating economic growth and improvements in living standards. The contribution of technological change to economic performance was difficult to measure precisely but "by raising the productivity of labour, capital, land and other natural resources, technology has had a dominant role in stimulating economic growth". The general proposition could be applied to particular sectors. Microelectronics had been responsible for major improvements in the productivity not only of labour but also of capital, particularly via the use of computers. Microelectronic technologies had increased productivity in engineering; for example, computer numerically-controlled (CNC) tools and

Box 14: The emerging technologies

Microelectronics

Defined in the report to refer to four overlapping activities, microelectronics is the technology associated with large and very large-scale integrated circuits, particularly microprocessors and memory chips:

- components (semiconductors; integrated circuits)
- information processing (computers and related software)
- information transfer (telecommunications)
- other electronic applications (factory automation, instrumentation etc)

The key characteristics of this set of technologies are:

- digital logic leading to rapid information processing through a 'universal language'
- devices that are programmable, leading to numerous applications
- increasing density of 'microchips' reduces costs, through miniaturisation
- these features contribute to simultaneous handling of complex information as in flexible manufacturing systems (FMS) and computer-aided manufacturing (CAM)
- increasingly there is a linkage beyond manufacturing processes to integrate design, manufacture, management and control, as in 'just in time' systems
- synergy between different technologies as in related telecommunications and computer developments: leading increasingly to a seamless concept of information 'technology' instead of separate sectoral issues (i.e. the range of telecommunications and information activities centred around microelectronic devices which permit the storage, transmission and manipulation of data in digital form at low cost and great speed).

Biotechnology

The application of scientific and engineering principles—particularly those used in microbiology, biochemistry, genetics, biochemical and chemical engineering in the processing of materials by biological agents (micro-organisms, enzymes, living cells).

Biotechnology can be conveniently sub-divided into taditional and modern.

Traditional biotechnology has been concerned with such matters as: use of fermentation organisms; plant and animal breeding including high yield-ing plant varieties; antibiotics and vaccines; sterilisation and pasteurisa-tion of foods; biological control of pests.

Hightech or *modern* biotechnology includes genetic and cellular manipu-lation (including 'cloning'); enzyme production and reaction; fermenta-tion related to large scale growth of living organisms. Actual and potential areas of application include:

- health (drug development)
- agriculture (genetic engineering of plants; nitrogen fixing; animal husbandry through embryo transplants; changes in genetic character-istics and hormone control)
- manufacturing (using micro-organisms for low temperature chemical processes)
- energy (for biomass conversion)
- waste control.

New materials

There has been a stream of new materials from metallurgy and petrochemi-cals. What is ''new'' is the speed with which a new generation of materials is emerging with improved purity, durability and strength and capacity for forming close to final shape; and also the shift from petrochemicals and metals to polymers and ceramics. Among the key developments are:

- engineering ceramics
- high strength, low alloy steel
- powder metallurgy
- new polymers
- composites (of new fibres—such as carbon, brass and polyamide with polymers, metals, ceramics and cements)
- joining technologies (laser welding, diffusion bonding)

New energy technologies

Major innovations are being made in processes and products:

- energy conversion (use of microelectronics based control to reduce losses)
- new end uses (heat pumps and fluidised-bed combustion)
- integrated energy systems (combined heat and power)
- renewable energy sources (biofuels; wind; tidal and other ocean energy; new forms of hydro including mini hydro; solar power).

computer-aided design (CAD) could raise labour productivity two to three times. In the services sector, the productivity of labour and capital was being raised by the use of automated equipment. Information technology had already created several new service industries, e.g. to transport economically vast amounts of information through telecommunication channels. At the same time it was modifying the relationship between goods and services, increasing the service content of goods. The full effects of biotechnology had not yet been realised but its traditional forms had already increased agricultural production, e.g. by contributing to the development of high-yielding varieties of cereals. Modern biotechnology had potential applications in animal health, energy and food production, pharmaceuticals and industry, and could create new products very quickly.

What was often most revolutionary—and growth stimulating—about these new, frontier technologies was that they converge with other new technologies, the Group pointed out. In particular computer and communications technologies transformed not only specific processes but also the organisational structures of firms and industry. This pervasiveness was facilitated in turn by the exceptional fall in the costs of transmitting, storing and processing information, and by the technologies' novel capacity to integrate and control industrial and services activities. Microelectronics also combined well with biotechnology and traditional technologies to enhance their capabilities to extend their applications into new fields.

Almost all the evidence for the growth stimulating effects of new technologies derived from developed economies. The impact on developing countries had so far been superficial or, in some cases, negative, as in the replacement of natural rubber and textile fibres by new products. But there were examples, usually localised, of positive consequences: the use of superabsorbent synthetic polymers to retain water in soil; the use of 'micro hydro' technology in hilly and increasingly in flat areas; and the 'blending' of microelectronics technology with traditional manufacturing to increase efficiency.

Impact on employment

Emerging technologies were important too for employment, although their impact was uncertain because of difficulties in measuring long-term employment gains from increased economic growth, and in isolating the employment impact from other factors, notably economic policy. Quantitative studies had generally been of limited value as they had been confined largely to short-term developments in the microelectronics sector of developed countries. Noting these difficulties, the Group emphasised the need for caution in reaching conclusions; there was no predetermined link between technological change and employment. The Experts concluded that "it is not possible to estimate —and probably not very useful to speculate—what the aggregate effects of technology are likely to be on employment levels in developed or developing countries... what can be said however is that there will be major structural changes involving the loss of existing jobs with consequential costs to the individuals concerned and a need for measures to assist adjustment''.

Notwithstanding these major reservations, some studies showed interesting results. The impact of technology varied both according to the time period and the type of labour being observed. In the short term the employment impact had often been negative, particularly in industries where new processes based on microelectronics could readily be substituted for more conventional, labour-intensive operations—motor vehicle manufacture, printing, insurance, banking, etc. However, in the long term, new, improved products and services, in computer software, for example, were creating considerable demand for labour.

In the developing countries, employment was lost when mechanical processes replaced labour and when new competing products like high fructose corn syrup—a substitute for sugar—were developed. On the positive side, renewable energy generally created more jobs than energy from fossil fuels or nuclear power, and increased supplies of energy in rural areas could create additional employment, e.g. in food processing and bricklaying. In agriculture, more labour was being employed, bringing marginal lands under cultivation with improved varieties of food grains and multiple cropping. The use of microelectronic devices in management, accounting and marketing could raise efficiency by reducing delays and thus increasing employment.

The new technologies tended to increase the demand for technical and managerial skills and decrease the demand for more physical and unskilled tasks in many sectors including electronics and banking. The Experts noted that ''The broad thrust of new technologies is to create a large, generally unsatisfied, demand for highly skilled workers in particular areas such as programming, product development and equipment maintenance... However the main anxieties... appear to be among the less skilled''. Such 'deskilling' could affect vulnerable groups (for example, women workers in the services sector) and also widen the gap in status, pay and security between groups of workers, with women, older workers and new entrants to the labour force being particularly disadvantaged by rising skill requirements.

In developing countries, the Group observed, the shortage of skills might be such as to restrict the diffusion of new technologies. However the new computer based information technology also provided opportunities for improving education and training systems: more people can be trained in convenient locations, providing for greater access.

Working conditions
The effect of new technologies on working conditions had both positive and

negative elements, the report noted. Such technologies could reduce or eliminate hazardous and tedious work, making for safer and cleaner environments. But they could also increase monotony, stress and other health problems. The spread of visual display units (VDUs), for example, had been accompanied by stress and other harmful effects; the operation of nuclear power plants could involve dangers to workers and society as a whole.

New technologies also modified the organisation of production through both centralising decision-making and dispersing production. Information systems offered the potential for home working for what are currently 'office jobs'. On the whole, new technologies increased the flexibility of production systems and work patterns. This might enhance job satisfaction through, say, work sharing and home working. But the manner of their introduction might deny this advantage, as is evident from the concern expressed about isolation from other workers, heavier work loads, etc.

There were many issues affecting labour rights which were leading to the demand for adequate consultation with labour when new technologies are introduced. Here, as in other spheres, there were threats as well as opportunities from new technologies. Data information networks, for example, were used by some firms and governments to supervise people at work, enabling the centralised collection and storage of other information, e.g. on trade union activities, on computerised personnel records.

International trade
Trade helped to diffuse new technologies but also created some problems, in particular for developing countries, said the Menon Group. Raw material exporters faced the prospect of substitutes emerging from biotechnology and new materials technology. Manufacturers might also lose their comparative advantage as a result of a reduction in the importance of labour costs because of process innovation. The emergence of new and better products, with shorter product cycles, might offer less scope for production in developing countries.

The potential to benefit from the positive features of new technologies varied. In the electronics sector a few developing countries were enlarging their share of a rapidly expanding segment of world trade. The expansion of these industries in developing countries was based essentially on low labour costs. In the Asian newly industrialising countries wages were generally below US levels; some input costs were cheaper and infrastructure was subsidised; and there was less control over working conditions, allowing for longer working hours, and less resistance to new work methods. However, in many low-income developing countries with a shortage of skills and limited infrastructure, production costs were higher than in developed countries, though a few market niches existed for radios or pocket calculators, for example, which such countries could exploit.

There were also sectoral variations in the *textile and clothing* industries. The use of techniques based on microelectronics had led to some processes being relocated to developed countries. This movement had been limited so far, mainly because of the technical difficulties of automating garment assembly operations. But in the long term developing countries' export prospects could be affected by flexible manufacturing systems and automation of all assembly stages. The Menon Group pointed out that developing countries could react by some restructuring, and possibly retooling, of their industries. Moreover the increasing range of new products of new technologies was creating many niches which developing countries could exploit.

One consequence of cheaper communications was the establishment of *new export-oriented services* in developing countries, e.g. computers, keypunching services, computer software services, typesetting and editing services. But new technologies also created barriers to market entry. For instance, countries which could not have information about their tourist resorts included on the tourist industry networks might find their potential visitors going elsewhere. Overall, developing countries were likely to increase their imports from developed countries of the more traditional services such as banking and insurance and new services such as data services and transmission. With falling communication costs, developing countries' firms have had their designs, calculations and routine research data processed in developed countries. Significantly also, those developing countries currently enjoying the most rapid rates of growth of their manufactured exports were precisely those that had traditionally tended to show a strong position in the services trade. With the growing links between the services sector and industrial development, the state of services infrastructure would increasingly be a determinant of comparative advantage.

In *engineering*, exporters of conventional equipment might be faced with falling demand but exports from developing countries might grow if developed country producers shift production of older or lower technology equipment to these countries. By contrast, efficient production of high-tech equipment usually required a minimum scale and domestic capability in electronics design, engineering and R&D. There were also strong links between producers and users of sophisticated equipment which required the support of an international marketing and after sales service. These factors limited the access for developing country exporters.

Biotechnology opened the prospect of efficient import substitution in energy and food, and new seed varieties were expected to be developed whose cultivation required less inputs of chemical fertilizers and pesticides, the report went on to point out. However, biotechnologies leading to increased use of synthetic substitutes adversely affected exports of other primary commodities. Genetic engineering firms in developed countries had been producing medicinal chemicals, pesticides, flavourings and essential oils from tissue cultures rather than from plants exported by developing countries. But these techniques could also be used by developing countries to diversify their exports and to reduce costs, as Malaysia had done with plant cloning of rubber trees to shorten the time taken to mature.

New materials technologies had been producing a range of substitutes for traditional products. The use of optical fibres as a substitute for copper had begun in some applications, and new materials based on ceramics, plastics and composite materials were starting to compete with traditional minerals and metals.There had also been growing economy in the use of raw materials through an improved recovery rate of minerals from bacterial leaching of ores, and, through recycling, of such materials as paper, glass, copper and lead.

Social impacts

Technological change was part of a far-reaching social process; its impact was not simply economic, the Group said. This was especially true of information technologies. The centralisation of decision-making that it permits could greatly increase governmental control and mass surveillance. Computerised information on health, social security or criminal activities could also be misused. The issue of privacy had developed an international dimension as information could be transferred from one country to another to circumvent national data protection laws. Information technologies could also create problems for national and corporate security and present opportunities for large-scale crime.

With respect to health, new biotechnology had great potential for producing better medicines and expanding food supplies, but genetic engineering could present dangers to the health and safety of plant and animal life. Health, safety and environmental concerns also existed with respect to nuclear energy, toxic wastes (including waste from electronic industries) and the creation of micro-organisms harmful to animal and plant life.

Policies for managing technological change

Given the two-sided nature of much new technology, with its capacity for both favourable and unfavourable effects, what can governments do to influence its adoption? The required actions range from strategic decision-making to practical policies on, for example education and research.

Strategy

The Menon Group argued that the inevitability of technological change did not mean that societies and governments need to adopt a passive or deterministic attitude towards it. There were options in terms of the speed and direction of technological change and policy choices to be made. It suggested that all societies must have some capability to forecast, assess and monitor the impact of technological change. In this way adjustment problems could be at least anticipated and perhaps reduced.

Technological forecasting and evaluation needed adequate information to be useful; but even then technological selection was a highly skilled task and most developing countries at present did not have the required specialists. It was the Group's view that governments could try to meet this problem through a collaborative approach on a regional or international basis.

The Group further suggested that, in order to provide an overview of technology policy, and each government should establish a mechanism to co-ordinate its technology activities, possibly an independent unit close to the Head of Government or Cabinet.

In the development of an indigenous technological capacity, governments had to make the initial fundamental decision as to the most useful point of entry. This would vary according to needs and costs, the report observed. In most low-income countries agriculture, especially food crops, was likely to be a priority, while microelectronics might be a priority in developing countries with a large industrial base and extensive communications. Small island economies, because of size and inadequate infrastructure, might identify some limited areas in microelectronics and microbiology and promote certain activities on a sub-regional basis. For such countries, a major export crop would be a natural focus for special attention.

Education and training

To make effective use of new technology, high priority had to be given to education and training. The range of needs, which would vary according to each country's requirements, included mathematical education and exposure to computers in schools; technical awareness programmes, including for those outside the formal economy e.g. small farmers; the provision of specialised skills like those possessed by system designers and programmers and management; training to use information technology.

As many small developing countries had at best limited facilities for training and retraining, governments had a role to play in making the most of available resources, and in providing and upgrading facilities, making changes in educational curricula, establishing regional training institutions and encouraging enterprises to expand training including on-the-job training and providing workplace training for students from training institutions. The Group felt that regional co-operation could be an important mechanism for dealing with these issues.

The report noted the critical importance of financing and discussed several possibilities. The transfer of high technology from abroad could be accompanied by the obligation to provide training. A system of fees or loans could be used to discriminate in favour of the required disciplines. Firms could be induced to train workers by tax relief and subsidies, possibly financed by a levy on the industry in question.

Indigenous research and development
Selecting the area in which to concentrate limited R&D resources would present a difficult policy choice. The Group felt there was little scope in most countries for fundamental work; R&D would therefore largely involve adaptation of technology, including its blending with new technologies. Priorities were likely to include ways of modernising traditional technologies without reducing their employment potential, and R&D on products and services of special interest to the poor where purely commercial returns were inadequate.

In some developing countries the results of research had failed to reach expectations and there had been limited commercial interest. Several measures were considered in the report to ensure that scarce resources are efficiently used. These included the establishment of clear priorities for the work of public sector research institutions; collaboration between research institutions in different centres; a high proportion of contract research; and a dialogue between technologists and the business community to help research to be marketed.

Assistance for technological diffusion
In many developing countries there was a weak link between invention and innovation. To remedy this, the Group said that governments could catalyse private sector activity through credit schemes for small farmers and extension services involving experienced engineers. Commercialisation of research could be promoted either through the sale of technology to private enterprise or by official research institutions.

A suitable climate for innovation
Innovation required the right economic conditions for risk-taking and investment. These were difficult to achieve even in most developed countries and would be doubly difficult in many developing countries with limited infrastructure and vulnerability to severe external shocks.

Venture-type capital could play a crucial role in commercialising the results of R&D, the Experts pointed out. Venture capital financing was spreading rapidly in some developing countries—India and Thailand, for example—and developed country venture capital companies were internationalising their operations. There were obvious benefits in establishing strong ties between venture capital companies and government agencies responsible for technological development.

The report suggested that innovation could be rewarded by fiscal incentives such as tax holidays, tax deductions and accelerated depreciation allowances. Ideally, the incentives should be oriented towards fostering risk-taking and investment without encouraging labour saving; they could be selective to avoid costly benefits to many firms not needing them. Governments, as important purchasers of new technology, could stimulate innovation in local firms through their procurement policies. But the Group warned that it was crucial to avoid costly protection.

Innovation was more likely to occur in conditions of optimism and economic expansion. Efficient market mechanisms and clear macroeconomic priorities facilitated innovation and avoided the use of inappropriate technology, the Group said. In many developing countries technology imports had been reduced to allocate scarce foreign exchange to debt servicing, and to food and energy imports. Distortions in labour, capital and foreign exchange markets with overvalued foreign exchange impeded the creation of a rational technology policy.

Social priorities

It was the view of the Group that commercial innovation of technology geared to satisfying private demand might not meet social needs. Most of the population, playing an insignificant role in the money economy, would hardly benefit from lower prices and better quality in products brought about by technological change. A policy which incorporated new technologies for basic needs could reduce the cost of necessities and the insecurity of low-income groups. These technologies could include: cheap energy for rural households, e.g. biogas, windmill and solar power; drought and pest-resistant high-yielding strains of cereals; improved health services; mass literacy campaigns; and disaster warning systems through satellite detection.

An important additional criterion when considering technological change should be the impact on the environment, the Group said. New technologies could assist environmental protection—biotechnology, for example, could help maintain a better genetic balance in animal and plant life—and were available to recycle waste. New energy technologies could reduce the dependence on fossil fuels and nuclear power. There were also dangers to the environment: to the air and water from pollutants and to the land from the use of new chemicals. The Group said that governments could minimise the side effects of new technology on the environment through policies relating to natural resource conservation. A good example would be policies to promote the use of plants without harmful effects on agricultural land. Arid and semi-arid plants had been identified as an alternative to synthetic chemicals as potential commercial sources of insect attractants, repellents and toxicants.

With respect to health and safety impacts, the report said new products were emerging whose properties and long-term consequences were very imperfectly understood. The policy priority should be greater research and monitoring by independent bodies involving the creation of at least a minimum number of health, safety and protection staff.

Adjustment policies

Technology change, whatever its benefits in aggregate, necessarily inflicted some costs, and adjustment policies might be necessary to compensate for their uneven distribution. These policies could not be separated from the general macroeconomic policy which must create an environment favourable to mobility and change.

Education and employment-related policies were seen as of crucial importance to efficient adjustment. In the developed countries many measures had been tried, such as continuing education for adults to adapt to future scientific demands, portable pensions, and housing entitlements. Retraining was crucial to adjustment but it demanded a level of resources which might be prohibitive for developing countries. Only modest adjustment assistance might be available to regional policies aimed at arresting decline and disparities in development. The most effective measures were the establishment of infrastructure and provision of fiscal incentives, differentiated on a regional basis.

New technologies presented developing countries with peculiar problems of policy adjustment. Labour-intensive technology could face competition from emerging technologies which could destroy traditional occupations at great social cost (e.g. the replacement of handwoven by factory made fabrics). But they could be made to co-exist with traditional technologies by 'blending', thus preserving employment and possibly enhancing efficiency. The report said governments could play a useful role in undertaking or supporting 'blending' R&D and demonstration projects to encourage small users. They could also ensure that the cost of new technology was not too high for small-scale users.

The adjustment problems that arise for commodity exporters could be mitigated by the provision of R&D and other assistance to develop new products from the same materials (e.g. livestock feed from cane by-products) or suitable alternative crops and to diversify into goods and services making greater use of skilled labour and advanced technology. In the view of the Group, the prospects for the low-income developing countries, in spite of protectionism, lay in concentrating on the growing demand for new products which—with low labour costs—they were ideally placed to supply. These include products with individual styling or requiring complex hand-manufactured operations, or where labour costs still remained a large proportion of total costs.

Importing technologies

There were several ways of importing technology that make different demands on indigenous capacity, the Group said. Managing technology imports required making the most appropriate choice among the options available.

Direct purchase of technology required a strong base in information collection and other supporting infrastructure. It was therefore unlikely to be viable for small states. An alternative was to import hardware while trying to ensure it was accompanied by the transfer of technology, training and software. Frequently, however, machinery imports led to a continuing dependence on foreign suppliers for operating and maintenance assistance. To avoid this there must be a capacity to assess technology imports and to ensure the provision of appropriate software and systems.

The *foreign investment* option was increasingly favoured by many developing countries because it required the foreign investors to take an equity risk. Some developing countries like India were more selective and allowed foreign investment only when it was considered indispensable for technological transfer. The attraction of foreign investment was that capital, technology and management were all present in the same 'package'—though there was no guarantee that training, R&D, and technology adaptation would take place without supportive domestic policies.

Technology could also be obtained by some form of *technical collaboration* agreement without foreign ownership. A potential disadvantage was that the lengthy process of evaluating licensing could delay the absorption of technology. Licensing also required local expertise and financial resources that may not be available, and it might not always provide access to the emerging technologies.

Joint ventures had elements of both technical collaboration and foreign investment. Most successful joint ventures, however, involved producing for the domestic market rather than export, and were in mature industries rather than newer ones.

The report pointed out that countries that lack trained personnel might find it necessary to import them through consultancies, management and service contracts, or to resort to education and training abroad and technical assistance. Technological transfer was important to develop a local absorbtive capacity.

Inter-governmental co-operation

In view of the great disparities in technological capacity, the Group felt that co-operation between countries could have an important role. *Technical assistance*, including the establishment of training institutes and scholarships, could help relieve the shortage of skills as could the establishment of joint training institutes, probably on a regional basis. A more important influence than either of these was the migration of skilled workers from developing to industrialised countries. In some cases this had compounded skill shortages though there could be benefits when migrants returned home with greater technological experience. Either way it was the immigration policies of industrial countries rather than their aid programmes that were more likely to influence skill transfers.

Joint R&D efforts were justified, the Group said, by the existence of substantial economies of scale and common problems and needs. There was a particular need for co-operation among small states. Among the examples of successful collaborative efforts were those of the International Rice Research Institute in Manila in developing new seed varieties. An International Centre for Genetic Engineering and Biotechnology (ICGEB) has been established, with training in industrial microbiology, agriculture and health among its activities. Sub-regional networks were also being devised to tap into broader regional networks, e.g. a proposed Caricom network to link into the Latin American-Caribbean Network for Microelectronics and the ICGEB.

Several international organisations had assisted developing countries in formulating technology policy. Developing countries could also provide mutual support on policy by exchanging experiences in negotiating contracts or in managing new technologies and could implement common technical standards, the Group said. Institutional mechanisms for carrying this out had been established under UNIDO.

The development of *South-South trade* could identify appropriate technology, particularly for the least developed countries. Using technologies adapted and tried in other developing countries could reduce the need for costly trial and error procedures.

One unresolved issue in North-South negotiations was that of an international *code of conduct* for the transfer of technology. Since the mid-1970s UNCTAD had been trying to bring such a code into being. It had not so far been possible to strike the delicate balance between improving access to new technology for developing countries and ensuring that foreign companies were not discouraged from transferring their technologies.

A further issue concerned copyrights and counterfeiting. Counterfeiting had spread to high-tech goods such as computers and related software. Firms in the developed countries wanted to recoup their research and development costs but were reluctant to reveal details of their new products, through patents or otherwise. Developing countries, on the other hand, were seeking greater and concessional access to patent information. This issue loomed large in the Uruguay Round of negotiations as it affected trade (see Chapter 7).

Areas for Commonwealth co-operation

The Commonwealth Secretariat was seen by the Menon Group as having an important role to play in the management of technological change, subject to the need to avoid duplication with other agencies and to the Secretariat's resources constraints (see Box 15).

The Group's proposals for Commonwealth action have been adopted in various ways in the work of the Secretariat. An important element has been a series of *regional meetings*. The first, in Trinidad and Tobago, held in collaboration with UNESCO and the Caribbean Community, focused on how

---

Box 15: Recommendations by the Menon Group for action by the Commonwealth Secretariat

For most Commonwealth countries it was extremely difficult to keep up to date with the rapid development of emerging technologies and to evaluate their likely impact. The Menon Group felt that the Secretariat might perform a useful role (complementing the work of other agencies) in *monitoring developments and disseminating information* in an easily readable form to decision-makers in the Commonwealth. The Secretariat was also encouraged to help Commonwealth countries collect data to assess the *economic and social impact* of new technologies.

The Commonwealth was seen as playing an important role by organising *training or exchange programmes* for creating a better awareness of new technologies and their impact. Policy-makers confronted with the problem of choice needed information on the systems available. The Group suggested that a particularly useful role could be played by the Commonwealth Industrial Training and Experience Programme in providing training to the less developed small island states and to countries in special need in sub-Saharan Africa. Co-financing could be explored from manufacturing companies and international agencies. The combination of satellite communication and the English language medium could achieve more cost-efficient education and training systems, especially in higher and specialist education, throughout the Commonwealth.

The Group also saw merit in the Commonwealth setting up an advisory panel of experts who could be drawn upon as the need arose. As well as being able to provide advice on technology forecasting or assessment, the panel would be able to help Commonwealth developing countries to develop technology institutions and improve contacts between them.

Table 7: Characteristics related to technological capacity in selected countries

Categories/Countries	Population (thousands) 1988	GNP Total at market prices (mn. US $) 1988	GNP Real growth rate (per cent) 1980-88	GNP Per capita US$ 1988	Numbers of Scientists and engineers Total	Numbers of Scientists and engineers As a % of total labour force ++	Number of scientists and engineers in research and development — MRE — Total	Number of scientists and engineers in research and development As of % of total labour force ++	Research and development expenditure as a % of GNP	Patents in force 1984
	(1)	(2)	(3)	(4)	(5)	(6)	(7)	(8)	(9)	(10)
I. Major developed economies										
United States	245,871	4,863,674	3.1	19,780	3,431,800l	3.44	728,600m	0.72	2.8p	1,192,322
Japan	122,433	2,576,541	4.0	21,040	7,046,000l	12.49	496,145m	0.86	2.8p	439,489
United Kingdom	57,019	730,038	3.0	12,800	n.a.	-	86,500h	0.33	2.3p	222,558
II. Medium or small, open developed economies										
Canada	26,104	437,471	3.4	16,760	1,291,210k	11.81	37,853o	0.33	1.5p	405,247
Australia	16,506	204,446	3.1	12,390	383,368k	6.03	29,236o	0.43	1.4p	49,458
New Zealand	3,339	32,109	1.6	9,620	47,249b	4.31	n.a.	-	0.9i	n.a.
III. Newly industrialising outward-looking countries										
Hong Kong	5,674	52,380	7.3	9,230	83,200k	3.29	n.a.	-	n.a.	n.a.
Korea, South	42,593	150,270	9.2	3,530	94,171k	0.67	32,117m	0.22	1.8p	11,979
Malaysia	16,921	31,620	4.0	1,870	26,000l	11.36	n.a.	-	n.a.	n.a.
Singapore	2,639	24,010	7.0	9,100	38,259j	3.56	3,361q	n.a.	0.9q	9,098m
IV. Populous developing countries with substantial technology base										
India**	813,990	271,440	5.5	330	697,600g	0.27	85,309p	n.a.	0.9	24,140e
China**	1,083,889	356,490	10.5	330	n.a.	-	n.a.	-	n.a.	n.a.
Brazil	144,369	328,860	3.4	2,280	541,328a	1.80	32,508l	0.06	0.4	10,953i

V. Low-income countries with limited technology base									
Ghana	14,040	5,610	2.0	400	6,897a	0.21	4,084f	0.11	n.a.	730
Kenya	23,021	8,310	3.9	360	16,241l	1.56	361e	0.04	n.a.	1,831
Sri Lanka	16,565	7,020	4.3	420	7,457c	0.18	2,790o	n.a.	0.2	734
Tanzania	24,739	3,780	2.2	160	n.a.	-	n.a.	-	n.a.	2,079j
Bangladesh	108,851	18,310	3.6	170	23,500d	0.09	n.a.	-	n.a.	891
Nigeria	110,131	31,770	-1.0	290	22,050j	n.a.	2,200g	n.a.	0.3g	359e
VI. Small, open developing countries with limited technology base									
Jamaica	2,429	2,610	-0.7	1,080	5,963a	0.95	18p	n.a.	0.0	648
Mauritius	1,048	1,890	6.1	1,810	7,256m	3.75	267o	0.12	0.6	186
Seychelles	68	260	2.5	3,800	900m	5.14	18m	0.10	1.3	48
St. Kitts/Nevis	43	120	4.9	2,770	135a	1.04	n.a.	-	n.a.	n.a.
Trinidad & Tobago	1,241	4,160	-5.8	3,350	3,314a	0.98	275n	n.a.	0.8	1,900e
Tuvalu	8r	5k	n.a.	680l	n.a.	-	n.a.	-	n.a.	n.a.
Samoa, Western	168	100	n.a	580	350g	0.92	140h	0.37	n.a.	13k

Please note: Data in columns 5 to 9 exclude law, humanities and education.

MRE: Most recent estimate (see below for the years concerned).

n.a.   Not available.

**   Excluding social sciences and humanities.

++   Estimates in columns (6) and (8) correspond to the periods indicated in columns (5) and (7) respectively.

a 1970; b 1971; c 1972; d 1973; e 1975; f 1976; g 1977; h 1978; i 1979; j 1980; k 1981; l 1982; m 1983; n 1984; o 1985; p 1986; q 1987; r mid-1987.

Sources: World Bank, World Development Report, 1989; World Bank, Atlas, 1989; United Nations, Statistical Yearbook, 1982; United Nations, Statistical Yearbook, 1983/84; United Nations, Statistical Yearbook 1985/86; UNESCO, Statistical Yearbook 1984; UNESCO, Statistical Yearbook, 1987; UNESCO, Statistical Yearbook, 1988; UNESCO Statistical Yearbook, 1989.

small states could maximise their capacity for technology management through collaboration and organisation of priorities. It also looked at several Caribbean 'models' of technology development institutions, particularly at the Caribbean Industrial Research Institute (CARIRI) which is a successful example of an R&D centre with a strong bent for industrial applications.

The second meeting, in Zimbabwe, addressed the question of how low-income African countries, many of them beset by economic crises and enforced cuts in research activities and in investment, could adopt a long-term, technological perspective. Several apparently successful examples were described of attempts to introduce basic technology forecasting and assessment, as in Mauritius. The third seminar, in Malaysia, drew on the experience of such countries as Malaysia, India and Singapore where indigenous technological capacity has been already well developed—although in different ways—and sophisticated systems of forecasting, assessment and monitoring have been built up.

Arising from the Group's recommendation for an advisory panel, the Secretariat has evolved a programme of advisory services based on sharing experiences among member countries. This has found expression in the Science Council's project on Commonwealth Strategic Management and Planning of Science and Technology (COMMANSAT). The success of COMMANSAT contributed to an important step forward in the work of the Secretariat, as shown by the following extract from the communique issued by the Commonwealth Heads of Government Meeting in Kuala Lumpur in 1989:

> Heads of Government endorsed the Malaysian Government's proposal for the establishment of a Commonwealth Consultative Group for Technology Management (CCGTM), based on the approach of the Commonwealth Project on Strategic Management and Planning of Science and Technology and its Integration in National Development , with a small support unit within the Secretariat. They noted that this unit would draw on, and develop, the work of the Commonwealth network of specialists and managers in the field of technology management and would enable the Secretariat to provide an advisory service to governments.

The Secretariat is now establishing the CCGTM network and this could turn out to be a valuable legacy of the Menon report.

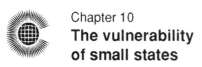

Chapter 10
The vulnerability
of small states

The economic and security problems of small states became important international concerns as decolonisation accelerated in the 1960s and 1970s, bringing a large number of such states to independence. These problems were of direct concern to the Commonwealth as the proportion of small states in its membership was high—and increasing. As a result, they became a subject of regular attention at the biennial meetings of Commonwealth Heads of Government and the annual meetings of Commonwealth Finance Ministers. These discussions were of considerable value in securing greater international recognition of the needs of small countries. They also led to a special programme of assistance to small states within the Commonwealth.

When Commonwealth Heads of Government met in New Delhi in October 1983, they were acutely aware of the peculiar vulnerability of small states which had been brought dramatically to the world's attention over the preceding months with events in Grenada. Commonwealth leaders therefore felt that the problems of small states—including their special security problems —deserved wider consideration. They accordingly asked the Secretary-General to undertake a study of the special needs of such states. To do so, he brought together, in a Consultative Group, 14 persons who had gained wide knowledge of the problems of small states as a result either of their positions within these countries or of extensive diplomatic or academic involvement (see Annex). Chief Justice Telford Georges of The Bahamas, an eminent jurist who had worked in both the Caribbean and Africa, was the Group's chairman. The Group considered the vulnerability of small states in all its relevant aspects—military, political, economic, technical, social and cultural. Its report, *Vulnerability: Small States in the Global Society*, contained some eighty recommendations to provide a basis for international co-operation.

While the security aspects were a special concern of the study in the context in which the Consultative Group was set up, the Group made a particular point of examining the economic underpinnings of security. In keeping with the focus on international economic relations of this volume, this chapter is concerned mainly with the economic dimensions of the Group's report. It first examines the evolution of the concept of smallness, considers the Commonwealth's growing collective concern over small states, and then discusses the contribution of the Consultative Group's report and developments at the Commonwealth and global level subsequent to the Group's report.

The concept of smallness

The relationship between country size and economic prosperity received little attention until a 1957 meeting of the International Economic Association. This concluded that the minimum population required to provide a home market large enough for a country to benefit from economies of scale in production was 10 to 15 million. External trade was therefore seen as having special significance for smaller countries. But it was considered to be more risky due to a number of factors, including political uncertainties, changes in market access, fluctuations in currency, differential rates of inflation and differences in tastes. However, it was felt that these difficulties, including those imposed by small size and the problems involved in securing scale economies, could be overcome by establishing customs unions or free trade areas among groups of countries. To obtain the full benefits of such arrangements, participating countries would need to co-ordinate their monetary, fiscal and other economic policies.

Since that meeting, there have been many discussions on small states. Their focus has changed from viability, through dependency, to the special disadvantages springing from vulnerability.

Viability

In the 1960s, with a large number of small countries becoming independent, their viability was given attention at various forums. At a conference organised by the Institute of Commonwealth Studies of London University in 1962, it was felt that any national entity which could maintain its separate existence was ipso facto viable. The advice to small states was to resolve their problems by undertaking some form of economic integration, preferably with prosperous partners but also with countries at the same or similar levels of economic development.

There was an effort to define smallness using the notions of area, population, accessibility, economic resources, market size and degree of political development. But no agreement was reached, and the meeting concluded that smallness was a comparative and not an absolute concept.

At that time, the UN was also concerned with the viability of small states.*

---

* The League of Nations had been concerned, too. When it was formed four small European countries—Liechtenstein, Monaco, San Marino and Iceland—were debarred from admission by reason of limited area, small population and geographical position.

In 1965, the UN Secretary-General said that the limited size and resources of small states could pose a difficult problem for the role they should try to play in international life, and that Member States might wish to examine more closely the criteria for admitting new Members in the light of the long-term implications of the then present trends. In 1967, he said that while

> It is of course, perfectly legitimate that even the smallest territories ... should attain independence ... it appears desirable that a distinction be made between the right to independence and the question of full membership in the United Nations.... I would suggest that it may be opportune for the competent organs to undertake a thorough and comprehensive study of the criteria for membership in the United Nations, with a view to laying down the necessary limitations on full membership.

On a proposal by the United States, the Security Council in August 1969 appointed a panel of experts to study the question of membership of small states. Though the panel was expected to report to the General Assembly in the same year, the issue was not placed on its agenda. Parallel deliberations at the Security Council also faded out as a result of strong opposition from several members who considered the matter complex and delicate. None of the small states was consequently debarred from UN membership.

A study on the role and participation of small states and territories in international affairs, published in 1971 by the United Nations Institute for Training and Research, concluded that there were many ways to define a mini-state or mini-territory, but they were all more or less arbitrary. The use of a single variable was considered to be too narrow. In its view there was no real need for a rigorous definition for the purposes of UN technical assistance.

Dependency

In the early 1970s the focus of discussion shifted from viability to dependency. The reliance of small states on foreign trade became the centrepiece of attention only with the advent of dependency theory. The economies of small states were generally considered to be more dependent and peripheral than most, and it became fashionable to write about small dependent economies. This was regarded as satisfactory as long as it was understood to mean that such economies were both small and dependent. However, it became misleading when small states were held to be dependent only because they were small. The thrust of the dependency analysis was to identify a number of factors, including the role of foreign investment, the position of certain social groups, and the tradition of monoculture, which are capable of explaining under-development and economic weakness, quite apart from the fact of small size.

The dependency of small states was also the theme of a conference organised by the Institute of Development Studies at the University of Sussex and held in Barbados in 1972. Contributory factors were considered to be: weaknesses in political leadership; relatively high trade/GDP ratios; domination by foreign banks and corporations; strong foreign cultural influences; and relatively large aid flows. The suggested escape route was regionalism. The conference did not produce an unambiguous definition of size, concluding that it should reflect the purpose for which it is being used.

Special disadvantages
In the mid-1970s, the focus of discussions moved to specially disadvantaged groups such as islands, land-locked and least developed countries. In the UN, island developing countries became the subject of many resolutions, particularly after the adoption of UNCTAD resolution 98 (IV) in May 1976, which called upon the international community to undertake special programmes to assist these countries.

The emphasis on island developing countries complicated the debate on the problems of small states. Scepticism was expressed by certain developed countries as to whether island developing countries as such have special needs and problems. A panel of experts convened by UNCTAD in 1973 expressed even stronger reservations: ''Many of the problems of large developing islands are not dissimilar from those of large developing mainland countries, and in this respect they do not require separate consideration in their situation as islands''.

A conference organised by the Australian National University in 1979 examined the broad objectives of island developing countries of the Pacific and Indian Oceans. These were considered to be maintaining political independence, increasing living standards, promoting greater economic self-reliance, and preserving the values, traditions and integrity of island societies. Smallness was examined according to the criteria of population, area and GDP, and islands classified as small, very small, and micro. The participants agreed that the policy options would vary according to the category of country.

The special disadvantages of small states were also the theme of a meeting convened by the Commonwealth Secretariat in 1981. This suggested that in contrast to larger countries, small states were likely to suffer from several disadvantages: difficulties in developing manufacturing and banking sectors, insufficient skills for development projects, a tendency towards monoculture and undiversified output, rigid production and land distribution structures, and high costs associated with instabilities in commodity trade and capital inflows. One of the main conclusions was that only such sectors as services, that are not generally subject to increasing returns, could provide a long-term development path for small states which are not very favourably placed in terms of natural resources or land/man ratios.*

* See Bimal Jalan, ed., *Problems and Policies in Small Economies*, London: Croom Helm, 1981, p.4.

The Commonwealth meeting considered two approaches to identifying small countries, viz. a composite index incorporating area, population and GNP; and a critical minimum size of economies in terms of employment and investment, below which a positive rate of growth in labour productivity in manufacturing cannot be maintained. The validity of the first approach was questioned on the grounds that there was no logical basis for assigning weights to the three variables of the index. Considerable difficulties were envisaged in obtaining comparable data for countries under the second approach. However, there was broad agreement on the use of a population of five million as a working definition for studying the problems of small states.

Since then, the trend has been to set lower population limits to define small countries. A cut-off level of one million has been used by the Commonwealth for the purpose of the Secretariat's special programme of assistance for small states. This limit was also adopted by the Commonwealth Consultative Group* when it undertook its study in 1984.

The Commonwealth's concern

Concern about the factors that hamper the progress of small states came increasingly to be voiced within the Commonwealth during the 1970s. In 1977, Finance Ministers called for special measures to assist these states. Meeting in Barbados, they stressed the fragile nature of small states' economies, citing their "extreme dependence on exports and imports, high dependence on capital inflows and in some cases the lack of natural resources". Ministers asserted that special measures to help small states should at least parallel those being considered in favour of least developed and land-locked countries.

The needs of small states were a central topic of discussion among Commonwealth Heads of Government of the Asia/Pacific region when they met in 1978. In calling for special measures and relationships to assist small states to realise their development potential, the twelve leaders saw that the need for such assistance would grow "with the achievement of independence by a number of very small Commonwealth countries in the years immediately ahead". Their agreement that "systematic programmes of assistance" should be established for small states as a matter of priority reinforced the call made by Finance Ministers in Barbados. They asked the Secretary-General to examine ways in which assistance might be given to small states on a

---

* In view of the focus on security issues, the Commonwealth Group decided to include two larger states, Jamaica and Papua New Guinea, because of their integral links with small states in their respective regions. A total of 31 Commonwealth states were included for purposes of the study.

Commonwealth-wide basis and to seek general Commonwealth support for such assistance.

The Secretary-General prepared detailed proposals to assist small states overcome the "disadvantages of small size, isolation and scarce resources which severely limit the capacity of such countries to achieve their development objectives". These were considered by Commonwealth Senior Officials at their meeting in Kuala Lumpur later in 1978. Elaborated in the light of their discussions, the proposals were put before Heads of Government at Lusaka in 1979. Their endorsement cleared the way for a special programme of assistance to be put into operation. It involved the Secretariat reorienting its work to take greater account of the needs and concerns of small states in economic affairs, education, health, management, food production, and science and technology; these issues were also given higher priority in Secretariat assistance through the Commonwealth Fund for Technical Co-operation (CFTC).

This special programme of assistance had been in operation for some three years when in October 1983 the US military intervention in Grenada put the vulnerability of small states into sharp focus. Commonwealth leaders meeting in New Delhi within a few weeks of the action were deeply disturbed by the further evidence of small states' fragility. Their communique noted that:

> Time and again in their discussions Commonwealth leaders were recalled to the special needs of small states, not only in the Caribbean but elsewhere in the Commonwealth. They recognised that the Commonwealth itself had given some attention to these needs in the context of economic development but felt the matter deserved consideration on a wider basis, including that of national security. Recalling the particular dangers faced in the past by small Commonwealth countries, they requested the Secretary-General to undertake a study drawing as necessary on the resources and experience of Commonwealth countries, of the special needs of such states, consonant with the right to sovereignty and territorial integrity that they shared with all nations.

The Consultative Group set up by the Secretary-General to undertake the study decided to draw as widely as possible on the views not only of Commonwealth governments but also on other informed opinion within member countries; it held a series of colloquia to canvass opinion in different regions of the Commonwealth. The Group's report, publicly released in 1985, gained wide acceptance as an authoritative study of the factors contributing to vulnerability in small states and signposting directions in which such states (and the international community) should move to reduce their vulnerability.

The many aspects of economic vulnerability

Although the concept of vulnerability was widely used in analyses on the condition of small states in the 1980s, there was a tendency to concentrate on their political vulnerability. It was left to the study by the Commonwealth

Group to draw attention to vulnerability in all its aspects, economic and cultural as well as political.

The economic vulnerability of small states is usually associated with such characteristics as a narrow resource base, specialization, small internal markets, openness and a shortage of skills. The report made a range of recommendations to alleviate the resulting problems (see Box 16, pages 188-9). Some small states face additional problems such as remoteness from major markets and sources of supply, or are prone to natural disasters. Although the per capita income in small states is on average higher than in most other developing countries, their narrow and fragile economic structure constrains them from achieving self-sustaining economic growth (see Table 8, page 197). A particular contribution of the report was that it highlighted the persistence of structural problems even when incomes are increasing. It stated that "to regard income levels as an indicator of their economic advancement is to use a flawed measurement".

Visible trade

A principal feature of small states is their openness (see Table 9, page 198); a small domestic market and a narrow resource base increase the significance to them of international trade. For instance, in 1988, the proportion of merchandise imports to GDP was nearly three-quarters in small states, whereas it was only about one-fifth in developing countries as a whole. Although openness is sometimes considered a positive influence on economic growth, the Commonwealth Group concluded that it was not by itself a sufficient condition for growth, as borne out by the experience of many backward areas in developed countries.

A narrow resource base and a small domestic market have led small countries to specialise in a few products to secure scale economies in marketing, distribution and transportation, as well as in production. For example, the Group found that five product groups accounted for about half the exports of small states as a whole and for over four-fifths of some of them. The level of output required to take advantage of export market opportunities for a particular product usually absorbs a much larger proportion of the resources of a small country than a large one.

Openness and specialisation have contributed to small states' vulnerability to external economic shocks. The study found that between 1980 and 1982, export earnings (in nominal terms) had fallen by 38 per cent in Tonga, 34 per cent in Vanuatu, 27 per cent in Guyana, 24 per cent in Western Samoa and 15 per cent in Lesotho. In such countries there was little scope for domestic counterbalancing or stabilizing action. Hence small states have a special interest in improvements in earnings stabilisation schemes such as the IMF's Compensatory Financing Facility (CFF) and the Lomé Convention's STABEX.

**Box 16: Commonwealth Consultative Group on Small States :
Main recommendations for international action***

The international community has a special obligation to provide an external environment which could assist small states in promoting self-reliant and stable development and in strengthening their economic independence. That environment does not now exist and the situation is being made worse by the current difficulties experienced in multilateral co-operation. Areas of special importance to small states are: trade liberalisation; official flows from multilateral and bilateral sources, in particular concessional flows; technical co-operation; balance of payments support, including export earnings stabilisation; disaster preparedness and relief.

The provision of special support for small states should be approached pragmatically through securing better international recognition of their problems and needs and through categorisation of small states, formally or informally, in specific areas as the need arises.

ECOSOC should review as early as possible the criteria for inclusion of countries in the Least Developed category to take account of the special structural and developmental problems of small states.

Aid agencies should continue to recognise the special needs of small states for concessional capital. The World Bank should adopt more flexible criteria for

* On international economic policies (viz. recommendations 47-59 of the report).

Small states have received preferential access to markets under various trading arrangements, e.g. the Lomé Convention between the African, Caribbean and Pacific countries (ACP) and the European Community (EC); the South Pacific Regional Trade and Economic Co-operation Agreement between the Pacific islands and Australia and New Zealand; and the Caribbean Basin Initiative (CBI) launched by the United States. However, the Commonwealth report warned: ''Where only one major state enters into an arrangement with small states, as in the CBI, the possibility exists that it can eventually overwhelm its captive partners by political influence and leverage, while simultaneously reducing economic benefits''.

Considering their small domestic markets and the dangers of certain bilateral arrangements, removal of protectionist barriers in important markets is of particular interest to small states. The Group recommended that these states be exempted from access ceilings under the Generalised System of Preferences (GSP) and such protectionist measures as the Multifibre Arrangement (MFA), orderly marketing arrangements and voluntary export restraints.

---

graduating small states from its lending, especially from IDA. The IFC should significantly extend its support to smaller projects. It should also assist regional and national development banks to expand their operations in this area. The latter should do more to provide venture capital for small projects.

The IMF should review the functioning of its Compensatory Financing Facility to improve its effectiveness in stabilising foreign exchange earnings, giving special attention to the needs of small states.

The agreement to establish a Common Fund for commodity price stabilisation should be implemented as early as possible. Its modalities should reflect the special interest of small states.

Small states should be freed from all limitations that apply to their access under the Generalised System of Preferences, and exempted from all organised marketing arrangements and voluntary export restraints. Small states should be excluded from the export restrictions adopted in any renewed MFA.

The Codes of Conduct on relations between transnational corporations and host countries, which are under negotiation, are of special interest to small states Increased international assistance should be given to small states in dealing with foreign business ventures.

International arrangements on disaster preparedness and relief measures should be considerably improved.

International institutions should be more supportive of regional co-operation arrangements involving small states.

In recent years, a decline in food production per head has meant increasing resort to food aid in many small states. This can increase vulnerability as it exposes them to the political influence of donor governments. Their problems of agricultural development have been compounded by their inability to realise economies of scale relating to research, extension, procurement and distribution of inputs, as well as transport and marketing. The Commonwealth Group noted that product specialization and regional co-operation offered some scope for alleviating these problems.

Invisible trade
A large proportion of the foreign exchange receipts of small states, particularly islands, come from services (invisible trade). Between 1984 and 1986, average export earnings from services as a proportion of those from goods (visible trade) were over 60 per cent for 20 island states in the Commonwealth. This was partly due to the attraction of islands as tourist destinations; in 10 of the 20 states gross receipts from tourism were larger than those from merchan-

dise exports. Another reason is the strategic location of many island states. This makes them particularly suitable for providing logistic services as staging posts and refuelling stations and for siting communications and meteorological and other observation facilities. They have also been found suitable by major powers for basing military or para-military facilities, but countries run the risk of being reduced to client status through such arrangements.

Other types of invisible export include offshore financial services, which are concentrated in the Caribbean; the provision of educational facilities; and the issue of postage stamps, which is the main source of foreign exchange of Tuvalu. Emigrants' remittances are an important source of foreign exchange for a number of small states including Grenada, Western Samoa and Tonga among islands and Botswana, Lesotho and Swaziland in Africa among those which are landlocked.

Issues related to trade in invisibles tend to get less attention than merchandise trade in international trading or financial arrangements in favour of developing countries. For instance, the EC's export earnings stabilisation (STABEX) arrangement does not cover invisibles. Since 1979, the IMF's CFF has been extended to cover shortfalls in receipts from travel and workers' remittances, but only two island countries, Barbados and Jamaica, have made drawings in respect of a fall in earnings from tourism and none in respect of workers' remittances. Difficulties in providing precise information appear to prevent greater use of the CFF to cover a decline in earnings in these areas.

Transport problems
Apart from size, a particular disadvantage for many small islands is their remoteness. While continental developing countries, however small, can and often do connect with the highway, water or electricity networks of a neighbouring country, this option is not usually open to islands. Shipping services are thus essential for island states, in view not only of their high dependence on international trade, but also of their frequent archipelagic nature. In many island states the volume of trade would not justify the massive investment and reorganisation needed to operate or provide facilities for modern means of sea transport, e.g. container-cellular vessels. Many of them have therefore had to subsidise their shipping services. Similar developments have been occurring in civil aviation where the advent of bigger, faster and longer-range aircraft has resulted in airlines ceasing to fly to ports of call serving many small islands.

Capital flows
Because of high unit costs, small states' infrastructure (e.g. airports, roads, harbours, administration, health, education, agricultural extension and research) tends to absorb a bigger share of national resources than in larger

countries. This increases the cost of their goods and services. The development assistance they receive needs therefore to be more concessional than for larger countries at the same level of income.

Most small countries have in fact been receiving assistance with a high level of concessionality, although this may also reflect such factors as their historical ties or strategic position. In view of the political risks of heavy dependence on bilateral assistance, the Consultative Group suggested that multilateral institutions should have an important role in meeting the capital needs of small states. However, access to concessional finance from some of these institutions such as the World Bank Group is constrained by eligibility criteria based on per capita income. For small states which normally have very limited access to private finance, this poses a special problem. The report therefore suggested that no small state should be made to 'graduate' from the International Development Association (IDA) or the International Bank for Reconstruction and Development (IBRD) unless there is assurance of adequate access to alternative sources of finance, and that in any case transitional arrangements should be put in place.

Although direct foreign investment is in theory another source of finance, the report noted that ''one of the main problems confronting the very small states, especially those not richly endowed with natural resources, is the difficulty in attracting the interest of transnational corporations''. A more immediate problem for small states was to ensure that those foreign operators who do wish to establish businesses on their territory do not plan to use them as a cover for criminal or other anti-social activities.

Exclusive Economic Zones

Islands have the possibility of taking advantage of the resources of the sea. These resources can enhance their self-reliance in food and possibly in energy, as well as provide valuable exports. As a result of the Third UN Conference on the Law of the Sea, island states have acquired exclusive economic zones (EEZs) extending over vast areas of ocean.

Most small islands, however, do not have the capacity to exploit their ocean resources, since this usually requires sophisticated technology. As a result, the foreign exchange income from their EEZs is likely, over the medium term, to consist mainly of rents from leasing fishing and prospecting rights to foreign companies. In the management of EEZs, island states need external support in such areas as negotiating with foreign companies, the surveillance and enforcement of economic rights, and the development of land bases related to exploiting EEZs. The Commonwealth report suggested that increased regional co-operation as well as interregional exchanges of experience in these matters would be fruitful.

Environmental dangers

A consequence of the geographic isolation of many islands is the fragility of their ecosystems. Their ecological balance is increasingly threatened by exposure to economic development, technology and tourism. An understanding of the possible effects of external influences on island ecosystems, as well as on their economies, calls for research and continued monitoring that is clearly beyond the capability of small countries.

The likely effects of changes in climate expected to result from the 'greenhouse effect' are of particular concern to many small states (see Chapter 13).

Natural disasters

Small states are particularly vulnerable to natural disasters. Because of the area covered by a tropical cyclone or earthquake, their effects are much greater for a small state than for a larger one with a wider variety of products and back-up facilities and services. An event which in a large country might be merely a regional disaster, becomes a national calamity in a small country.

Tropical cyclones have been responsible for a high proportion of the economic and human losses among small islands. In the Pacific, the damage caused to Vanuatu in early February 1987 by hurricane Uma is estimated at $280 million, which is about twice the country's GNP. The damage caused to Jamaica in 1988 by hurricane Gilbert was enormous. To alleviate the effects of such disasters, the Commonwealth report recommended strengthening the UN relief agencies, especially the United Nations Disaster Relief Organisation. It also noted the catalytic role which non-governmental organisations could play in mitigating the suffering caused by such calamities.

Human resources

Small states face a number of human and institutional problems caused mainly by diseconomies of scale. Principal among these problems are the high per capita costs and manpower requirements of providing the whole range of government services, including those involved in national security, political representation abroad, negotiations with foreign interests, and the operation of central banks. These essential services impose a heavier burden on the governments of small states—than those of larger countries.

Their human resource constraints seem to have slowed down their project identification, formulation and implementation; reduced their ability to deal expeditiously and efficiently with aid donors; and, as a result, lowered their capacity to absorb and utilise effectively whatever financial and technical support is available. Administrative weaknesses have also reduced the capacity of small states to counter illegal operations such as drug trafficking, particularly those originating from abroad. Multi-island states have the special need to administer and provide services to outlying islands.

Stronger Commonwealth support

Commonwealth leaders discussed the Consultative Group's study in October 1985 at their Nassau Summit. Welcoming the report, they expressed the hope that it "would help to increase international awareness of the link between the well-being of small states and wider concerns of peace and security, and that this would enlarge the possibilities for creative responses". They stressed that action to reduce the vulnerability of these states "should not diminish their status as independent, sovereign and equal members of the world community". Efforts should be made to realise "a global environment safe for small states and conducive to their economic viability". Heads of Government agreed that a special meeting of Commonwealth Officials should be convened to enable governments to consider ways to promote action in the directions the report had outlined.

At this and subsequent meetings of officials it was agreed that action to implement the report's recommendations would need to be taken at many levels. The Commonwealth Secretariat, in liaison with other international agencies, would have a continuing important contribution to make, both in meeting the needs of small states and in articulating their concerns internationally.

The Commonwealth's special programme of assistance to small states, started in 1979, has since been reshaped to reflect the priorities identified in the report. It includes activities relating to training, regional collaboration, macroeconomic management, debt and financial management, trade negotiations, industrial development, management development and the control of commercial crime. As a result, the CFTC devotes more than half its resources to the support of small states. It gives them priority in meeting requests for experts and training; two-thirds of the serving CFTC experts are in small states while half the trainees financed by it are nationals of small states. Secretariat support has also taken account of the important role that regional co-operation can play in lowering the vulnerability of small states. It has accordingly given extensive technical assistance to regional organisations like the Caribbean Community, the Organisation of Eastern Caribbean States, the South Pacific Commission and the South Pacific Bureau for Economic Co-operation.

To help small states work effectively with other developing countries in combating protectionism, they have been helped in the Uruguay Round of multilateral trade negotiations. A Trade Adviser stationed in Geneva has been of special assistance to small countries without permanent offices in Geneva. The Secretariat has also helped small states to improve their competence in dealing with such matters as exchange rate instability, structural adjustment and fluctuations in capital flows, and to improve their access to international capital markets and foreign investment. It has organised symposia to develop exchange rate management policies, and recently provided an Advisory Group to assist Guyana to develop its macroeconomic policies for recovery. Its efforts to establish a Commonwealth Equity Fund are intended to be of special value to countries with emerging stock markets (see Chapter 8).

In keeping with the recommendation of the Consultative Group, the Secretariat has continued to assist small states overcome weaknesses in dealing with transnational corporations. External debt is not yet widely regarded as a critical major problem for small states. However, it is a serious constraint to adjustment and development in an increasing number of them. The Secretariat has developed a comprehensive assistance package to help small states and others to establish national debt recording and management systems.

Over two-thirds of the industrial projects assisted by the Secretariat's Industrial Development Unit have been in small states. The Secretariat is also supporting small countries' export promotion efforts. Many small island countries have been helped to resolve issues relating to the development of small firms. The Secretariat has assisted several small islands to delimit their seas, advised on marine surveillance systems, and helped to negotiate contracts with foreign fishing fleets, upgrade marine products and find new markets. It has also provided training for staff in most of these fields.

To strengthen management development in small countries, the Secretariat has conducted workshops on ways to improve national planning processes and to cope with the effects of natural disasters and sharp falls in commodity prices. It organises training courses to help small states overcome severe shortages of legal drafting skills, and has promoted the establishment of regional legal units in the Eastern Caribbean and the Pacific. The Secretariat is supporting efforts by law enforcement agencies to prevent organised and commercial crime. As most small countries find it difficult to provide a full range of education and training facilities, the Secretariat has organised workshops on community financing of schools, improving technical and vocational teaching, and organising small schools; it has also prepared technical publications and facilitated information and training links between the education systems of these countries.

Global improvements

There is in the UN system a growing recognition of the economic vulnerability of small states. Most of the UN's global agencies have developed special programmes to help such countries, as recommended by the Commonwealth report. Some agencies have accorded them special status in respect of certain programmes. In the UNDP, for example, this has resulted in additional resources being provided for 50 small states during 1987-91. The Commonwealth Group considered that assistance to meet the needs of these countries should also be provided through the UN regional economic commissions, regional development banks and other regional and sub-regional institutions. Some have done so, and particular attention is being given by the three regional development banks to the development of small states in their regions.

UNCTAD has a specific mandate to act as a focal point and catalyst for special action in favour of island developing countries. It has given technical assistance to these countries through regional and, in some cases, national projects, with financing mostly from UNDP. It has also facilitated cross-regional exchanges of information and experience between island developing countries in a number of ways. These have included holding seminars, workshops and regional conferences on such topics as sustainable develop-memnt and environmental management in small islands, the generalized system of preferences, and the transfer of technology. An expert group meeting in May 1988 re-appraised the problems of island developing countries and agreed on recommendations to guide the international community in helping these countries' development efforts. As a result UNCTAD and other UN agencies have modified their programmes of special assistance to island developing countries, although policy implementation seems to have been slow in view of some skepticism among certain donor governments as to whether this category of countries has special needs and problems.

Recognising that in view of their economic vulnerability small states required special treatment, the UN Committee for Development Planning agreed in March 1988 to review the eligibility criteria used to define 'Least Developed Countries'. This review will consider whether account should be taken of the special structural and development problems of small states, as suggested in the Commonwealth report.

The issue of 'graduation' from access to support from the IBRD and IDA remains of continuing concern for small states. The Secretariat and Commonwealth Governments in 1986 provided support to the Eastern Caribbean states in their effort to retain eligibility for concessional loans from the World Bank Group. The states concerned have now secured greater recognition of their case and their graduation from IDA has been put in abeyance.

The need for improved arrangements to protect small states against the sudden shocks to which they are so vulnerable was pressed by the Commonwealth Group. It made two recommendations: to improve the effectiveness of the IMF's CFF in stabilizing export earnings; and to bring the Common Fund for commodities into operation. The IMF reviewed the CFF and in August 1988 agreed on the modalities of a new facility—the Compensatory and Contingency Financing Facility (see Chapter 4). This combines the old CFF with a new 'window' to provide additional support to countries if their adjustment programmes are thrown off-track by unexpected changes in the exogenous components of export earnings, import prices and international interest rates. Other current account transactions, such as receipts from tourism and migrant workers' remittances, can be covered where they are of particular importance, as in small states. The IMF has also recently permitted purchases of Fund resources, beyond the first credit tranche, without requiring planning and performance criteria, in cases of serious balance of payments difficulties caused by major natural disasters. It has been reported that several Caribbean countries have benefited from this policy.

The Common Fund for commodities entered into force in June 1989, and is expected to become fully operational by mid-1990 (see Chapter 6). Its Second Account could make a significant contribution to product and market diversification, in which small states have a special interest.

No progress has been made on the Consultative Group's proposal that small states should be freed from all limitations on market access in developed countries under the GSP; nor on its proposal that they should be exempt from protectionist measures inconsistent with the GATT. Small states, in so far as they are 'small suppliers', are however exempt from the restraints under the current MFA.

Conclusion

The large number of small states in the Commonwealth and the special attention given to their problems have led to the Commonwealth assuming a leading role in articulating and addressing these problems. A substantial contribution to this has been made by the report of the Consultative Group. Its conclusions and recommendations remain prominent in international discussions on these problems.

In some areas progress is being made, e.g. in recognising the special structural and financing problems of small states, and in evaluating the importance of per capita income in assessing their level of development. There is also renewed attention to the significance of regionalism for helping to deal with their problems.

Table 8: Size indicators of Commonwealth small states[a], 1988

Region/Country	Surface Area (sq km)	Population (thousand)	Population Density (per sq km)	GNP at Market Prices (mn US $)	GNP per Capita (US $)
CARIBBEAN					
Antigua & Barbuda	440	84	191	230	2,800
Bahamas	13,880	247	18	2,611	10,570
Barbados	430	255	593	1,530	5,990
Belize	22,960	182	8	264	1,460
Dominica	750	81	108	130	1,650
Grenada	340	102	300	139	1,370
Guyana	214,970	799	4	327	410
St. Kitts-Nevis	360	43	119	120	2,770
St. Lucia	620	145	234	220	1,540
St. Vincent & the Grenadines	340	122	359	130	1,100
Trinidad & Tobago	5,130	1,241	242	4,160	3,350
Jamaica	10,990	2,429	221	2,610	1,080
SOUTH PACIFIC					
Kiribati	710	67	94	40	650
Nauru	20	8	400	..	..
Solomon Islands	28,900	304	11	130	430
Tonga	750	101	135	80	800
Tuvalu	160	8	50	..	..
Vanuatu	12,190	151	12	120	820
Western Samoa	2,840	168	59	100	580
Papua New Guinea	462,840	3,804	8	2,920	770
AFRICA					
Botswana	581,730	1,164	2	1,191	890[b]
Gambia	11,300	822	73	180	220
Lesotho	30,350	1,673	55	690	410
Swaziland	17,360	737	42	580	790
INDIAN OCEAN					
Maldives	300	203	677	80	410
Mauritius	1,860	1,048	563	1,890	1,810
Seychelles	280	68	243	260	3,800
MEDITERRANEAN					
Cyprus	9,250	686	74	4,320	6,260
Malta	320	345	1,078	1,740	5,050
ASIA					
Brunei Darussalam	5,770	243	42	3,317	15,390[c]

[a] Countries included in the report of the Commonwealth Consultative Group on Small States.
[b] 1987
[c] 1986
.. not available
Sources: Compiled from FAO and the World Bank.

Table 9: Indicators of openness and export concentration of Commonwealth small states[a]

Region/Country	Merchandise Exports as a percentage of GDP		Merchandise Imports as a percentage of GDP		Number of Commodities Exported [b]	
	1980	1987	1980	1987	1970	1987
CARIBBEAN						
Antigua & Barbuda	55.1	13.1	107.2	96.0	18	19
Bahamas	17.2	15.4	68.7	50.0	41	16
Barbados	21.0	11.1	55.8	37.2	28	31
Belize	64.9	34.6	87.7	43.7	14	13
Dominica	17.1	60.0	82.0	48.3	12	12
Grenada	23.2	21.6	65.1	64.0	4	17
Guyana	65.8	74.1	65.4	59.6	22	32
St. Kitts-Nevis	63.2	39.7	118.4	82.8	..	..
St. Lucia	41.1	31.8	74.5	78.1	12	18
St. Vincent & the Gren.	36.2	39.2	89.5	63.7	7	15
Trinidad & Tobago	40.8	34.4	28.7	27.4	87	77
Jamaica	32.1	24.8	38.9	43.1	59	85
SOUTH PACIFIC						
Kiribati	11.5	8.1	80.0	69.0	2	6
Nauru	..	..	..	..	..	3
Solomon Islands	50.9	55.2	51.5	69.8	8	13
Tonga	..	..	..	..	9	11
Tuvalu	..	..	..	..	..	11
Vanuatu	31.0	27.1	62.8	75.8	10	10
Western Samoa	17.9	9.7	66.3	39.8	11	13
Papua New Guinea	40.5	38.7	40.1	40.0	24	35
AFRICA						
Botswana	56.0	74.1	77.0	52.9	..	..
Gambia	13.0	35.0	69.0	102.8	4	14
Lesotho	14.0	11.0	111.0	137.8	..	..
Swaziland	61.6	65.9	89.8	72.3	..	..
INDIAN OCEAN						
Maldives	26.0	33.1	88.0	68.9	..	..
Mauritius	38.0	59.6	54.0	67.1	9	42
Seychelles	14.0	2.1	67.0	42.7	7	8
MEDITERRANEAN						
Cyprus	22.5	15.9	49.7	39.8	49	106
Malta	44.9	38.2	77.9	71.80	32	58
ASIA						
Brunei Darussalam	93.4	86.8[c]	12.4	17.9[c]	7	7

[a] Countries included in the report of the Commonwealth Consultative Group on Small States.
[b] Number of products exported at 3-digit SITC level: this figure includes products which are greater than $50,000 in 1970 and $100,000 in 1987.
[c] 1985.   .. not available.
Sources: Compiled from IMF and UNCTAD.

Chapter 11
Women and
structural adjustment

The issue of women and development has been a matter of close concern to the international community for almost two decades, and the Commonwealth has played an active role in efforts to bring women into the mainstream of the development process.* The position of women has improved in almost all countries, as can be shown by various indicators. In the developing countries as a whole there have been increases in their life expectancy (from 44 years in 1950 to 61 years in 1980), access to education (from 37 per cent of primary school enrolment in 1950 to 44 per cent in 1980), and employment (from 37 per cent of the workforce in 1950 to 42 per cent in 1980). But they have shared in economic and social advances to a smaller extent than men have, and their position has remained significantly inferior to that of men. Recognition of this continuing disparity—and the discrimination which underlies it—has been an important influence on global efforts to bring women into the mainstream of development.

During the three decades between 1950 and 1980 economic growth in the Third World proceeded at a significant, if generally slackening, pace; per capita incomes in the low-income countries rose on average by 2 per cent annually and in the middle-income countries by 4 per cent annually. Social progress paralleled economic growth. But in the 1980s all that changed. Deteriorating terms of trade, increased developed country protectionism, high interest rates and a collapse of bank lending led to large deficits in developing countries' balance of payments. Added to this were chronic imbalances on their internal accounts, where large budgetary deficits helped fuel inflation. The result was a series of crises which in most developing countries meant that policymakers' attention turned increasingly towards the structural adjustment measures insisted upon by the IMF and the World Bank as a condition for medium-term balance of payments support designed to restore economic growth and development.

---

* A brief chronology of selected global and Commonwealth events concerned with women and development is given at the end of this chapter.

These adjustment measures are considered in a wider context elsewhere in this volume (see Chapters 3-5). They commonly include measures which, while not designed to have a disproportionately adverse effect on women, do have this impact. Cutting government expenditure has curtailed employment and reduced real wages in the public sector, including those areas in which women find much of their employment (e.g. in teaching, nursing and the lower grades of the civil service). Abolishing subsidies has raised the cost of basic needs such as food and fuel, healthcare and education, all of which bulk large in women's budgets. Increasing the rate of interest and otherwise restricting the flow of credit has further marginalised women producers. More generally, the asymmetries that typify gender differences in society have been magnified by the economic recessions and structural adjustments of the 1980s. They have meant that women almost always face more severe constraints and harsher choices in their time-use than do men.

Whatever the wider merits of the adjustment measures taken, there is no doubt that they were designed with little if any consideration of their human impact and took no account of women's specific needs and concerns. As a result they have checked and in some cases even reversed the progress in health, nutrition, education, employment and incomes which women in developing countries had been making during the previous three decades.

The Commonwealth Group's study

The problems faced by women and vulnerable groups during the 1980s have been given increasing attention by the Commonwealth. In 1985 the first meeting of Commonwealth Ministers Responsible for Women's Affairs identified the impact of structural adjustment on women as a priority issue. When they met again in 1987, Ministers recommended that an expert group be set up to study it, a proposal which was supported by Commonwealth Finance Ministers and approved by Heads of Government.

The Commonwealth Expert Group was set up in 1988 and chaired by Ms Mary Chinery-Hesse, a former Principal Secretary of Ghana's Ministry of Finance and Economic Planning who became Deputy Director-General of the International Labour Office (see Annex for list of members). The Group was asked to establish the extent of women's contribution to the economy and its implications for structural adjustment measures; examine evidence of the impact of these measures on women; consider alternative policies which would be more effective socially and economically; and put forward suggestions for influencing the international aid and finance institutions in the light of these findings.

To assist the Group's work, case studies (funded by the Canadian International Development Agency, UNICEF and UNDP) were undertaken in nine

Commonwealth countries,* and questionnaires sent to government departments and organisations in Commonwealth countries and to international organisations. The Group was able to compile a comprehensive and authoritative report, *Engendering Adjustment for the 1990s*, which covers many issues of current concern.

In its report, the Group noted that the ways women had been affected by structural adjustment depended on their role and situation in the economy and society, and the contribution they made to each. As producers, women had accounted for an expanding proportion of the labour force, being especially important in agriculture and the informal sector and increasingly so in manufacturing. Yet they continued to earn less than men, even for the same work, and were almost always without assets, especially land. Their economic contribution, moreover, was grossly under-recorded in official statistics: adding household work alone would increase estimates of world production by at least one-third. As managers of household consumption, women had had to ensure that their families' basic needs were met; but in general they had done so while having little control over the allocation of family income. As mothers, they were primarily responsible for their children's welfare and, as daughters, they were relied on for the welfare of aged parents and parents-in-law; they also played a large role as community organisers. The net result was that women consistently worked longer hours than men—16 hours a day in parts of East Africa, for example. Their health, education and general welfare had often suffered as a consequence.

The Group noted evidence that women had been generally ill-served by adjustment policies and programmes. Many of them had lost their jobs in the formal sector, and found it more difficult than men to gain another. In the few countries undertaking adjusting where women's employment in the formal sector had increased during the 1980s, the increase had by no means been commensurate with the need for more jobs. As food producers women had gained less than proportionately from the better terms of trade for agriculture, and any expansion of their agricultural wage-earning opportunities had not kept pace with the extra numbers seeking such work. The result of these changes in employment and in the labour force had been to force many more women into insecure jobs in the informal sector, where there had been a drastic decline in earnings (often much greater than the fall in other sectors), even for longer hours of work. Yet despite the meagre returns, women's informal sector earnings had been crucial to the survival of poor families during the crisis of the 1980s, especially in Africa, the Caribbean and Latin America. Overall,

---

* Bangladesh, Jamaica, Malaysia, Nigeria, Sri Lanka, Tanzania, Trinidad and Tobago, Zambia and Zimbabwe.

however, their lack of access to resources, e.g. land and credit, and to support services, chiefly for looking after children, the elderly and the sick, together with the increased pressures on their time and energies had meant that, in general, women had been unable to take advantage of the productive opportunities that had opened up through structural change.

The Experts found that women's role as home managers had been adversely affected by the reduction or abolition of subsidies on food and other basic goods, while their role as mothers had been made more difficult by reduced social services. The effects had often been catastrophic. In Ghana, for example, at the peak of the crisis in July 1984, it was reported that even upper middle civil service salaries could cover barely 10 per cent of the minimum nutritional diet of a five-person household. As early as 1982, per capita health expenditure had been only one-fifth of that in 1975/76, and the country lost half its doctors between 1981 and 1984. In Zambia in 1985, despite free primary education, parental expenditure on basic items necessary for one child to attend school was over one-fifth of average per capita income. Children's health and education had suffered accordingly, particularly if they were members of female-headed households which were among the worst affected.

Women's own welfare had also suffered. Their use of time, always subject to special demands as they tried to undertake each of their main roles, had been made even more difficult by their diminished resources and the need to spend longer hours searching for income from employment outside the home, and cheaper food for their families. Their health had been adversely affected by increased hours of work and by reduced availability of food and healthcare facilities. Less healthy women were less efficient and less productive; as a result national income and national welfare were both below their potential. In total, therefore, the Group found the structural adjustment programmes adopted to have reduced the resources available to women in their roles as home managers, mothers and community organisers, while making additional demands on them as producers. The trade-offs for women undertaking their multifarious roles, it concluded, had become almost impossibly difficult, for poor women especially.

The Group acknowledged that awareness of the problems which the poor and the vulnerable faced as a result of stabilisation and structural adjustment programmes was increasing among international agencies and governments. Both the IMF and the World Bank had become more conscious of the human costs of adjustment. A number of UN bodies had provided some support for poverty alleviation measures related to adjustment programmes, as had some bilateral aid agencies and international non-governmental organisations (NGOs). Certain developing country governments had also acted, seeking at least to maintain expenditure on key sectors—such as primary healthcare, primary education or nutrition—of benefit to the poor.

While the Experts welcomed these new orientations, they noted that it was a case of too little and too late; in general, these approaches had not been given the resources and priority they deserved. Moreover, attention was rarely given to women as a specific category, and virtually no compensatory measures had been taken that were directed specifically to their needs. Any benefits women had gained had been only incidental. The measures had not prevented devastating setbacks in such crucial areas as maternal and child health services, basic education and training, childcare, and the provision of credit, extension and other support services to help women as producers.

The Group, like others, acknowledged the difficulty of separating the impact of the stabilisation and structural adjustment programmes from the fundamental problems that had necessitated them. It nevertheless was able to conclude that

> Women have been at the epicentre of the crisis and have borne the brunt of the adjustment efforts. They have been the most affected by the deteriorating balance between incomes and prices, by the cuts in social services, and by the rising morbidity and child deaths. It is women who have had to find the means for families to survive. To achieve this they have had to work longer and harder. Yet they have no role in the design of adjustment programmes which have in consequence ignored their needs and concerns.

These findings, based on the country studies and other material available to the Group, have been underscored by the analysis of others, such as the UN's 1989 *World Survey on the Role of Women in Development*. These issues have been raised at various fora and in sundry reports. UNICEF's publications— *Adjustment with a Human Face*, and *The Invisible Adjustment: Poor Women and the Economic Crisis*—have provided graphic evidence of the difficulties faced by women as a result of the crisis and of the adjustment measures implemented to resolve it. The April 1989 report by the UN Economic Commission for Africa (ECA), *African Alternatives to Structural Adjustment Programmes: A Framework for Transformation and Recovery*, and various documents for the March 1988 Khartoum Conference convened by ECA on the Human Dimension of Africa's Economic Recovery and Development also show the damaging effect of the crisis and the ensuing adjustment on human resources.

The Commonwealth report called on the international financial institutions, aid agencies and governments to rethink their adjustment policies and pro- grammes. ''We are convinced'', the Group noted, ''that short-term stabilisa- tion measures have too often been in conflict with long-term development goals, and have caused hardships severe enough to invalidate the process. It is only by recognising the economic necessity of protecting the social base, par- ticularly as it affects women, and by incorporating these concerns into policy, that adjustment can achieve the desired results. In other words, adjustment policies which fail to incorporate women's concerns fully are not only unjust and cause unnecessary hardship but also imperil the effectiveness of the policies themselves.'' The solution required a fundamental rethink of the gender aspect of adjustment. ''The problem of existing adjustment is not its omission of a few projects for women—but its failure to take adequate account of the time, roles, potential contribution and needs of half of each country's population''. The remedy was seen by the Group as requiring a broader approach to adjustment. This should emphasise social equity and economic growth as well as efficiency; institutionalise women's concerns and involve them at all levels of decision-making; provide a supportive international economic environment; and ensure regular and effective monitoring of the gender impact of adjustment. It demanded action by governments, international agencies and non-governmental organisations.

The Group set out six general areas for action (see Box 17, pages 206-7). Its specific recommendations to support women in their four main roles were in keeping with the objectives of the Nairobi Forward-looking Strategies for the Advancement of Women, adopted by the United Nations in 1985, and also with the conclusions and recommendations of the UN-convened Interregional Seminar on Women and the Economic Crisis, held in Vienna in October 1988.

Broadening the approach to adjustment

The recommendations called for women to have greater access to productive resources—credit, foreign exchange, infrastructure, marketing, training, extension and technical services, technology, and land; and for adjustment programmes that take account of the employment needs of women. Governments were asked to design adjustment programmes which:

- ensure that a certain proportion of bank loans are secured by women, and establish special credit arrangements to help them overcome existing disadvantages, including requirements for collateral;
- guarantee that some foreign exchange is reserved for priority sectors of special concern to women, so that they can purchase vital imports;
- provide more feeder roads and small-scale decentralised means to generate energy and obtain access to water, so as to help those small enterprises in which women find their greatest employment and reduce pressure on women's time use;
- take care that the disbanding of state marketing enterprises does not reduce opportunities for small producers, including women, to sell their output and acquire inputs; encourage women's participation in marketing, including marketing co-operatives, so that they retain more of the income from selling their products;
- restore and expand training budgets, with special schemes for retrenched employees, especially from the public sector; reorient programmes to provide women with technical and entrepreneurial skills; experiment with

innovative delivery systems for non-formal training, especially of women;
• provide women with adequate access to agricultural extension services
and give more emphasis to the activities in which women specialise, such as
food crops; increase government support for technical services and repair
centres which women can use in establishing and operating manufacturing
and other non-farm enterprises;
• promote more long-term R&D into activities or goods of special interest
to women as producers or consumers;
• reform inheritance and land tenure laws to remove gender inequalities and
improve their implemention; protect communal land rights (e.g. for grazing) from privatisation through promoting group ownership; and
• incorporate special measures to employ women (for example, through
public works schemes), assist or otherwise compensate women and other
workers who become unemployed as a result of structural adjustment (including grants for setting up small businesses); ensure satisfactory labour
standards for those still at work and review them regularly to ensure
adequacy.

The Group also called on governments to protect the environment in which
women live and work; safeguard their access to fuelwood, food and drinking
water; and institute legal reforms to protect their human rights. Women should
participate in decisions on the use of forestry resources and the distribution of
water through irrigation systems. Governments should enact and enforce
reforms ensuring equality before the law in all aspects of women's daily lives.

The report pointed out the vital need for women to have sufficient access
to basic goods and services to be able to carry out satisfactorily their roles as
home managers and mothers, which provide critical support to the operations
of the monetary economy and the nurturing of the human resource base. It
therefore recommended that the prices of staple food and fuel should be
maintained at levels that low-income families could afford; and that health and
education budgets should be restored and expanded. Governments were urged
to encourage group action as this enhanced the ability of women to gain access
to productive resources and basic goods and services and was particularly
effective in enabling women to obtain credit without providing collateral and
to use common land for grazing.

Improved data collection, monitoring and evaluation were seen as of critical
importance to effective policy-making. The report recommended more accurate, regular and prompt gender-disaggregated data; a better conceptual basis
to data so as to reflect women's full contribution to the economy and the
household; and more and quicker dissemination of information.

Institutionalising women's concerns
Implementing this broader approach to structural adjustment would require

Box 17: Six areas for action by governments, international agencies and non-governmental organisations

I. Broaden the approach of governments and international agencies to structural adjustment, so as to:
(i)   incorporate women's concerns in the basic objectives of adjustment, as part of a more general widening of adjustment objectives to focus on human needs, environmental protection and sustainable development in the long term;
(ii) take account of women's special needs in and contributions to economic production; household management; child rearing and caring (and often caring for the aged); and community organisation, by incorporating measures which:
  (a)   increase women's productivity and ease their time burdens in all their roles;
  (b)   enhance women's opportunities for remunerative and productive work by ensuring greater access to credit and key services, and implementing employment creation schemes tailored towards women's needs; and
  (c)   restore momentum to women's advance in the longer term by giving priority to education, health and other goals for women in the 1990s.

II. Institutionalise women's concerns through strengthening official machinery by:
(i)   placing women's bureaux in strategic areas of a country's decision-making processes;
(ii) establishing women's units in key economic ministries and development agencies, and ensuring that they participate fully in all decision-making related to structural adjustment and other concerns of women; and
(iii) setting up Parliamentary and administrative committees to review legislation and programmes to ensure that all concerns of women are adequately addressed.

III. Involve women fully at all levels of the decision-making processes; introduce anti-discrimination and affirmative action legislation to assist in breaking down the gender segmentation of the workforce; implement measures to ensure women have equitable access to education, training and employment opportunities, and receive equal pay for work of equal value and equality of treatment in all aspects of the law; and undertake publicity and information campaigns to persuade men to bear a greater share of domestic and family responsibilities.

IV. Provide a supportive international economic environment for the broader approach to structural adjustment by:
(i) increasing external finance for areas supporting women during adjustment; targeting a specific proportion of aid flows to measures which directly benefit women; and initiating debt swaps in support of such measures;
(ii) increasing net resource transfers both from the public and the private sector through additional aid flows and debt write-off by aid donors; lower interest rates, substantial debt reduction, and additional financial flows from the private sector; improving access to developed countries' markets, especially for labour-intensive manufactures where women are heavily involved; and supporting primary product prices.

V. Ensure the provision of:
(i) accurate, regular and prompt gender-disaggregated data on critical economic and social indicators (including access to land and credit, rates of employment and earnings, levels of education, morbidity, mortality, and nutrition); and ensure that the data on women's work and employment reflect the full extent of their contribution to the economy and the household (including home-based work);
(ii) facilities for regularly monitoring the impact of adjustment programmes and disseminating the results; and
(iii) detailed surveys and analytical case studies so as to help design more appropriate policies and programmes which mitigate any adverse effects and realise opportunities for improvement.

VI. The Commonwealth to:
(i) take steps to initiate and secure joint sponsorship with appropriate UN organisations for a small international meeting of high-level national and international officials involved in structural adjustment policies. This meeting should seek a consensus on the policy goals for a broader adjustment strategy, fully reflecting women's interests, and focus on ways in which such a strategy would be implemented;
(ii) encourage regional meetings and workshops so as to foster intensive discussions and actions on the issues discussed in the report.

political commitment, translated into administrative and institutional action; it would also require that women should be enabled to have greater control over their economic and social roles. The key elements of this process were the empowerment and organisation of women themselves; affirmative action to incorporate them fully into all decision-making processes; institutionalising their concerns; and educating the public on 'women's issues'. Specifically the report recommended that:

- government departments formulating, negotiating and implementing structural adjustment policies and programmes establish women's units as an integral part of their administrative structures and consult women's affairs ministries, national bureaux and other women's organisations;
- women's affairs ministries, national bureaux and other women's organisations be strengthened in their ability to undertake economic analysis and project appraisal techniques;
- women's organisations concerned particularly with economic issues be adequately financed;
- other women's groups be assisted to collect and disseminate information relevant to structural adjustment, to lobby and to promote improved policies for women in this area; and
- international financial institutions (especially the World Bank) involve their women and development units more fully in the design, implementation, monitoring and appraisal of structural adjustment policies and programmes.

A supportive international environment

While stressing that some of their recommendations would cost little or nothing, and that all would pay for themselves in the long term, the report admitted the need for some financing in the interim. Most of this could be generated internally by reorienting expenditure, raising taxes on luxuries, or reforming the tax system. But some external finance would be needed in many cases. An external environment more conducive to sustained economic development and more supportive of adjustment would help.

The Group went on to urge developed countries to meet as soon as possible the internationally accepted targets for official development assistance (ODA); to direct a higher proportion of their multilateral ODA to agencies whose activities are of particular value to women; and to allot a specific proportion of their bilateral ODA to projects and programmes of special benefit to women. It called for the expansion of IMF and World Bank resources to assist debt reduction and meet growing development needs; and for greater resources and attention to be given to integrating women's concerns in the design, implementation, monitoring, appraisal and follow-up procedures of adjustment programmes. The Group also said that the current negotiations on international trade policy should pay greater attention to the interests of women and the poor, especially in developing countries.

Follow-up to the report

The Expert Group's report was considered at the meetings of Commonwealth Finance Ministers (Jamaica, September 1989) and Commonwealth Heads of Government (Malaysia, October 1989). Finance Ministers called on governments and international institutions to pay particular attention to its recommendations in formulating adjustment programmes. They accepted the need for more intensive Commonwealth discussion of the report within regions and commended for priority attention a Commonwealth initiative to secure a small international meeting of representatives of selected governments and international organisations to consider how adjustment strategies could be framed to take the needs of women into account.

Heads of Government, while accepting the need for structural adjustment, expressed concern that economic difficulties in several countries were adversely affecting the already disadvantaged position of women. They commended the Group's approach and emphasised the need to redress the socio-economic inequities facing women. They stressed the importance of totally integrating women into the development process, and providing them with equitable access to education, training, credit, land and employment, so as to facilitate their full participation in both the public and private sectors. Highlighting the Group's six general areas for action (see Box 17), they endorsed the Finance Ministers' recommendations for regional discussion of the report and for Commonwealth action to promote an international examination of ways to design adjustment strategies so as to take women's needs into account. They also recommended that Commonwealth Ministers Responsible for Women's Affairs should give further consideration to the report when they meet in Ottawa in October 1990.

Plans have since been made for three Commonwealth regional meetings as well as for the international meeting. At these and similar events, a video produced by the Secretariat at the Group's request (and with financial support from UNICEF, UNIFEM and UNFPA) will be shown. The accounts of women's lives under adjustment in Ghana and Jamaica, told on film by the women themselves, lend support to many of the conclusions and recommendations of the Expert Group. The video has been distributed to women's bureaux and other agencies in the Commonwealth, and organisations in many countries have been using it along with the report. The Secretariat is preparing for publication the country studies on which many of the Group's conclusions were based.

The issues of women in development in general, and women and structural adjustment in particular, will continue to receive international attention. The first update of the World Survey on the Role of Women in Development, presented to the UN General Assembly in October 1989, will be considered by the Commission on the Status of Women in 1990. There are also plans for an NGO meeting on women and structural adjustment in 1990 to which the Commonwealth Secretariat will make an input. In 1994, a world conference will be held to assess progress in the advancement of women and appraise implementation of the Nairobi Forward-looking Strategies. It will provide an occasion to look at developments relating to the recommendations of the Expert Group, and to see whether adjustment in the 1990s really is being engendered as far as women are concerned.

The portents do not, however, look good. The report of the Commonwealth Group, in a chapter entitled ''So Little Action'', showed that there was still a very long way to go to achieve the broader approach to adjustment, fully incorporating women's needs and concerns, which the Group advocated. Too little has happened so far to make that judgement out of date.

Chronology of events

1975 UN proclaims International Women's Year.
World Conference on Women (Mexico City) highlights
- inequality in opportunities and rewards between women and men
- inadequate recognition of women's roles in and contributions to the economy, and of the obstacles to their full participation as agents and beneficiaries of development efforts
- paucity of data and research on women's conditions and needs.

1976-85 UN Decade for Women: equality, development and peace, with subthemes of employment, health and education.

1977 Commonwealth Heads of Government call for greater attention to the integration of women in development programmes.

1979 Commonwealth Heads of Government agree that a focal point is needed within the Commonwealth Secretariat to respond to identified needs and priorities of governments in the field of women and development and help the Secretariat plan its programmes to take full account of the needs of women. Women and Development Programme created within the Commonwealth Secretariat.

1980 World Conference on Women (Copenhagen)
- elaborates on the obstacles facing women
- agrees on the need for international consensus on measures to help the advancement of women.

1985 Commonwealth Meeting of Ministers Responsible for Women's Affairs (Nairobi) agrees to develop national policies on women and development, and to integrate these into national development plans; to enhance the status and effectiveness of national machinery for women; and to open up opportunities for women at the policy-making level.

World Conference to Review and Appraise the Achievements of the UN Decade for Women (Nairobi) outlines Forward-looking Strategies for the Advancement of Women, 1986-2000.

UN General Assembly requests update on the World Survey on the Role of Women in Development, to focus on emerging issues (including adjustment policies) impacting on women's role in the economy.

1987 Commonwealth Meeting of Ministers Responsible for Women's Affairs (Harare) adopts Commonwealth Plan of Action, under which all parts of the Secretariat are to pay attention to gender issues in their work and seek to ensure that women benefit equitably from the training and technical assistance provided by the Secretariat.

Commonwealth Heads of Government approve Commonwealth Plan of Action.

1988 Commonwealth Expert Group on Women and Structural Adjustment established.

1989 World Survey on the Role of Women in Development examines inter alia the effects on women of external debt and adjustment and calls for adjustment policies to be designed and implemented in ways that minimise any harmful impact on the poor.

Commonwealth Finance Ministers welcome the Expert Group's report, and call on governments and international institutions to pay particular attention to its recommendations in formulating adjustment programmes.

Commonwealth Heads of Government commend the Group's approach and highlight the six general areas for action outlined in its report.

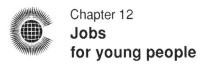

Chapter 12
Jobs
for young people

Youth issues were discussed at a Commonwealth forum as early as 1969 when Heads of Government, meeting in London, considered the possibility of pooling resources and working together to support national youth programmes.* This led to their deciding, in 1973, to establish a Commonwealth Youth Programme (CYP) administered within the Commonwealth Secretariat. Among the objectives of CYP was the promotion of productive activities, in their widest sense, with a view to reducing unemployment among the young and alleviating its ill effects. A Youth Study Fellowship Scheme and Youth Project Fund were set up within the CYP to assist toward the achievement of these ends.

The issue of unemployment first figured in a substantive manner at the 1981 meeting of Heads of Government in Melbourne. Their decision at that meeting that Commonwealth Ministers of Employment/Labour should have regular meetings reflected the fact that tackling unemployment had by then become a preoccupation of governments. Concern over persistent high unemployment was voiced at all meetings of Ministers of Employment/Labour from their inception, and it was on their recommendation that Heads of Government in 1985 decided that an expert group should study youth unemployment.

Rise of unemployment

Although youth unemployment did not become a central concern of policy-makers until the world recession of the mid-1970s, the problem has long antecedents, particularly in the developing countries. During the 1950s and 1960s it had not been much documented or researched, being subsumed in the wider issue of general unemployment and underemployment. It was generally held that, in developing countries, unemployment and inadequate incomes were largely the result of an insufficiency in skills, technical know-how, investment resources, and infrastructure, and that once the process of growth

---

* 'Youth' are defined in this chapter as being between 15 and 24 years of age

had taken off, employment opportunities would improve. The basic development strategy in most countries was to concentrate efforts on expanding the modern sector of the economy as the main engine of economic growth. It was thought that unemployed and underemployed persons in the traditional, rural sector and the urban, informal sector would eventually be drawn into productive employment in rapidly expanding modern industrial and service sectors.

Despite the achievement of relatively high rates of economic growth—averaging 5-6 per cent a year in many developing countries during the 1950s and 1960s—the number of jobs did not keep pace with the growth of the labour force. This was partly because the rapidly expanding modern sector was based largely on activities marked by high capital intensity and high labour productivity compared with other sectors. Also, fast rates of population growth (averaging 2-3 per cent and in some countries in Africa as much as 4 per cent a year) greatly exacerbated the problem. At the same time, the slow rate of labour absorption in agriculture, the increasing inequalities of income between the urban and the rural sectors, and the rapid expansion in education led to a large influx of people into urban areas. Since the modern sector did not offer sufficient jobs, most of these migrants were forced to seek work in the informal sector. The majority were young people.

The perceived shortcomings of the strategy to spread the benefits of economic growth to most of the population through 'trickle-down' effects prompted the development of a 'basic needs' approach. This was spearheaded by the International Labour Organisation (ILO), which advanced it at the World Employment Conference of 1976. While continuing to support the development of the modern sector, it recognised that sector's limited capacity to absorb labour and sought to direct efforts towards raising incomes in the low-productivity sectors—the traditional and informal sectors which sustained most of the population.

Despite the greater attention given to basic needs, few governments attempted to implement a comprehensive redistributive strategy to foster development. In addition to political constraints, the hesitation was due largely to uncertainties over the trade-offs between policies intended to produce a more even distribution of income and wealth and those intended to accelerate economic growth. In any case, the implementation of the basic needs strategy was partly overtaken by events. The problems arising from the global recessions of the mid-1970s and early 1980s caused governments to concentrate on stabilisation and adjustment measures to overcome external payments and budgetary deficits, and the growing problem of external debt and debt-servicing.

Policies towards youth

While youth unemployment became an issue of central concern only during the mid-1970s, youth affairs had been the subject of a range of policies and measures implemented within countries and at the international level for a much longer period. Many governments (and non-governmental organisations) had started national and community youth service schemes to absorb young people productively and to promote national cohesiveness. Work within the UN led to the convening of the first World Youth Assembly in 1970, to strengthening channels of communication with youth organisations, and to the establishment of the UN Volunteer Programme in late 1970. The designation of 1985 as International Youth Year, with the theme of participation, development and peace, gave added stimulus to policies and activities of relevance to young people.

With the continuing rise in unemployment in both developed and developing economies during the 1970s and early 1980s, attention was given not only to the imbalance between the number seeking work and the available work opportunities, but increasingly to the structural imbalance between the skills, education, and experience of the workforce, and the requirements for labour. Thus, education and training came to the forefront of public attention (for example, the 1980 International Labour Conference considered a special report, Training : the Challenge of the 1980s), while the integration of young people into working life became a central issue. As a result, a great variety of programmes and schemes were offered relating to general education, vocational preparation and training, and work experience, targeted initially at the unemployed in general but later increasingly at unemployed youth.

Over the period 1975-85, major programmes concerning youth unemployment were launched not only by international agencies like the ILO, but also by many national and regional organisations. These were supported in most instances by substantial research and by meetings which recommended action. Noteworthy among the latter was the OECD High-Level Conference on Youth Unemployment (December 1977) which generated many studies; the European Community carried out similar activities related to its member countries. However, in the developing countries, where the problem of youth unemployment had become even more acute, it was much less documented, largely because of the lack of detailed data.

Study by a Commonwealth Group

In early 1986, acting on the decision by Heads of Government, the Commonwealth Secretary-General established an Expert Group of ten persons with extensive experience of policies and practices relating to employment and labour, education and training, and youth affairs (see Annex). The Chairman was Mr Peter Kirby, who had led a similar enquiry in Australia a few years earlier.

The Group's terms of reference were to analyse the factors causing youth unemployment and their effects; examine relevant government policies; and make specific recommendations to assist governments in reducing youth unemployment on a sustainable basis.

It decided to consult young people through two surveys. One was conducted through interviews, using an identical questionnaire, with some 5,000 young people in four countries in different regions of the Commonwealth. The other relied on a questionnaire sent to a sample of the readership of the CYP's quarterly News Service. Replies to the first survey indicated that the respondents saw economic factors as the predominant cause of youth unemployment. They indicated that lack of money was one of its more serious effects, leading to a sense of inferiority or to crime. Social phenomena, including vandalism and drug abuse, were cited as among the effects of unemployment in more than half the replies. Although there was general ignorance of the success of government initiatives, one-tenth of the respondents cited broad economic policies as being particularly effective, one-eighth identified economic initiatives relating directly to employment creation, and just over one-quarter mentioned initiatives relating to education, training and vocational guidance. Suggestions for government action included the provision of skills training, on-the-job training and work experience (to overcome the drawbacks of new entrants), the provision of credit, and the creation of more opportunities for youth in self-employment or agriculture, and in industry, through the opening (or reopening) of factories.

The Experts, who completed their report, *Jobs for Young People: A Way to a Better Future*, in April 1987, examined youth unemployment within the broader context of general unemployment. They noted that in Commonwealth developing countries the scale of the problem was generally much greater than in industrial countries. Considerable variation was found in the nature and especially the extent of open unemployment. Recorded unemployment rates among young people ranged widely—from 40 per cent in Jamaica to 3 per cent in Cyprus, for example (see Table 10, page 216). Nonetheless there were many factors in common. Youth generally comprised the largest proportion of the unemployed, and the youth unemployment rate was typically two-and-a-half to three times the adult rate. Among youth, the economically and socially disadvantaged (e.g. children of landless labourers and of the urban poor) bore a disproportionate share of the unemployment, although this was not always revealed in official statistics of open unemployment where the most visibly unemployed tended to be the more educated youths who aspired to wage employment. The unemployment rate among young urban women was generally higher than among young urban men, especially in the Caribbean. Young

Table 10: Estimated rates[a] of open unemployment in total and among youth in selected Commonwealth countries, 1985 (per cent)

Country	Total unemployment			Youth unemployment		
	Total	Males	Females	Total	Males	Females
Jamaica	25	15	36	40	26	58
Seychelles	21	15	28	31	25	40
Barbados	17	13	21	32	26	39
Mauritius	17	17	17	29	31	26
Trinidad & Tobago	16	15	20	31	30	34
United Kingdom	12	14	10	20[b]	22[b]	18[b]
Canada	10	10	11	17	18	15
India	9	10	6	22[b]	23[b]	16[b]
Australia	8	8	8	14	15	13
Singapore	4	4	4	6	6	7
Hong Kong	4	4	3	5[b]	6[b]	5[b]
New Zealand	4	4	4	6[b]	6[b]	5[b]
Cyprus	3	2	3	4[b]	3[b]	5[b]
Ghana[c]	1	1	1	2[b]	3[b]	2[b]

(a) Total unemployment as percentage of total labour force, and youth unemployment as percentage of youth labour force.
(b) Figures relate to the age group 20-24 only.
(c) Figures relate to 1980.
Sources: ILO: *Yearbook of Labour Statistics, 1986* Tables 1, 9A and 9B; and *Economically Active Population Estimates and Projections,* 1950-2025, Vols I-V, 3rd ed. Geneva, 1986.

people with middle-level education (i.e. those finishing secondary school) generally experienced higher rates of unemployment than the illiterates or the highly educated, although the problem of the educated unemployed, including graduates, was a growing one in many developing countries.

In the developed countries, as in developing countries, youth comprised the largest proportion of the unemployed when grouped into ten-year age-bands, and their rate of unemployment was also two and a half to three times as high as those for adults. Unemployment was also unequally distributed, with socially and economically disadvantaged groups, racial minorities and immigrants being more seriously affected. In contrast to developing countries, however, young people with little schooling fared least well in finding jobs.

Moreover, female youth unemployment rates in the developed countries were generally slightly lower than those of males. While young people tended to be unemployed for shorter periods than adults, they could expect to be unemployed more frequently. Among the youth who had jobs, there was some shift out of full-time into part-time work.

The Kirby Group held that the problem of youth unemployment was closely linked to that of general unemployment. The latter was essentially the result of slow economic growth relative to the growth of the labour force - though the nature of the problem differed greatly as between developed and developing countries. In Western Europe, there had been increasing difficulties in reconciling the objectives of economic growth, full employment and price stability, as well as in dealing with structural imbalances in the world economy. A growing element in unemployment could be considered 'structural', i.e. caused by a failure to adjust to rapid changes in technology and international competitiveness, and by a lack of effective measures to counter local mismatches between the skills and other labour characteristics available, and those in demand.

Slow economic growth had been transmitted to developing countries through depressed commodity prices and growing debt burdens. But the causes of unemployment were not all external. Many developing countries had deep-rooted domestic problems, arising on the one hand from a rapid rise in the labour force— the product of high population growth— and on the other from a basic lack of investment and skills.

The Experts considered that the significantly higher unemployment rates for youth could be explained partly in terms of the advantages of accumulated knowledge and experience which those who had held jobs had over those joining the labour market. The disadvantage of the newcomer was considerably increased where the work was skilled and experience counted. In the developed countries, especially, the skill levels demanded of young people were rising, as employment was growing largely in the services sector, particularly in activities making intensive use of information technology. Considerable investments in education or vocational training were required. In developed countries, the failure of wage and non-labour costs to adjust sufficiently to reflect the relative disadvantages—actual or perceived —of employing youth was seen as a further contributory factor. In the developing countries, the impact of high population growth was seen as a crucial problem. The very high numbers entering the labour market each year were likely to exceed the increase in jobs generated in these countries. In addition, expansion in the number of young people being educated led to rising aspirations as well as to mismatches, both between skills and work opportunities and between the location of those possessing the skills and the most favoured employment opportunities (see Boxes 18 and 19, pages 218 and 219).

Box 18: Mismatches between skills and work opportunities

The mismatching of skills with available jobs can have very marked impacts on young people at this crucial stage of their lives. It may occur partly because education and training are insufficiently adapted to the rate of technological change. In developing countries, resource limitations are an additional constraint since it costs more to provide courses in scientific and technical subjects than in other subjects, and teachers are in short supply. The 'paper qualifications syndrome' (where progressively higher qualifications are called for without reference to labour market conditions) also remains significant in many developing countries.

Two examples within the Commonwealth of initiatives to overcome educational mismatch are *Britain's Technical and Vocational Education Initiative (TVEI)* and Sri Lanka's Life Skills Programme. The TVEI aims to encourage young people to acquire skills and qualifications of direct value to work by making available technical and vocational education to all 14-18 year olds in schools and colleges. Work experience is provided from 15 years and vocational specialisation may begin after 16 years of age. Courses last four years and wherever possible are expected to lead to nationally recognised qualifications.

Sri Lanka's Life Skills Programme, beginning at Junior Secondary level, aims to promote a positive attitude to the world of work, facilitate the acquisition of domestic and other skills relevant to a range of vocations and provide activity-based learning experiences. The curriculum consists of over 80 short 'learning events', based on skills of survival, maintenance and improving the quality of life. They relate to : agriculture and gardening; electricity; wood and metal-work; ceramics and weaving; home economics and a miscellaneous group including maintenance of bicycles and other machinery. Teachers are expected to choose events from the topics specified and to complete 10-12 each year.

The prospects for youth employment in the medium term, the Group found, were considerably worse in developing countries than in developed ones, largely because of demographic trends. In fact, youth unemployment was likely to become a less difficult problem in the developed countries. Between 1985 and the year 2000, for example, people aged 15 to 24 years were projected to increase by over 125 million (or 16 per cent) in the developing countries, but to diminish by 11 million (or 6 per cent) in the developed countries (see Table 11, page 220). Moreover, the increase in the developing countries' youth population was likely to be accompanied by an accelerating

---

Box 19: Mismatches between location and most favoured employment opportunities

Mismatches between the location of most youth and that of the most favoured types of employment occur in both developed and developing countries. In the developed countries the majority of youth and of jobs are already found in urban areas. There is, however, regional mismatching when youth are immobile and there is structural change, such as the decline of heavy industries. In the developing countries the greatest increases in youth population occur in rural areas. Rural-urban migration exceeds employment availability in the cities. Rapid population increases in some countries, especially in Africa, suggest that these problems will intensify in the future. To counteract this trend various Commonwealth countries have adopted schemes to promote youth employment in rural areas:

• National community service programmes, such as *Malawi's Young Pioneers* (centred on a 10-month leadership/agricultural training course aimed at self-employment in agriculture) and *Botswana's Rural Brigades* (which place school-leavers in a one-year programme of service in rural areas to assist in primary school teaching, agricultural/livestock extension, literacy teaching and communal and social work);

• Measures to improve rural youths' access to productive inputs such as training, credit, land, technology and advice. One non-formal training programme imparting craft skills is *Kenya's 'village polytechnics'* which focus on carpentry and masonry for boys and tailoring/dress-making and home economics for girls. A successful rural credit programme (not confined to youth) is *Bangladesh's Grameen Bank* which issues loans, without collateral, to the landless poor in rural areas. Performance has been outstanding, with almost 97 per cent of loans being repaid on time.

---

shift from rural to urban areas; the proportion of their youth living in urban areas is projected to rise from 36 per cent in 1985 to nearly 50 per cent by the end of the century. Rising educational levels were expected to exacerbate the problem, particularly in the formal sector. These three major factors together presaged a continuing vast shift from formerly disguised, rural underemployment to more open, urban unemployment. This was likely to present enormous political and social difficulties unless remedial action was taken.

The extent of the problem can be seen from Tables 11 and 12 (pages 220 and 227). The first refers to total youth, the second to economically active youth.

Table11: Projections of youth population

Year	Youth (millions) 1970	1985	2000	2025	as % of total population 1970	1985	2000	2025
Developed countries	175	186	175	180	16.7	15.9	13.7	12.9
Developing countries	492	755	881	1,117	18.6	20.6	18.2	16.4
Africa	67	106	168	334	14.0	19.1	19.3	20.7
Latin America	54	82	104	127	18.9	20.2	19.0	16.4
North America	390	44	40	46	18.6	16.7	13.6	12.9
Asia	390	584	623	670	18.6	20.7	17.6	14.8
China	158	237	188	185	19.0	22.4	15.0	12.6
India	100	149	184	180	18.0	19.7	19.1	14.6
Japan	20	17	16	17	19.0	14.2	12.5	12.6
Arab countries[a]	12	20	32	51	18.8	19.6	14.5	18.9
Europe	71	77	67	63	15.5	15.7	13.1	12.1
Oceania	3	4	5	5	17.7	17.9	15.5	14.3
USSR	40	44	48	52	16.7	16.0	15.1	14.1

(a) Western South Asia region, excluding Israel, Cyprus and Turkey, but including Iran.

Source: ILO *Economically Active Population Estimates and Projections, 1950-2025,* Vol. I-V, 3rd ed. Geneva, 1986.

Table 12 shows that in developing countries, which are often unable to absorb productively 20-30 per cent of their young people, some 34 million youths are projected to enter the labour market between 1985 and 2000, and a further 105 million by 2025. The influx could be higher if, as a result of adverse economic conditions or for other reasons, governments fail to maintain school enrolments or parents the level of family support. In that case some of the 378 million youths not projected to enter the labour market before 2000 might do so (compare Tables 11 and 12).

The Group's recommendations

The Experts proposed to governments a package of measures from which a choice could be made in the light of a country's particular needs (Box 20 on page 223). Their belief that youth unemployment was only a part—albeit a crucial one—of the larger problem of general unemployment led them to propose that its basic solution be sought in policies to promote faster, non-inflationary economic growth.

Table 12: Projections of economically active youth

	Economically active youth (millions)				as % of total economically active population			
	1970	1985	2000	2025	1970	1985	2000	2025
World	424	580	604	712	26.5	26.8	21.9	19.5
Developed countries	105	111	101	104	22.0	19.5	16.4	16.4
Developing countries	319	469	503	608	28.5	29.4	23.5	20.2
Africa	42	61	94	181	28.4	28.5	29.6	27.8
Latin America	27	41	51	63	29.7	29.3	25.5	20.5
North America	23	28	25	28	24.0	21.5	17.0	17.7
Asia	262	374	365	370	28.1	28.8	21.7	17.5
China	133	196	152	140	31.1	31.7	20.0	17.3
India	55	74	87	80	24.6	25.3	22.6	15.7
Japan	12	8	8	8	22.6	13.3	12.5	13.1
Arab countries[a]	5	8	13	22	29.4	27.6	26.5	21.8
Europe	45	46	39	37	22.1	20.4	16.4	16.1
Oceania	2	3	3	3	28.0	25.9	21.4	19.7
USSR	24	27	27	29	20.5	18.9	17.4	16.6

(a) Western South Asia region, excluding Israel, Cyprus and Turkey, but including Iran.

Source: ILO *Economically Active Population Estimates and Projections, 1950-2025*, Vol. I-V, 3rd ed. Geneva, 1986.

In the developed countries, where the problems were expected to ease in the longer term due to declining youth populations, the Kirby Group recommended that governments should use a variety of measures to influence labour markets. These should include policies to reduce mismatches, mainly of skills, between labour supply and demand, particularly by expanding training programmes; to introduce special job creation and training programmes to help the long-term unemployed; and to reduce taxes on employment. The Experts wanted such initiatives to be focused selectively on young people, especially those in disadvantaged groups or living in depressed areas, where unemployment was likely to last a long time.

In the developing countries, the Group emphasised the need for structural adjustment programmes to reduce labour imbalances; those between urban and rural areas, which had promoted migration out of the countryside and acted as a disincentive to agriculture, were deemed to be especially harmful. These programmes should include setting realistic prices for locally grown food and measures such as land reform to promote small-scale farming. The Group also recommended more support for the urban informal sector, through credit, training and infrastructural development, as well as the removal of fiscal, price and other distortions that encouraged the adoption of technologies which were capital intensive rather than labour intensive. It particularly recommended that industrial countries should remove protectionist barriers against developing countries' manufactures, especially those that were labour intensive.

The Experts indicated that temporary job programmes had a role to play, although as far as youth were concerned, their value depended heavily on their training content. They did not, on the whole, consider the agricultural resettlement schemes or national community service programmes implemented in many developing countries to be cost-effective ways of dealing with youth unemployment, particularly as only a minority of young people were involved. They believed that in view of the need to promote self-employment, in the developing countries especially, young people wishing to set themselves up in enterprises — individually or in groups — should be given the maximum possible help by way of training, credit, advice and extension services. This was particularly important for young women and for those especially disadvantaged, for whom further assistance was needed. Sexual equality in access to employment (as well as education and training) was seen as a basic objective.

Examining the role of education and training, the Group stressed that literacy, numeracy and problem-solving abilities were life-skills which made people more adaptable and employable. Basic education should include a vocational element related to the local economy. Countries, particularly in the same region, should collaborate in producing low-cost vocational materials, improving teacher training, developing distance-learning capabilities, and providing continuing education.

The Group drew attention to the large gap in detailed information, in terms of both factual material and assessments, on the many youth employment schemes. To help fill this void, it recommended a range of Commonwealth initiatives. The Commonwealth Secretariat's research capacity should be enhanced. Mechanisms should be established to identify and assess the various types of employment initiatives being undertaken in the Commonwealth. The results of this work should be disseminated so that others in the Commonwealth could benefit. Further, the Secretariat, with the CYP taking the lead, should organise exchange visits and on-site training courses through which those responsible for youth employment could learn from the experience of those operating successful schemes. It was also suggested that the Secretariat should focus more of its training resources on officials responsible for employment policies and programmes, particularly those directed mainly at youth. Finally, the Group recommended the creation of a Commonwealth Youth Enterprise Fund, administered by the Secretariat through the CYP, to

Box 20: Selected recommendations of the Expert Group

For developing countries

The informal sector should be regarded as a priority area, given the crucial role which it will have as a residual source of employment for growing numbers of unemployed youth in developing countries; governments should assist it to overcome disabilities in such areas as credit and training.

Every possible help should be given to young people seeking to set themselves up in individual and group enterprises, in both urban and rural areas, through credit and extension services. This is particularly important in view of the need and scope for self-employment in developing countries.

A major effort should be made by international agencies and governments to disseminate knowledge of existing non-formal training practices, such as village apprenticeships; and to exchange experiences, so as to produce training materials suited to low-cost productive activities which young people may enter in large numbers.

Programmes of structural adjustment, particularly those carried out under IMF and World Bank auspices, should specifically address the issue of how the imbalance between urban and rural areas can be reduced to discourage undesirable migration, promote employment and reduce poverty in the country as a whole.

For developed countries

Some form of education, part-time or full-time, should be made available until at least age 18. It is important to ensure that early school-leavers, especially disadvantaged youth, are encouraged to continue to study and do not move suddenly from the structured world of schooling into a vacuum - without a job, without training and without counselling.

Industrial countries should remove protectionist market access barriers on manufactured goods from developing countries since these act to inhibit employment generation by labour-intensive technologies.

help young people who lacked capital, skills and experience to undertake self-managed innovative activities.

The Experts set their recommendations in the context of a 'Youth Entitlement', based on the need of young people to have a role and status in society and ensuring that all of them are given adequate preparation for adult working life. An 'Entitlement' would cover the set of services and institutional arrangements which together would support youth in making informed choices and so facilitate their progress through school into the world of work. These services include: education, particularly ensuring relevance of curricula to work prospects and enterprise in general; career guidance and counselling; labour market information; work experience opportunities; basic training linked to life-skills instruction; access to further education and training, particularly to informal training; validated and generally recognised credentials covering all skills and occupations; and access to support in alleviating the ill-effects of unemployment. While recognising that not all governments would be in a position to commit themselves fully to such a comprehensive programme, the Group suggested that it should become an objective to which they should aspire and that its elements might be introduced incrementally over a period of years.

Finally, the Group stressed that despite the scale of the youth unemployment problem, particularly in developing countries, the energies and economic potential of youth should be seen positively, as a potentially dynamic element in the development process. If societies were willing to invest in young people, its report said, that investment would be repaid many times over.

Action by the Commonwealth

Commonwealth Ministers of Employment/Labour, who considered the Group's report at their meeting in June 1987, endorsed the Group's general approach and commended the report to Heads of Government. Ministers, like the members of the Group, placed considerable emphasis on self-employment in the rural areas and in the urban informal sector. They generally supported the Group's proposals on education and training, although several of them thought that the education systems should be oriented more towards self-employment requirements, and that training in agriculture should be supplemented by training in artisanal and engineering skills to enable young people to work in both urban and rural services. They welcomed the report's concept of a 'Youth Entitlement', although acknowledging that not all countries would have the resources to realise it immediately.

The report was also considered by Commonwealth Ministers of Education, who met in Nairobi in July 1987 and had chosen the vocational orientation of education as the main theme of their meeting. The conclusions they reached were in line with the Experts' recommendations (such as the need to provide pupils with the basic skills for working life; to encourage those who leave school early to take advantage of opportunities to resume their education or to retrain; and to expand science and technology education). The Education Division of the Secretariat was asked to make case studies of selected programmes to develop entrepreneurial skills in Commonwealth countries, to serve as a basis for exchanging experiences and for preparing curriculum guidelines for developing similar programmes in other Commonwealth coun-

Box 21: Programmes for tackling unemployment, with special reference to youth

Case studies were made of ten programmes and schemes considered to have had a positive impact in overcoming unemployment in different developed and developing Commonwealth countries. Although by no means embracing all relevant policy areas, the studies together provide a range of possible strategies which governments could consider in their own contexts.

Three of them cover education and training initiatives—*Britain's Youth Training Scheme (YTS)* (which provides an integrated programme of training, education and work experience of one or two years' duration, for all 16 and 17 year olds); *Britain's Vocational and Educational Initiative (TVEI)* (see Box 18); and *Jamaica's HEART programme* (see Box 22).

Two others are aimed at self-employment viz. the *Enterprise Allowance Scheme (EAS) in Britain*; and *India's Scheme for providing Self-Employment to Educated Unemployed Youths (SEEUY)*. Both are country-wide programmes. EAS is designed to help Britain's unemployed, of all ages, to start up their own business or become self-employed, by providing them with a weekly allowance during the crucial start-up period; over 100,000 were assisted in 1988 alone. The SEEUY includes a government package of assistance, notably credit, but also counselling advice and assistance with marketing, to help some of India's 250,000 educated unemployed youths undertake self-employment ventures in industry, commerce and services. Self-employment provision is also an element of the *Grameen Bank in Bangladesh*, which provides loans to the rural landless (largely women) without the requirement of collateral (see Box 19).

Zimbabwe's Organisation of Rural Associations for Progress is a non-governmental organisation which aims to promote self-reliance in rural development. It does so by helping village groups to organise and promote the sharing of expertise, skills training, information and resources, and by providing them with technical and financial support.

The promotion of small industries as a means of creating jobs, including jobs for young people, particularly females, was examined in relation to *Tonga's Small Industries Centre*. This provides infrastructure facilities and a package of investment incentives to small enterprises to promote employment, training and exports.

Finally, two examples of employment initiatives, centred on job placement activities, were taken from Australia and Canada, revealing the value of developing such mechanisms at the local level.

Each of the ten studies drew lessons or guidelines which could be of value to other countries.

tries. The most far-reaching recommendation of Education Ministers, however, was that a Commonwealth institution should be established for co-operation in distance education, with the ultimate aim of enabling any learner in any member country to follow any distance-teaching programme available from any bona fide college or university in the Commonwealth. Ministers proposed that this institution should devote a considerable part of its activities to supporting vocationally oriented education and training. They felt that such a development would undoubtedly make a significant contribution to the implementation of the Expert Group's proposals on preparing young people for the world of work. The Commonwealth of Learning, based in Vancouver, was set up in November 1988 with a core budget of £12-15 million for the five years 1989-93.

Heads of Government, who considered the Kirby Group's report at their meeting in Vancouver in October 1987, asked the Secretariat to make an early start in collecting and disseminating material on member countries' employment policies and to give priority attention to supporting study visits, including tripartite missions, to encourage exchanges of experience. The Secretariat duly undertook a series of case studies on effective and replicable employment initiatives in Commonwealth countries (see Boxes 21,on page 225 and 22 on page 227) which were presented to the June 1989 meeting of Employment/Labour Ministers. The Secretariat's Fellowship and Training Programme arranged study visits to youth employment programmes and more specialised activities such as careers advisory services by officials responsible for youth employment in Trinidad and Tobago (to Singapore and Malaysia), Nigeria (to Malaysia and Indonesia) and Hong Kong (to Australia). In addition, around one-sixth of the 3,500 trainees supported by the Fellowship and Training Programme in 1987/88 were on courses in entrepreneurship and small business management.

Heads of Government also asked the Secretary-General to draw up a detailed plan for the Commonwealth Youth Enterprise Fund recommended by the Group. The CYP, as part of a reorientation of its activities, is doing this. The Fund could be based on its existing Youth Project Fund, which provides seed capital and, where necessary, training and consultancy services in parallel with CYP's work on youth enterprise development. Some 20 studies have been carried out in various regions of the Commonwealth to test the elements of a unified enterprise strategy, based on the experiences of countries of different size and economic conditions. In addition, CYP's regional centres have organised workshops to study young people's needs in entrepreneurship, self-employment and business management.

The central preoccupation of many policy-makers in developing countries, including those concerned with labour and employment, has moved on to the effects of the debt crisis. A key concern has been to ensure that the structural

---

Box 22: An integrated system for vocational training in Jamaica

The Human Employment and Resource Training Programme (HEART), together with its co-ordinating body, the HEART Trust, is the umbrella under which all national training programmes in Jamaica fall. Launched in November 1982, HEART is intended to develop, encourage, monitor and provide finance for vocational training schemes; provide employment opportunities for trainees; direct or assist the placement of persons seeking employment in Jamaica; and promote employment projects. It includes a school-leavers' programme, building skills programme, apparel and sewn products programme, craft training and agricultural skills training. The school-leavers' programme, for those with at least two passes in school certificate examinations, provides one to three years of on-the-job training in private sector firms including some of Jamaica's largest corporations. Those school-leavers for whom placement is not immediately possible attend evening classes in business studies and upgrade their academic standards and so increase their suitability for employment. The building skills programme provides training for graduates of technical/comprehensive schools, high schools and secondary schools, and industrial training centres. The programme offers training in the most modern techniques of carpentry, masonry, plumbing, welding, and electrical installation. HEART seeks also to foster the use of indigenous natural resources by its craft skills and apparel and sewn products programmes, and by providing a wide range of training in agricultural practices. Funding is based on a three per cent levy on the salary bill of private sector employers, less any expenditure they incur on stipends to HEART trainees they employ.

---

adjustment measures instituted by governments, often as a condition for receiving financial assistance from the IMF and the World Bank, do not aggravate unemployment, particularly among those in the vulnerable groups (of whom youth are an important segment). Several international conferences have been held on this matter; for example, in addition to the many meetings on structural adjustment held under the auspices of the IMF and World Bank, the ILO held a High-Level Meeting on Employment and Structural Adjustment in November 1987. Within the Commonwealth, an Expert Group on Women and Structural Adjustment examined the impact of such strategies on women (Chapter 11). But no consensus on the best mix of policies appears to have emerged. Youth unemployment is not an issue for which easy solutions are available, and the problems it brings to developing countries seem likely to be around for a long time to come.

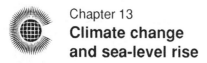

Chapter 13
Climate change
and sea-level rise

The idea that a manmade accumulation of 'greenhouse gases' might lead to a warming of the earth, and to climate change, is almost a century old; but it is only very recently that the reality and severity of the problem have been recognised by more than a small group of scientists and impinged on public opinion and on policy-makers.

The matter was first raised in a Commonwealth context at the Meeting of Heads of Government in Vancouver in 1987 in a discussion on environmental issues based on the report, *Our Common Future*, of the (Brundtland) World Commission on Environment and Development. President Maumoon Abdul Gayoom of Maldives spoke of the vulnerability of his own archipelagic country. There had already been serious flooding due to exceptional storm surges, he said; with most of the land less than two metres above the sea, the whole future of the islands—and others with comparable topography—could be threatened by global warming and sea level rise. His intervention, and that of President Hussain Muhammad Ershad of Bangladesh on the issue of flooding, led to the decision that the Commonwealth should commission an examination of the issues. An Expert Group was later established under the chairmanship of Dr Martin Holdgate, Director-General of the International Union for Conservation of Nature and Natural Resources (see Annex for list of members).

The Group published its report, *Climate Change: Meeting the Challenge*, in July 1989 at a time when global warming had come to command priority attention as an international issue. The report featured prominently in the discussions among Commonwealth leaders at their Meeting held a few months later in Kuala Lumpur. The growing concern about environmental matters was reflected in the Commonwealth leaders' Langkawi Declaration issued from the summit, and the subject is likely to be a focus of attention for many years to come.

Two areas in particular were highlighted in the Holdgate Group's report. One is the need for all countries to prepare for climate change: this will require more active research and monitoring, dissemination of information to create public awareness, and the preparation of realistic strategies to deal with problems. Many developing countries will need technical assistance to undertake these activities; some assistance is now being organised within the Commonwealth. The second point emphasised by the Group is the need for restrictions on greenhouse gas emissions. Some reduction in emissions would occur indirectly if certain measures that are environmentally important in any event are adopted: increasing energy efficiency and conservation; developing alternative, renewable sources of energy; phasing out the use of chlorofluoro-carbons (CFCs); and halting deforestation. But, in addition, the international community is rapidly moving towards a Convention governing climate change which would almost certainly entail some direct restrictions on greenhouse gas emissions. Several Commonwealth countries are closely involved in the preparatory process.

A substantial number of small states in the Commonwealth are not contributors to global warming but could be seriously affected by it. A meeting of Ministers from 17 small island states held in Maldives in November 1989—with support from the Secretariat and the Australian Government—to discuss the question of sea level rise, underlined the importance of small states' being effectively represented in global negotiations on this issue and the value of the Commonwealth as a forum for articulating their concerns.

Growing global concern

While the Holdgate Group was asked to address the specific issue of global warming and climate change, there has been growing concern in the Commonwealth about environmental degradation in general. The report of the World Commission on Environment and Development—to which the Secretary-General contributed as one of the Commissioners—was a milestone in the search for understanding about the environment, in a global context, and in particular in explaining the links between the environment, economic development and poverty. "Poverty is a major cause and effect of global environmental problems", it argued. It was therefore futile to attempt to deal with environmental problems without a broader perspective that encompasses the factors underlying world poverty and international inequality, said the Commission. Noting that developed countries with 25 per cent of the world population consume 80 per cent of the world's commercial energy and have, on average, 10 times the per capita consumption of commercial energy of developing countries, its report warned that the greenhouse effect caused by the burning of fossil fuels might "by early next century have increased average global temperatures enough to shift agricultural production areas, raise sea levels to flood coastal cities and disrupt national economies".

The Commission also provided a normative approach to environmental issues in terms of 'sustainable development'. This incorporates an essentially optimistic view of the possibilities of environmentally sustainable forms of economic growth lifting living standards and reducing poverty-induced environmental stress, as well as of the possibilities of technological advance leading to more frugal use of resources.

The Commonwealth Expert Group made it clear from the outset that, like the World Commission, it did not share earlier 'gloom and doom' attitudes about the environment; but believed that policies to combat global warming did not necessarily preclude economic growth.

While the Group was carrying out its work, popular awareness was growing of environmental issues in general, and global warming in particular. Specific events—such as the disastrous floods in Bangladesh and the drought in the North American grain belt—added to the feeling that manmade changes lay behind environmental disasters. This concern was reflected in the Queen's Commonwealth Day Message in 1989, in which she said:

> The threat to the environment takes many forms, of which some are so far-reaching that it is difficult to grasp them. We hear, for example, of the possibility of radical changes in our climate leading, among other things, to a rise in the sea level, with all that that would mean for small islands and low-lying regions. The Commonwealth has a particular part to play in facing up to such issues as these.

Specifically in relation to climate change, the Group had to take account of a rapidly rising tempo of public concern, reflected particularly in the work of scientific and intergovernmental organisations. Key events were the two Villach Conferences of 1985 and 1987 which helped to consolidate a scientific consensus on climate change; the 1988 Toronto Conference which produced an influential 'call for action' including internationally agreed reductions in carbon dioxide emissions; the passing by the UN General Assembly om December 1988 of a resolution on the protection of the global climate; and the 24-nation conference on climate change, held in the Hague in March 1989. There was also the rapid progress made in negotiating, ratifying and strengthening the Montreal Protocol on CFCs. Building on existing programmes of scientific work carried out under the auspices of the UN Environment Programme (UNEP), the World Meteorological Organisation (WMO) and the International Council of Scientific Unions, an important new initiative was launched in 1988: the Intergovernmental Panel on Climate Change (IPCC). The IPCC was asked to provide an authoritative assessment of the scientific work, assess the impact of climate change and formulate strategies for responding to the problem. Its report will be placed before the World Climate Conference to be held in November 1990.

A challenge to the Expert Group was to fulfil its own mandate while relating its activities to the rapidly evolving work of these other institutions. It chose to do this in several ways: by concentrating on the policy implications of climate change rather than seeking to extend scientific research; by focusing on the consequences for developing countries in particular; and by making an original contribution through selective case studies. These studies, supported financially by the Australian Government, looked in detail at the socio-economic implications of sea-level rise for Bangladesh, Guyana, Maldives, and a group of Pacific islands—Tuvalu, Kiribati and Tonga. They also surveyed work being carried out on climate change in relation to Africa and reviewed the implications of climate change and sea-level rise for major habitat types such as forests and mangroves. The Experts were also concerned to ensure that Commonwealth scientific networks, and such gatherings as the meetings of Commonwealth Meteorological Officers, should be used to project a Commonwealth dimension.

The scientific evidence

The Group considered that its task was to take note of the scientific evidence rather than to elaborate it. It was helped in its review by advice from Dr Richard Warrick of the Climate Research Unit at the University of East Anglia and from Professor Gordon Goodman and Miss Jill Jager of the Beijer Institute. They had all made important contributions to the work of the Intergovernmental Panel on Climate Change (the IPCC), the Villach Conference and the World Climate Programme (a joint programme of the WMO and the UNEP). It became clear that a consensus on climate change had emerged embracing most of the scientists working in the field—though there still remain large gaps in the modelling of global warming and some differences in the interpretation of data.

The consensus starts with an acknowledgement that some global warming has taken place over the last century, perhaps by 0.5°C as a global average. Sea-level rise also appears to have occurred—of perhaps 10-15cm over a century. The fact that the second half of the 1980s saw several of the warmest years ever recorded provided corroboration for the general proposition of global warming (as well as creating through popular awareness of climatic abnormalities, a growing sense of alarm about it). The trend has varied from country to country: some countries have become cooler; in others, land movements have caused the sea level to fall. It is only the world average that is relevant to the global warming argument.

There is also a theory to explain the trend in terms of the build-up of greenhouse gases. Roughly 55 per cent of the contribution to the greenhouse effect over the last 40 years is attributed to carbon dioxide; 23 per cent to the rapidly growing concentration of CFCs; and the rest mainly to methane and nitrous oxide. Roughly 50 per cent of greenhouse gases comes from the energy sector, 15 per cent from deforestation, 25 per cent from industry (essentially CFCs) and the rest from agriculture. The energy sector is therefore the key source. Scientists are still groping towards a deeper understanding of the 'carbon cycle' and, in particular, the role of the oceans as a 'sink' for carbon dioxides. The complexities of the atmospheric system, particularly cloud processes, are also very imperfectly understood. Nonetheless, a broad consensus now exists on the mechanisms by which global warming occurs.

Prediction is even more difficult than historical analysis since it depends on future human behaviour as well as on natural processes. Some increase in emissions of carbon dioxide is inevitable, not least because of the rapid growth of energy consumption in the developing world, which, with China, now accounts for just over 20 per cent of emissions. CFC emissions on the other hand could be reduced as the Montreal Protocol takes effect and substitutes are developed.

A global projection that appears to command widespread support in the scientific community was put to the Group. According to this, likely trends in greenhouse gas emissions suggest that the carbon dioxide equivalent concentration in the atmosphere will be double its preindustrial levels by 2030 (they are now just under 50 per cent above those levels). This change is consistent with global warming of 1.1-1.9°C by that date and—even assuming all emissions stop in 2030—a further, delayed warming leading to a 1.5-4.5°C rise in temperature. Longer-term projections suggest even greater warming and some scientists argue that the range cited above is conservative.

The Holdgate Group pointed out that "while a few degrees Celsius may seem a small increase to the layman, a change of such magnitude over 50 years is in fact unprecedented in recorded human history". The earth has warmed by, perhaps, only 4-5°C since the coldest point of the last Ice Age; this extent of warming could now take place in well under a century and, on some projections, in only half a century.

On the implications of global warming for particular regions—let alone countries—the report was circumspect. The scientific evidence does not permit forecasts to be made for them with any precision. The furthest it is possible to go is to say that "the greatest warming should occur in winter in high latitudes... in general wet areas could become wetter and dry areas drier. Extreme events could become more common. There seem good reasons for believing that tropical storms could increase in intensity".

One prediction on which scientists broadly agree is that global warming will raise sea levels as a result of the thermal expansion of sea water and the melting of glaciers. A 'best guess' for a global average is 17-26cms by 2030 but, given the lengthy time-lags, much greater increases will be experienced over a longer period. Although topographical detail will determine the precise local effects, it is clear that such an increase could have far-reaching consequences for densely populated low-lying regions such as deltas as well as atoll islands. In some cases the loss of land is the main danger; in others there will be a greater risk of storm surges and flooding.

The social and economic impact

While stressing the scientific and behavioural uncertainties, the Group endeavoured to sketch out some possible consequences of its predictions. It was particularly concerned to dismiss the expectation that gains and losses from climate change would simply cancel each other out. It stressed the need for all societies to adjust: "It is the fact that projected climatic change is so rapid in historic terms that causes such concern and threatens a costly process of adjustment. Greater climate variability and more extreme events also have costs", the report said. Costs were likely to be unevenly distributed and would fall particularly hard on developing countries. They are more dependent on agriculture and natural systems. Their environment is also often already under serious stress because of poverty and rapid population growth. And they are less able to finance the costs of adjustment.

The Group's report pointed to particular dangers for natural ecosystems which are unable to adapt quickly enough: "Forest tree species can probably disperse at most by two kilometres a year which is less than the speed at which natural frontiers of different forest types... would move with global warming". Species extinctions would probably increase. As for agriculture, the effects would differ greatly, depending upon local temperature and rainfall, the capacity of farmers to adapt their crop patterns and practices and also the changing economic environment, including the structure of incentives. Some pessimists predict severe global food shortages; optimists point to laboratory tests indicating faster plant growth with higher concentrations of carbon dioxide. The Group felt that the scientific evidence was too flimsy to endorse either viewpoint but stressed the particular dangers for marginal, rain-fed farming areas—as in sub-Saharan Africa—where environmental stress is severe and farmers are unable to cope with climatic extremes and new demands.

The Group highlighted the particular problems which climate change would pose for infrastructure projects with a long gestation period. Often big projects have to be planned years, sometimes decades, ahead. Climate change could undermine the assumptions, of rainfall in particular, on which the plans are based. This particularly affects water supply, irrigation and hydro power projects but all forms of construction specifications could be invalidated if there were large changes in temperature and rainfall. In some fields research is only just beginning into the impact of climate change. One such is health where even quite small variations in temperature could change the conditions in which particular diseases flourish. Some of the most worrying consequences of climate change could be where adverse environmental conditions are further aggravated, leading to mass migration with all the political stresses that this would induce.

The report gave detailed attention to the possible consequences of sea level rise based on country case studies. Some of the conclusions are summarised in Box 23. In particularly vulnerable countries with coral atoll islands, e.g. Maldives, the long-term viability of whole communities is threatened. In low-lying delta areas, as in Bangladesh, millions of lives are at risk from storm surges. The impact of higher sea levels cannot be considered in isolation from the adjustment options. There are a limited number of ways that small island communities can diversify their food and water supplies and provide defences against the sea. The Group's study suggested that in Bangladesh controlled flooding could help, through siltation, to raise land levels. Guyana could construct stronger sea defences. However, the options were severely limited by resource constraints and, in some cases, physical difficulties such as the virtual impossibility of building defences on shifting deltas or large numbers of small coral islands.

Responding to the dangers

The Experts approached their policy recommendations by stressing several ideas of fundamental importance. The first was that developing countries, while being particularly vulnerable to climate change and sea level rise, faced the constraints imposed on them by poverty and the need for rapid economic growth. The burden of action to reduce emissions was therefore likely to fall on the developed rather than the developing countries.

The second consideration was the high degree of uncertainty about the magnitude, timing and—even more—the local impact of climate change and sea level rise. Some governments have used uncertainty as a reason for postponing action. The Group argued strongly that, while more scientific research and information were certainly needed, "to do nothing...is the wrong approach and, could prove the most costly in the long term". Action was required to prepare for adaptation and preventive measures. But, given the uncertainty, it seemed to the Group that immediate priority should be given to measures that are justified on wider environmental grounds in any event: stopping deforestation and promoting reforestation, phasing out CFCs, promoting energy conservation and efficiency.

The Group made a series of recommendations designed to reduce uncertainty, including a call for more intensive research on climate modelling and more detailed and comprehensive monitoring. Research priorities will be highlighted by the IPCC when it publishes its report June 1990.

The Group set out in detail the needs of Commonwealth countries in respect

Box 23: The threat of sea level rise

The various case studies commissioned for the Expert Group identified some specific dangers from sea level rise:

- Storm surge risk: even where sea defences exist analysis shows (e.g. for Netherlands) that a 50cm rise could raise tenfold the probability of surges overstepping defences.
- Ecological damage: sea level rise would outstrip the capacity of existing mangroves to adjust (only 10-25cm a century), or corals (about 8cm a century).
- Agricultural: losses from sea flooding (or the threat of it) in coastal areas, especially deltas, and sea penetration of root crop beds (on coral atolls).
- Flooding of urban and industrial developments: at sea level together with flooding of airports on bay landfills, salt erosion of underground pipes, flooding of hazardous waste sites.
- Water supply affected by saline intrusion into waterbearing aquifers.
- Beaches lost to more rapid erosion.

In **Bangladesh**, if the sea were to rise 1 metre 15 per cent of the land would be flooded displacing 10 per cent of the population and causing the loss of 15 per cent of GDP; the risk of disastrous storm surges would rise; inland areas would be flooded from the 'back water effect'; the Sunderban mangrove forest would be destroyed; and there would be much damage to infrastructure including water supply and industrial facilities.

In **Maldives** almost all habitation, industry and infrastructure lie within 0.8 to 2 metres of mean sea level (msl). Most immediately vulnerable are the international airport (1.2m above msl and barely defensible), reclaimed land (which has added 70 per cent to the area of Male, the main island) and taro crop agriculture.

In **Guyana** most of the population live below 0.5 metres above msl and a large part of the agricultural area is under 1.5 metres above msl. Sea level rise would necessitate improved sea defences and, increasingly, a shift from gravity to pump drainage.

Some low lying **Pacific Islands** (Tuvalu, most of Kiribati, Tokelau, some of Tonga and the northern Cook Islands) rise to a maximum of 2 to 3 metres above msl. The Tonga island of Nuku'alofa could lose 15 per cent of its area from a 50cm rise and 38 per cent from a 1.5 metre rise in msl. Greater storm surge damage (and more severe hurricanes) could threaten Tuvalu, the Cooks and Tonga. Fresh water supplies and traditional food supplies are at risk.

of climate monitoring in particular. These include filling gaps in the observations in WMO's climate computerised data management system; more ozone monitoring sites; more observation sites for the Global Sea-Level Observation System of the International Oceanographic Commission; more comprehensive cyclone and flood warning systems; strengthening archives under WMO's historical data rescue project; and augmentation of the World Climate Research Programme. The Group argued forcefully that donor countries could make available highly cost-effective technical assistance in these areas. It also recommended that information should also be provided to the public whose awareness of the dangers of climate change would help to achieve the changes in consumption that may be necessary to reduce carbon dioxide (and CFC) emissions.

It was the Group's view that there was no alternative but to contemplate some degree of adaptation since ''it is already too late to prevent significant warming''. It believed that in many fields there was considerable scope for adaptation, and said: ''Some of the worst consequences of climate change and sea level rise can be avoided by adjustment in patterns of development, in the location of activities... and in consumer preferences...''. The case studies of atolls showed the scope for changes in diet and food production, construction standards, water allocation, preventive health, storm defences and coral conservation. The work on 'coping mechanisms' in African farming showed that farmers already had many options in adjusting to climatic variability—though they are under considerable stress—and that long-term research on crops could reveal new possibilities. Disaster preparedness strategies, necessary in any event, would be given added importance by the probable implications of climate change. The Experts were conscious that adaptation is not possible in many contexts, is particularly difficult for the poor and becomes progressively more difficult with large climatic changes. Nonetheless it recommended that all governments ''should evaluate how to adapt within their own national circumstances'' and that ''developing countries be helped to carry out such reviews''.

A third area of recommendations relates to action ''to reduce emissions of greenhouse gases and bring their concentrations towards stability''. The Experts accepted the need for reductions in emissions though they recognised the difficulty of setting precise targets for 'acceptable' rates of global warming. They focused specifically on the energy sector, which is expected to contribute over 50 per cent of global warming in the period to 2030. Analysis of the various long-term energy scenarios showed that only by a strenuous commitment to energy efficiency and conservation by industrial countries in particular would it be possible to curb global emissions while allowing economic growth to take place in developing countries. Energy conservation was seen as the most efficient and economic way of reducing carbon dioxide emissions. A useful role was also seen for substitution of renewable fossil energy, for substitution among fossil fuels (gas for coal), and for afforestation (and for halting, or slowing, deforestation where possible). National action to reduce emissions would almost certainly need to be supplemented by internationally agreed measures negotiated as part of the proposed Climate Convention—in the manner of the Vienna Convention and Montreal Protocol on CFCs—and the report strongly endorsed action along these lines.

The Experts recognised that while the Commonwealth, even taken as a whole, was not a large contributor to greenhouse gas emissions, its institutions —both technical and political—were sufficiently strong to be able to "guide the world by its example". A Commonwealth Plan of Action was suggested to translate that hope into practice (see Box 24 on the following page).

The Langkawi Declaration and other developments

The Report was reviewed in detail—in the context of a discussion of environmental issues—when Commonwealth Heads of Government met in Kuala Lumpur in 1989. This was the first occasion at any Commonwealth summit when a session was devoted specifically to the subject of the environment. The report served as one of the main inputs to the Summit's Langkawi Declaration on Environment; relevant extracts from the Declaration are in Box 25, on page 240.

Shortly after the Kuala Lumpur meeting, the President of Maldives convened a conference in Male of small developing coastal and island states to develop a common approach to climate change and sea level rise. The Commonwealth Secretariat, together with the Australian Government, supported the meeting to which 17 countries sent representatives, mostly ministers. The meeting established an Action Group, initially with representatives from the Caribbean, South Pacific, Mediterranean and the Indian Ocean regions, to oversee the implementation of its decisions and recommendations, to co-ordinate a joint approach on the issues of climate change, global warming and sea level rise and follow up on global and regional response.

It also recognised "the urgent necessity to take initial measures to create a monitoring infrastructure", and decided to seek the establishment of a climate and sea level programme and a monitoring network as an important component within the global measuring systems bearing in mind the specific interests of small developing island states, and to apply to the appropriate United Nations Agencies (in particular WMO, UNEP, UNESCO) for assistance in its implementation.

The next important step in the development of international responses

---

Box 24: Summary of action plan for the Commonwealth

1. Co-operation in research and evaluation
Exchange scientific knowledge, co-operate in research and evaluation and participate actively in the work of the Inter-Governmental Panel on Climate Change.

2. Co-operation in monitoring
A series of routine measurements of the climate at a network of points over the earth's surface is essential. Many small countries in particular need assistance to establish the recommended programme of climate monitoring and climatic hazard warning.

3. Co-operation in public information and awareness
The new initiative for co-operation in distance education could be a valuable means to facilitate the dissemination of balanced information on climate change.

4. Assisting adaptation
All members of the Commonwealth should review their "sensitivity to likely climate and sea level changes, and so avoid unwise public and private investment". Commonwealth technical assistance should focus on:
- small island and other low lying states
- assisting countries to develop effective disaster preparedness systems
- studying the 'coping mechanisms' of marginal farmers in rainfed agricultural regions.

5. Co-operation in reducing rate of increase in greenhouse gases
Co-operation and technical assistance is needed for:
- energy efficiency and conservation
- greater use of, and research on, renewable energy sources
- phasing out of CFCs
- sustainable use of forests, agroforestry, social forestry and afforestation
- promotion of fuel substitution notably toward natural gas.

6. Co-operation in the development of new technology for greenhouse gas control. In particular:
- CFC substitutes
- cost-effective small-scale renewable energy systems
- energy efficient technologies

7. Co-operation in international action
Commonwealth members should work together to implement and strengthen the Vienna Convention on the Protection of the Ozone Layer and the Montreal Protocol on Substances that Deplete the Ozone Layer, and to develop the proposed Framework Convention on Climate and its subsequent Protocols.

8. Machinery for co-operation and assistance
The Action Plan should be accepted as a priority within the technical assistance programmes of the Commonwealth.

---

to the greenhouse gas phenomenon will be the publication, in mid-1990, of the report of the IPCC. The Commonwealth report has been considered by the IPCC and its work will very probably be reflected in the Panel's conclusions. The IPCC report will help the World Climate Conference in November 1990 to map a way forward. Meanwhile discussions are proceeding on the negotiation of a climate convention and several Commonwealth countries—Canada, Malta and the United Kingdom—are prominently involved in them. As part of its growing involvement in environmental issues, the Commonwealth Secretariat expects to be assisting member governments in this process.

Box 25: Extracts from the Langkawi Declaration related to climate change and sea level rise

Recognising that our shared environment binds all countries to a common future, we, the Heads of Government of the Commonwealth, resolved to act collectively and individually, commit ourselves to the following programme of action:

- support the work of the UNEP/WMO Inter-governmental Panel on Climate Change (IPCC);
- call for the early conclusion of an international convention to protect and conserve the global climate and, in this context, applaud the efforts of member governments to advance the negotiation of a framework convention under UN auspices;
- support the findings and recommendations of the Commonwealth Expert Group's report on Climate Change as a basis for achievable action to develop strategies for adapting to climate change and for reducing greenhouse gas emissions, as well as making an important contribution to the work of the IPCC;
- support measures to improve energy conservation and energy efficiency;
- promote the reduction and eventual phase-out of substances depleting the ozone layer;
- promote afforestation and agricultural practices in developed and developing countries to arrest the increase in atmospheric carbon dioxide and halt the deterioration of land and water resources;
- support low-lying and island countries in their efforts to protect themselves and their vulnerable natural marine ecosystems from the effects of sea level rise.

Annex
Membership of Commonwealth Expert Groups

Towards a New International Economic Order (1975-78)
Mr Alister McIntyre *(Chairman)* Grenada
Prof.A.D. Brownlie	New Zealand
Mr Sidney Golt, CB[1]	Britain
Prof.Nurul Islam	Bangladesh
Mr Amir Jamal	Tanzania
Mr Peter Lai[2]	Malaysia
Mr L.M. Lishomwa[3]	Zambia
Sir Donald Maitland[1]	Britain
Mr S.S. Marathe	India
Prof.H.M.A. Onitiri	Nigeria
Dr David A. Simonda[3]	Zambia
Tan Sri Thong Yaw-Hong[2]	Malaysia

The Common Fund (1977)
Lord Campbell of Eskan *(Chairman)* Britain
Hon.G. Arthur Brown	Jamaica
Prof.Stuart Harris	Australia
Prof.Gerald K. Helleiner	Canada
Dr Lal Jayawardena	Sri Lanka
Mr W.R. Koranteng	Ghana
Mr K.M. Lamaswala	Zambia
Tengku Tan Sri Ngah Mohamed	Malaysia
Mr M.L. Rahman	Bangladesh
Prof.J. Rweyemamu	Tanzania

[1] Mr Golt succeeded Sir Donald Maitland as a member of the Group in December 1975.
[2] Tan Sri Thong Yaw-Hong succeeded Mr Lai as a member of the Group in March 1977.
[3] Dr Simonda succeeded Mr Lishomwa as a member of the Group in March 1977.

Co-operation for Accelerating Industrialisation (1977-78)

Mr L.K. Jha *(Chairman)*	India
Mr Maurice Abela	Malta
Mr R.D. Bakewell	Australia
Dr E.A. Essien	Nigeria
Mr Richard Kemoli	Kenya
Dr Kurleigh King	Barbados
Mr J.A.D. de Lanerolle	Sri Lanka
Mr John Marsh, CBE	Britain
Dr Pang Eng Fong	Singapore
MrR.A.Pillman	Canada
Mr Iddi Simba	Tanzania

The World Economic Crisis (1980)

Prof.H.W. Arndt *(Chairman)*	Australia
Prof.A.D. Brownlie	New Zealand
Sir Alec Cairncross	Britain
Dr William G. Demas	Barbados
Dr Lal Jayawardena	Sri Lanka
Mr William Jenkins	Canada
Mr Dominic Mulaisho	Zambia
Mr Ramon V. Navaratnam	Malaysia
Prof.H.M.A. Onitiri	Nigeria
Prof.Amartya Sen	India

Protectionism : Threat to International Order (1982)

Sir Alec Cairncross *(Chairman)*	Britain
Prof.Mohamed Ariff	Malaysia
Prof.Gerald K. Helleiner	Canada
Mr Satya Nandan, CBE	Fiji
Mr Philip Ndegwa	Kenya
Dr Eric M. Ojala	New Zealand
Mr Frank B. Rampersad	Trinidad & Tobago
Mr E. Olu Sanu	Nigeria
Dr Manmohan Singh	India
Prof.Richard H. Snape	Australia
Dr Augustine Tan, MP	Singapore

The North-South Dialogue : Making it Work (1982)
Mr B. Akporode Clark *(Chairman)* Nigeria
Hon. Bernard Chidzero, MP   Zimbabwe
Mr William D. Clark   Britain
Prof.Owen Harries   Australia
Dr Lal Jayawardena   Sri Lanka
Prof.Tommy T.B. Koh   Singapore
Sir Egerton Richardson, OJ,Kt.CMG Jamaica
Mr Lloyd Searwar   Guyana
Dr Arjun K. Sengupta   India

Towards a New Bretton Woods (1982-83)
Prof.Gerald K. Helleiner *(Chairman)* Canada
Prof.Conrad Blyth   New Zealand
Mr Kenneth Dadzie   Ghana
Dr William G. Demas   Barbados
Prof.Stuart Harris   Australia
Dr Lal Jayawardena   Sri Lanka
Sir Jeremy Morse   Britain
Mr Harry M. Osha   Nigeria
Dr I.G. Patel   India

The Debt Crisis and the World Economy (1984)
Lord Lever of Manchester *(Chairman)* Britain
Mr Alhaji Abubakar Alhaji   Nigeria
Mr Horace Barber   Jamaica
Mr Elasto Chalwe   Zambia
Mrs Chandra Hardy   Guyana
Dr Lal Jayawardena   Sri Lanka
Dr Lin See-Yan   Malaysia
Mr M. Narasimham   India
Mr Forrest L. Rogers   Canada
Dr Delphin Rwegasira   Tanzania

Technological Change : Enhancing the Benefits (1984-85)

Prof.M.G.K. Menon *(Chairman)* India

Dr Desmond Ali	Trinidad & Tobago
Dr M.N.B. Ayiku	Ghana
Mr Iann Barron	Britain
Mrs Shirley Carr	Canada
Dr David Gachuki	Kenya
Dr Linda Lim	Singapore
Sir Bruce Williams	Australia
Mr Carl Wright	Britain

Vulnerability : Small States in the Global Society (1984-85)

Mr Justice P.T. Georges *(Chairman)* The Bahamas

Prof.Elisabeth Mann Borgese	Canada
Mr Henry de B. Forde, QC, MP	Barbados
Mr Fathulla Jameel	Maldives
Mr Natarajan Krishnan	India
Dr Edgar Mizzi	Malta
Mr Lebang Mpotokwane	Botswana
Dr Robert O'Neill	Britain
Mr Olara Otunnu	Uganda
Sir Anthony Parsons	Britain
Mr Geoffrey Pearson	Canada
Mr Lloyd Searwar	Guyana
Mr Ata T. Teaotai	Kiribati
Mr Taniela H. Tufui	Tonga

Jobs for Young People : A Way to a Better Future (1986-87)

MrPeter Kirby *(Chairman)* Australia

Dr V.P. Diejomaoh	Nigeria
Dr Te'o I.J. Fairbairn	Western Samoa
Dr Dharam Ghai	Kenya
Mr Andre Juneau	Canada
Dr Azizur Rahman Khan	Bangladesh
Dr Joycelin Massiah	Barbados
Sir Richard O'Brien	Britain
Dr Prannoy Roy	India
Mr Carl Wright	Britain

Engendering Adjustment for the 1990s (1988-89)

Ms Mary Chinery-Hesse *(Chairperson)* Ghana
Dr Bina Agarwal   India
Dr Jamilah Ariffin   Malaysia
Ms Tendai Bare   Zimbabwe
Dr Dharam Ghai   Kenya
Ms Marjorie Lamont Henriques Jamaica
Dr Richard Jolly   Britain
Ms Hilda Lini   Vanuatu
Ms Iola Mathews   Australia
Ms Carolyn McAskie   Canada
Dr Frances Stewart   Britain

Climate Change : Meeting the Challenge (1988-89)

Dr Martin Holdgate *(Chairman)* Britain
Mr Jim Bruce   Canada
Mr R.F. Camacho   Guyana
Dr Nitin Desai   India
Dr F.U. Mahtab   Bangladesh
Dr Ophelia Mascarenhas   Tanzania
Dr W.John Maunder   New Zealand
Mr Hussain Shihab   Maldives
Mr Samuel Tewungwa   Uganda

Index